The CLASSIC SOUTHWEST

Readings in Archaeology, Ethnohistory, and Ethnology

EDITED BY

BASIL C. HEDRICK

J. CHARLES KELLEY

CARROLL L. RILEY

Southern Illinois University Press

Feffer & Simons, Inc.

Carbondale and Edwardsville

London and Amsterdam

Library of Congress Cataloging in Publication Data

Hedrick, Basil Calvin, 1932-   comp.
  The Classic Southwest.

    Bibliography: p.
    1. Indians of North America—Southwest, New.
2. Indians of North America—Southwest, New—
Antiquities. 3. Southwest, New—Antiquities.
I. Kelley, J. Charles, 1913-   joint comp.
II. Riley, Carroll L., joint comp. III. Title.
E78.S7H43   970.4'9   70-184966
ISBN 0-8093-0547-X

TO
ANNE
ELLEN
BRENT

Contents

INTRODUCTION

No cultural area in the New World has attracted more research in archaeology and ethnology than the American Southwest. Lying essentially within the states of Arizona, New Mexico, Colorado, and Utah, with extensions at times into adjacent areas of the United States and Mexico, this unique ecological and cultural area was inhabited by vigorous and culturally advanced aboriginal groups, as well as by a variety of more primitive peoples, when first discovered by Spanish explorers. Unlike the case in most areas of Mexico, many of these aboriginal groups succeeded in surviving Spanish domination and colonization without loss of their native cultures and even mounted a temporarily successful rebellion against their Spanish overlords in 1680. Although Spanish domination was reestablished before the end of the seventeenth century, many of the native groups survived as ethnic and cultural enclaves not only through the ensuing Spanish, and later Mexican, occupation of the Southwest, but throughout the later United States occupation of the area as well. When scientists began studies of the American Southwest in the latter half of the nineteenth century, they found not only intact native cultures, albeit acculturated by over three centuries of Spanish influence, but also the many ruins or archaeological sites representing centuries of aboriginal occupation and development. With great enthusiasm these early archaeologists and ethnologists committed themselves to the study of both the surviving native peoples and the archaeological remains. During the closing decades of the nineteenth and the first three decades of the twentieth centuries these devoted scholars described and made preliminary analyses of the cultures of most of the surviving ethnic groups and those represented by the more outstanding archaeological remains. They worked for the most part with inadequate funding and poor scientific resources, substituting very real participant observation among the living peoples and hard field drudgery in their archaeological field work for the advanced techniques and comfortable living circumstances of contemporary investigators.

Since World War II a great number of researchers have been at work in the Southwest, and a veritable flood of literature has appeared reporting their results. The students of living peoples now appear interested primarily in social organization or in applied anthropology. We have with us again a "New Archaeology," and some of its most enthusiastic advocates have told their students that anything published before 1960 is not worth reading. It is our impression that much of the basic data that must be used by the "New Archaeologists" and the social anthropologists alike were gathered by a small group of enthusiastic workers over some sixty years between 1880 and 1940, and that many of the basic inferences and the comprehensive syntheses upon which modern investigators in the American Southwest must depend were developed during this period. Without especial bias against the contemporary workers we feel that they and their students not only should, but must, read the significant papers written before 1960. Accordingly, in this book we have attempted to bring together for ready access some of the more significant and difficult to obtain papers on the archaeology, ethnohistory, ethnology, and folklore of the American Southwest written before 1960. Indeed, only two of the articles included here were first published after 1930 (1936, 1938); while six were published between 1880 and 1900; two were published between 1900 and 1920; and two were published in 1927. Choosing these articles included here from a great many available important papers has been a difficult task. In making our choice we have attempted to select those articles that first presented a new concept, or most succinctly stated a thesis, or presented a still significant body of data or durable synthesis or, occasionally, developed offbeat ideas or data which have largely been ignored or still remain undeveloped. By our choice we pay homage to a series of gifted researchers or recorders. Because we have had to reject as well as select from among the excellent papers available, we express our regrets that we have been unable to resurrect and honor the work of many others who deserved such attention. Perhaps our present efforts nevertheless will lead those who are totally devoted to the "New" to discover the great value—and their dependence upon it—of the "Old," and to explore still further the available riches of the past, now lying fallow.

For convenience and readability, type has been set in all papers. Editing has been minimal and confined mainly to removing incidental references to illustrations which have not been used. As an editorial policy we have found it necessary to delete most illustrations. Those researchers who find an article reproduced here to have especial value for their own work will be able to seek out the original publications for access to the illustrations which we have not reproduced. For greater value to the reader we have attempted to flesh out the bibliographical references in the several articles—only the gloriously inconsistent Bandelier is left with references more or less untouched. In the Strong article certain citation errors have been corrected and the bibliography has been merged with footnotes, thus preserving the over-all format of the book. This volume, then, like our earlier reader *The North Mexican Frontier* (Southern Illinois University Press, 1971) is intended for specialists in various disciplines who will have a quick, ready-at-hand reference to a variety of papers, some of which they will most probably not have on their shelves.

We acknowledge with gratitude the following people who have helped with the development of this book: Without D. Kathleen Abbass and Judith Grimes, these pages would still be only in our plans; their yeomanlike work is deeply appreciated by the editors. To Theresa Page, Jon Williams, Sue Vinson, and Maureen Oneill go our appreciation for their fine and loyal service in manuscript preparation.

In instances where the authors of works reproduced here are still living and available or where the works concerned were copyrighted and the copyright still valid we have obtained permission from the appropriate source for publication of the articles concerned in this book. Accordingly, special acknowledgment is made for permission to reprint the following works:

The Texas Folklore Society for permission to reprint "The Devil's Grotto" by Mody C. Boatright, from *Texas and Southwestern Lore* 6 (1927): 102–6.

The University of California Press for permission to reprint "Speculations on New World Prehistory" by A. V. Kidder, from *Essays in Anthropology: In Honor of Alfred Louis Kroeber,* ed. Robert H. Lowie, pp. 143–51, which was originally published by the University of California Press, 1936; reprinted by permission of The Regents of the University of California.

Our special thanks to Donald D. Brand for permission to reprint his article "Aboriginal Trade Routes for Sea Shells in the Southwest," from the *Yearbook of the Association of Pacific Coast Geographers* 4 (1938): 3–10, and for making corrections on the manuscript of that publication.

"An Elder Brother to the Cliff Dwellers" by T. Mitchell Prudden appeared in *Harper's Magazine* 95 (June–November 1897): 56–62.

A. F. Bandelier's "Fray Juan de Padilla, the First Catholic Missionary and Martyr in Eastern Kansas. 1542" was published in *American Catholic Quarterly Review* 15, no. 59 (1890): 551–65; "Alvar Nuñez Cabeza de Vaca: The First Overland Traveler of European Descent, and His Journey from Florida to the Pacific Coast—1528–1536" is from the *Magazine of Western History* 4 (1886): 327–36.

The article by C. F. Lummis, "The Penitent Brothers," is from *The Cosmopolitan* 7, no. 1 (May 1889): 41–51.

"Aboriginal Turquoise Mining in Arizona and New Mexico" by William P. Blake appeared in *American Antiquarian and Oriental Journal* 21 (1889): 278–84.

A. V. Kidder's "Prehistoric Cultures of the San Juan Drainage" was published in *Proceedings of the 19th International Congress of Americanists* (held at Washington, December 27–31, 1915), edited by F. W. Hodge, (Washington, 1917), pp. 108–33.

Also, we have reproduced here three important articles originally published by the American Anthropological Association in the *American Anthropologist*. They are "The Feather Symbol in Ancient Hopi Designs," 11 (January 1898): 1–14, and "Ventilators in Ceremonial Rooms of Prehistoric Cliff Dwellings," n.s. 10 (July–September 1908): 387–98, both by J. Walter Fewkes; and "An Analysis of Southwestern Society," n.s. 29 (January–March 1927): 1–61, by William Duncan Strong.

Basil C. Hedrick
J. Charles Kelley
Carroll L. Riley

Carbondale, Illinois
August 1971

The Classic Southwest

AN ELDER BROTHER TO THE CLIFF DWELLERS

T. Mitchell Prudden

This courtly, humorous, and sympathetic article written in 1897 is one of the first statements in print of the chronological position of the Basketmakers in the Basketmaker–Pueblo sequence. It is also notable for Prudden's (and the Wetherills') clear conceptualization of the use of stratigraphic position in archaeology as a means of determining the relative age of various cultural complexes—over a decade before N. C. Nelson deliberately employed the method in his excavations in the Galisteo Basin!

Aside from its historical significance for Southwestern archaeologists, however, the article has real value for its readable description of the San Juan area in the 1890s and its reminiscences of the famous Wetherill brothers, who first discovered and named the Basketmaker culture.

People rarely consider what an interesting experiment in the evolution of man was going on here in America when Columbus set out on his crazy adventure across the sea, nor how abruptly the experiment ended when the white race and the red race met. For most of us the history of America begins in 1492.

We, of course, all have some notion, framed partly from fact, largely from fiction, of the original possessors of our continent. But, after all, I fancy that most of us only dimly realize that back of the wars which made the country free, back of the struggle with forest and soil and forbidding wastes which made it rich, back of the bold adventures which made it known, stretch long ages, in which masses of dusky people, from one seaboard to the other, lived out their simple lives face to face with nature, won their way slowly through savagery to barbarism, and even here and there began to press eagerly through the portals which open toward civilization.

Then from countries in which mankind started earlier, or had more quickly scaled the heights of communal life, came the white men. The native advance was stayed, and soon the doors were closed forever upon a genuine American barbarism just shaping itself into a crude civilization in favored corners of the land. The Old World experiment in man-culture was grafted on the New, or, more frequently, replaced it altogether.

But here and there in the Southwest some small groups of red men, called Pueblo or village Indians, the wreckage of the abortive experiment in primitive man-culture in America, still survive. These Indians are mostly in Arizona and New Mexico, living in quaint stone or adobe houses in faraway fertile valleys or perched atop of great plateaus. Until within a decade or two they lived and thought and worshipped powers unseen in just such fashion as they did, and in the very places where they were, when the Spaniards found them, more than three centuries ago; and even in some instances they still do so.

These Pueblo Indians are not to be confounded either with the savages upon the Atlantic seaboard or in the eastern interior, with whom much of our early national history is concerned, nor with the nomadic tribes elsewhere in the land. Some of them present today a significant transition phase in the advance of a people from savagery toward civilization, whose study is of priceless value in the understanding of the science of man.

But each year—nay, each month—brings new ideas, new aims, new needs into the barbarian simplicity of this native life. Old traditions, old customs, old aspirations, are fading swiftly and surely in the presence of the white man. It is humiliating not only for an American, but for any educated human being, to realize that in this great, rich, powerful United States, boasting ever of its general enlightenment, there is neither the intelligent public spirit nor the sustained private devotion to the wider aspects of science to secure the myths and traditions and lore of those wonderful people before this page now open upon the Story of Man shall be closed forever. For nowhere else upon this planet does this particular illumining phase of human life exist, nor will it come again. There are many fields of science in which it does not make very much difference if the work which is waiting to be done shall wait a little longer. A decade more or less is of little importance in the end. But here delay is fatal.

The schoolhouses near the pueblos, the new requirements in food and dress, the new conceptions of the world, which begins for them to reach out beyond the cliffs upon the far horizon—these may all be very important to the material welfare of these waifs from the past, with a higher world culture pressing in upon them. But it means the speedy extinction of old customs in life and worship and ceremonial, which still are full of the spirit and practice of a primitive culture. It means that all natural things and happenings in their out-of-door world will soon lose their spiritual meanings, and that the quaint myths out of forgotten centuries will fade with the old folks who still may cherish them. When such people get on cotton shirts, need coffee and sugar, want rum, and begin to name their sons after the presidents—for it has come to this save in one or two faraway places—they will not continue long to send messages to the gods by rattlesnakes, nor propitiate the elements with feathers and songs.

It is not an untrodden way which must be followed if this treasure in the man-science is to be secured. The Bureau of Ethnology in Washington, under the direction of Major Powell, has done admirable work already. Cushing, Bandelier, Lummis, Stephen, Fewkes, Mrs. Stevenson, and others have rescued much. But the work should be more extended, more sustained, more amply supported, and must withal be quickly under way.

[Recently] the writer indicated the importance of a practical knowledge of the modern Pueblo Indians in forming a conception of the elder people to whom they are closely linked. For the later workers in American archaeology have finally made it clear that the Pueblo Indians are in all probability the descendants of the erstwhile mysterious Cliff Dwellers of America, whose architecture and industries and habits, and no doubt traditions and myths, they inherit. Some of the largest and most imposing of the old cliff dwellings are situated in southwestern Colorado and in northern Arizona, along the tributaries of the San Juan River. But from the Rocky Mountains to the Colorado River, and from the northernmost tributaries of the San Juan southward to Mexico, smaller cliff houses are abundantly scattered in the walls of the cañons. The ruins and burial places of the Cliff Dwellers in many parts of the country have been eagerly explored, and their ethnical position in the higher stages of barbarism has been established.

The purpose of this paper relates to some recent discoveries in the hot wonderland which lies along the San Juan River and its northern tributaries, mostly in southeastern Utah. It relates to people whom the Spaniards never saw—for the very good reason that they had long been buried safe under the sand before the Old World folks knew how "the other half lived," or even that there was another half. Buried, too, they were in a region into which those intrepid and heroic explorers were never lured by God's service or the color of gold.

But all these red folks, like their surviving types in the pueblos, lived no doubt in sympathetic touch with the spirit of the earth and air and sky; and so, before unveiling the secret which the parched earth has kept so long, I should like to give to the reader a passing glimpse of their deserted land.

As you go over the Rocky Mountains toward the west from Colorado Springs or Pueblo or Trinidad, you come into a region of jumbled ranges interspersed with mountain parks. The Colorado River, sweeping southwestward, has sculptured the wonderful valleys and sublime gorges known as the Grand Cañon. From the east the San Juan River, rising in the San Juan Mountains, and receiving from the north several tributaries, now mostly dry, joins the Colorado in southern Utah. North of the San Juan River, and between its namesake mountains on the east and the Colorado River on the west, lies a triangular region about as large as Massachusetts, Rhode Island, and Connecticut together, called the Northern San Juan Plateau Country. A few small peaks rise here and there above the plateau, while everywhere great cañons, wild and forbidding, or broad valleys with terraced sides, and lofty buttes or mesas rising gigantic from the bottoms, relieve the general level. The plateau region south of the San Juan River is the home of the Navajos.

There are two or three small villages along the upper reaches of the San Juan River. But for the most part the broad valley, bordered by imposing bluffs, is in summer a hot, bare, stifling stretch of desert, with the sullen, muddy stream sweeping silently through it. Only toward the end the river enters a profound chasm, and roars its way to the Colorado. But one town, Bluff City by name, with some two or three hundred of the Chosen, a solitary outpost and oasis of Mormondom, exists, and even thrives in a half-hearted way, as thrift goes in a desert, in the southeastern corner of Utah. This town, ninety miles from the railroad, is the metropolis of the San Juan Valley. A swiftly subsiding gold craze brought many adventurers to the valley a few years ago. But now only a few placer miners are left, struggling here and there against odds, far down the stream, picturesque and pathetic beside their rough sluices and quaint water wheels.

It is from Bluff that you most conveniently enter the country of which I write, and you see no fixed human habitation, and probably no white man, until you get back, brown, tired, and dusty, to Bluff again. The nearest railroad is at Mancos, in Colorado, and here at the Wetherills' Alamo Ranch one can obtain an outfit and most competent guides, hardy, bright sons of the household, and wise in the lore of the hills, for the rough trip by way of Bluff to the plateau of the Northern San Juan district. Access from Bluff to the plateau is mostly by dim and devious Indian trails, which meander along the rough bottoms of the cañons, or clamber toilsomely to the uplands, over whose bare or pine-clad surfaces they stretch tortuously away. Water is scanty at the best, its situations known only to a few, and in dry seasons long and trying marches must often be made to reach the hidden and meager pools and springs.

The explorer must secure hardy ponies or mules, accustomed to forage for themselves on the scantiest of herbage and capable, if need be, of sustaining life for a day or two on the willow twigs and rank dried weeds of the bottoms. The pack is intrusted to mules. A canvas wagon-sheet and a blanket must serve in lieu of tent and bed. It is no hardship, however, in this dry and bracing air, to sleep under the stars. Water, no matter what color or consistency it may possess, is the only thing which the traveler longs and strives and prays for, and for lack of this many an unwise adventurer in these arid wastes has left his bones to bleach beside the way.

The great cañons and their tributary gorges, which have been carved out of the plateau in the past, thousands of feet deep in places, by wind and sand and rain and mighty rivers, are now almost wholly dry, save when a cloudburst or a storm on the far mountains sends a mad torrent roaring down. But this soon passes, and in a few hours the horseman may be struggling along the parched bottom faint from thirst.

In the high country the great pines sing and moan in the wind at night and morning. The piñons and cedars on the lower levels murmur fitfully to the passing breeze. Small lizards rustle in the dried grass as they whisk from your presence. Prairie dogs here and there chatter and whistle at you as you pass. As night comes on, the howls and barks of the coyotes circling far above the camp are weird and mournful. But the great country stretching away for hundreds of miles has scarce a human habitation, few wild animals and birds, and these largely of the still kind, and so is mostly silent. It is very hot in the daytime, with the sun straight at you from above and back at you from the rocks as you ride. It is sometimes rather trying to stop at midday, unpack, and get dinner. Perhaps there is no shade for twenty miles, except under your mules—and your mules kick. But the air is so dry and bracing that a temperature of from 108° to 112° in the sun is never disheartening, as is the ordinary summer weather of our Eastern cities, with that combination of heat and moisture which so remorselessly saps the energies. And ever above is the marvelous sky. The nights are always deliciously cool. Altogether, the wanderer who doesn't mind the wholesome sunburn upon the skin and has a good supply of water, is about as free and comfortable and happy as good mortals deserve to be. How far away New York seems! And for the thousand unnecessary things which we gather about us in our winter thraldom and dote upon, how pitiful are they, if we deign to recall them! This is living. You get down to sheer manhood, face to face with the bare, relentless, fascinating old earth. And no memory of art rebukes your willing thraldom to the glorious pictures which momently rise and fade.

The tints of the cliffs in Monument Valley, south of the San Juan, shimmering through the hot haze of eighty miles; great sand columns which rise from the valleys, swaying pillars of pink and yellow and gray, now singly, now in groups, poising for hours, or gliding in stately fashion beyond the vision or melting away before you; the deep black shadows upon the broken faces of the cliffs; the dark moving acres of forest and bush and plain saved for a moment by drifting clouds from the pitiless thraldom of the sun—these, and a nameless witchery of the air, which makes all far things strange and beautiful, and which more than all else lures back the wanderer to these hot wastes year after year, dwell in the memory when the trials are forgotten.

This great desolate plateau, so inaccessible and so far from the usual routes of travel, is rarely visited save by cattleherders, and is inhabited only by a few renegade Utes, who in summer live in wickieups built of boughs and cultivate the few moist bottoms in the valleys. Even the best government maps are very faulty and practically useless for the location of water.

One of the great cañons, about fifty miles long and in places two thousand feet deep, with sheer cliffs overhanging the narrow winding bottom, and unnamed upon the map, is known to the herders as Grand Gulch. It harbors scores of large and imposing cliff ruins. But for the most part the ruined houses of the Cliff Dwellers in this region are small and widely scattered. Some are built in shallow caves far up the cliffs; some are under the overhanging rock near the bottom.

Explorations of these ruins and their adjacent graves show that these Cliff Dwellers were the same sort of folk as those who once inhabited the Mesa Verde in southwestern Colorado and the vast region stretching southward from the valley of the San Juan. The stone weapons, pottery, fabrics, etc., are similar, as are the skulls, which are short and flattened behind.

Richard Wetherill and his brothers, of Mancos, Colorado, have made many fruitful explorations of the cliff dwellings in this region. Part of their collections are now at the American Museum of Natural History in New York, some are in Denver, some in Philadelphia, some are in their possession at Mancos, and some are in private hands elsewhere.

Several persons from Bluff have gathered valuable material from these cliff ruins, part of which is in Salt Lake City, part dispersed without record.

But I must hasten to my purpose and speak of a remarkable discovery made by the Wetherills in their work among the cliff ruins and in the caves of cañon walls in the northern San Juan country, which has not, so far as I am aware, been yet recorded. In some of their excavations in this region the explorers were impelled, for what reason I do not know, to dig under the walls of the houses of the Cliff Dwellers and beneath their graves. Here, much to their surprise, they came upon another set of graves of entirely different construction, and containing relics of what appear to be a different group of people.

These older graves are in the floors of shallow caves. They are egg-shaped holes in the earth or sand, either stoned in the side, or lined with clay plastered directly upon the sand. The mummies of men, women, and children are found, often two bodies in one grave.

Sandals woven of yucca fibre upon the feet, a breechcloth of woven cedar bark, strings of rough beads around the neck, about the body a rudely constructed blanket of rabbit fur, enveloped in a yucca cloth, over the head a small flat basket, and a great finely woven basket over all—such was their burial fashion.

The graves never contain pottery, as those of the Cliff Dwellers are so apt to do, and the skulls of the people are narrow and long, and never flattened at the back. Bone implements, stone spearheads and arrowheads, twisted cords of human hair, well-formed cylindrical stone pipes and baskets filled with seeds and ornaments are found with the bodies.

Spear points between the ribs, stone arrowheads in the backbone, a great obsidian spear driven through the hips, crushed skulls and severed limbs—these secrets of the old graves show clearly enough that there were rough times in the cañons now and then, and that these old fellows were proficient in the barbaric art of killing men—the art toward which some of our wind-and-paper patriots would fain have us climb back.

Over these graves the rubbish heaps of the Cliff Dwellers have in places accumulated to a depth of two feet, showing a long residence above the graveyards, of whose existence they may well have been unconscious. In many places great rocks have fallen upon the graves.

The Wetherills soon recognized the ethnological importance of their discovery, and have provisionally named the people who buried in these older graves the *Basketmakers*.

There is no evidence that the Basketmakers ever built in these caves. While their graves are often found under the cliff dwellings, they also occur in caves in which the Cliff Men had no houses, and with the earth level and hard above them. The skull has great significance in the lore which anthropology gleans here and there the world over out of forgotten graves, and the difference in the form of the skull between the Cliff Dwellers and the Basketmakers would seem—I speak with the reserve which becomes a poacher upon anthropological preserves—to exclude their identity.

One need be a student only of the human nature of today to conclude that the newly found people were not mere intruders upon the domain of the Cliff Dwellers, vanquished, and hurriedly buried; for the solicitous care with which the bodies are furnished for their journey into "the country which is out of sight" forbids the notion.

It seems to me to be not without possible significance in determining the ethnical status of this new aborigine that no pottery of any kind has been found in his graves. He certainly knew the value of clay, for he plastered his graves with it. Students in the crude art of pottery making have been led to believe that the use of clay was preceded by the acquirement of considerable skill in basketmaking, and that from the earliest application of clay coverings or clay linings to baskets, to make them impervious or resistant to heat, the manufacture of pottery was gradually evolved.

Now if this old American did not know how to make pottery, he must, according to the widely accepted system of Morgan, be denied admission to the ranks of barbarism, and, in spite of the fact that he had discovered clay and just missed the achievement of a dish, be thrust sternly back among the savages. He might still be saved, however, by the creed of Tylor, if he knew how to till the soil; and though no agricultural implements were buried with him, as they often are with the Cliff Dwellers, he was thoughtful enough to stow away in his excellent baskets some corn and seeds. So, as far as I can see, while he is damned to savagery by the American doctrine, he is saved to barbarism by that of the Englishman. May we not give him the benefit of the doubt?

People who know about these things have told me that the stone hatchet fastened to a wooden handle by thongs is to be considered an implement of very high order, when you know, or guess wisely, about the genesis of inventions among people of the Stone Age. But I regret to say that while these Basketmakers possessed most excellent stone arrow and spear heads, stone hatchets are not found among their belongings. Nothing of this nature better than a crude pounding-stone, bearing the form of a natural unworked pebble, has been as yet unearthed. In the ruins and graves of the Cliff Dwellers, on the other hand, stone hatchets with wooden handles, or with grooves for the attachment of these by thongs, are common. This fact might perhaps be wisely adduced with the rest as evidence of the lower status of the Basketmakers.

The whole matter at present rests just here, until the various furnishing of their burial places shall have received systematic study and the country shall have been more widely explored. But one may hazard a guess that these Basketmakers were nomadic Indians who used the sheltered caves as burial places before the Cliff Dwellers settled the country and utilized the rocky shelters for their homes. There must in the old days have been many a fierce encounter up and down the rugged faces of the rocks when the Cliff Men met their foes with stone tipped arrow, axe, and spear—perhaps over the very spot where the elder folk, now still and crumbling in their unsuspected graves, had fought and lost.

To one who has traveled much in this southwest plateau country and knows not only just how dry it is, but also just how dry it is not, the residence of these early peoples in small scattered communities along the now remote cañons and valleys is neither surprising nor mysterious. Here were warmth and shelter the year round, and for those who had learned to build were houses half made already by the cave walls of the cliffs.

It does not require very much food for bare subsistence, and a very small patch of corn suffices for a family. While springs and pools are rare, there are a good many places, in valleys apparently dry the summer through, in which the seepage from the back country comes down some sag in the hills and furnishes moisture enough for a crop of corn. The beds of dry streams also, where sand is plenty, are often moist beneath the surface.

In fact, here and there all over the Cliff Dwellers' country today, in streambeds, mostly dry, or in low places in the bottoms, with no water visible, one comes across groups of Navajos or Utes camped beside little green patches of corn which seems to be growing out of the driest of sand banks. It is easier for the corn roots than it is for the humans to get enough drinking water, and the Indians are very clever today, as the older fellows doubtless were, in finding the few places here and there in which the deep moisture suffices for a modest crop of corn.

It has been the writer's good fortune, half on knowledge, half on pleasure bent, to journey over this desolate country under the skillful guidance of Al. Wetherill, to delve among the ruins of the cliff dwellings, to search through the opened graves of the Basketmakers, and so to gain a conception at first hand of the land they lived in, the old folks, and their graves. And it is with Richard Wetherill's permission that I record this interesting discovery of the Basketmakers which he and his brothers made some time ago. I am eager to do this because the enthusiasm, devotion, and practical knowledge which he has brought to his life work in the cause of American archaeology should find more general appreciation, and in the hope that means may be forthcoming from some quarter for the pursuit, under Wetherill's direction, of this promising research.

Will none of our great universities realize before it is too late that the treasure house of folklore among the Pueblo Indians is crumbling fast, and that these fields of American archaeology in the Southwest are wide and fruitful?

If you have seen the living Indian from his better side, which too often is the side away from the white man, have learned to admire the qualities which so well fit him for his life in the open, and have come to realize—not mayhap without a tinge of wistfulness—how close he stands in every act and purpose and sentiment to the powers above and to the presences about him, you may come to have an esteem, and even a certain dreamy affection, for the silent Cliff Dweller, so abounding that it shall include, bloody old warrior though he was, this new-found elder brother also.

SPECULATIONS ON NEW WORLD PREHISTORY

A. V. Kidder

This paper by Kidder, published in 1936, has stood the test of time. It is of course necessary to juggle certain dates (for example, it is now known that low-level agriculture appeared by perhaps 5000 B.C. rather than 1000 B.C.), and we now have a great deal of work in north Mexico by Kelley (1966, 1972), Ekholm (1939, 1942), Kelly (1938), DiPeso (1966), Kelley and Kelley (1969).

Nevertheless, the basic chronology of Kidder is valid, his tentative suggestion that the Southwest is a periphery of Mesoamerica may be regarded as proven, and his question as to the autonomy of New World civilizations is still vital—and unanswered today. (See Riley et al. 1971.)

All through the years that we excavated at Pecos we were bombarded with questions. Tourists visited our work in shoals, for the highway passes close by the ruin. We had people of every sort and their queries ran the entire gamut of human curiosity. But there was one that we always knew would, sooner or later, be asked by every visitor. From ranchman, movie director, hitchhiker, plutocrat, we had the inevitable "How old?" And our modest guesses that a thousand or, in moments of exaltation, fifteen hundred years would carry back to the founding of Pecos (it must be remembered that we were then in the pre-Douglass age) lowered our ruin, and with it ourselves, very perceptibly in popular estimation. We were often told that Pompeii (we got awfully sick of Pompeii) was older than that. What our visitors would have thought of us had they known then that everybody's old friend, 1066, would probably have seen the Pecos valley still untenanted by Pueblo Indians, one hates to contemplate.

This craving for antiquity is not confined to the traveling public. Archaeologists have it too, some, of course, much worse than others. And all of us, I think, have a sneaking sense of disappointment as the pitiless progress of tree ring dating hauls the Cliff Dwellers, and with

11

them the Basketmakers, farther and farther away from the cherished
B.C.S.

The same thing has been going on in Mexico, where Vaillant, un-
dismayed by the weight of lava flows, is lopping millennia from the
"Archaic"; and in the Maya field, Vaillant and Thompson, those Young
Turks of Central American archaeology, are almost indecently hauling
the revered Old Empire upward by two-hundred-and-fifty-year jerks.

Our ideas regarding the rate of Southwestern development have
been forced to undergo a thorough overhauling. The Maya, also, may
well have got on much faster than has hitherto been supposed. We miss
the comfortable amplitude of Old World dating. We have to stuff a tre-
mendous lot of cultural events into an ever shrinking chronological container. It is well, under such conditions, to back off, so to speak, for
a fresh view of the whole chronological situation.

We immediately encounter a paradox, for while the upper end of
our time scale is being distressingly compressed, its lower end is being
vastly expanded by the recent unequivocal determination of the high
antiquity of Folsom Man.

As everyone knows, the discovery of the European Palaeolithic
was followed by attempts to identify, in America, the traces of an occupation equally remote. The often ill-founded and sometimes prepos-
terous claims for the great age of man in the New World brought about
the then very salutary reactions of Holmes and Hrdlička. But these gen-
tlemen eventually swung so far to the right, they became so ultracon-
servative, their attacks upon any find suggesting even respectable age
were so merciless, that further purposeful search for early remains was
most harmfully discouraged; and palaeontologists and geologists, with
whom for the past forty years archaeologists should have been working
upon the problem of man's arrival in America, were actually frightened
away from participating in the investigation.

The discoveries of Figgins at Folsom, New Mexico, and by Harrington in Gypsum Cave, Nevada, have, however, not only reopened
the question, but have been followed by those of Howard at Clovis,
New Mexico; of Shultz in Nebraska; of Roberts in Colorado and Sayles
in Texas, which prove beyond possible doubt that man was present in
the New World contemporaneously with many mammals now extinct.
Whether these animals disappeared with the Pleistocene or whether they
persisted into postglacial times has not definitely been established. The
latter supposition seems the more likely. But it can no longer be questioned that human beings were here at the very least ten thousand years
ago. Antevs' recent estimate of fifteen thousand appears, indeed, to be

reasonably conservative. It is my personal opinion that the first migrations took place before the dawn of the Old World Neolithic.[1] If this be true, what was going on in North America during the millennia that intervened between the time of the pre-Neolithic Folsom nomads and, say, the Basketmakers who, according to the readjustments in our chronological estimates made necessary by tree ring dating, must now presumably be placed subsequent to the birth of Christ? And what was happening in Middle America and the Andean area between the Folsom epoch and the period of the well-developed farming, pottery-making cultures of those regions, the oldest of which, according to Vaillant and Kroeber respectively, are not earlier than the beginning of the Christian era?

In North America, hunting cultures apparently persisted. We shall, I believe, ultimately discover that there was a long, slow, and, in flint chipping at least, degenerative transition from Folsom to the cultures which were existing in North America when the maize-pottery complex spread north and inaugurated over wide areas a new era of sedentary agricultural life.[2] Strong's admirable excavation at Signal Butte, Nebraska, has already begun to fill the void. During those same millennia, somewhere in the south, there were being planted, both literally and figuratively, the seeds of aboriginal American civilization.

This last statement is made ex cathedra. Like most archaeologists in this country I am 100 percent American regarding the origin of the higher cultures of the Western Hemisphere. But we do not know for certain that we are right, and this matter of New World beginnings involves some of the most fundamentally important of all anthropological problems. Were, for example, such processes as agriculture, pottery making, metalworking, loom weaving, the recording of thought by written characters, discovered once and once only? Were they single and unrepeatable mutations, so to speak, of the superorganic? Or do all human beings possess an innate urge to take certain definite steps toward what we call civilization; and innate ability, given proper environmental conditions, to put that urge into effect? In other words, is or is not civilization an inevitable response to a law of human conduct?

There have been reams of writing upon psychic unity and upon diffusion as against independent invention. But the one question whose solution would do most to throw real light upon these and other anthropologically vital matters cannot yet be answered with full assurance. Why have we not progressed further in our research upon this outstanding problem of New World History?

There have been various hindrances. The study has many inherent difficulties and relatively few qualified persons have given it serious attention. But even more to blame is the fact that American archaeologists have been attracted by such spectacular remains as the cliff houses and mounds, the Maya temples, and Peruvian cemeteries. They have thus as a rule been concerned only with the latest manifestations of aboriginal culture; and in their quite natural predilection for interesting and striking finds they have been aided and abetted by the museums, which institutions have had the direction of practically all archaeological field work.

We have also been steered away from purposeful study of origins by the general trend of archaeological thought in America prior to about 1910. During several decades before that date it was the general fashion to connect all prehistoric remains with the peoples occupying, at the time of the Discovery, the regions in which such remains occurred. This was due to a healthy revolt against the still older tendency to see in Mound Builders and Cliff Dwellers and Toltecs mysterious races of vast antiquity. But the very commonsense attitude of our immediate predecessors resulted in a most unfortunate loss of historical perspective; speculation as to beginnings was, in fact, almost taboo. Archaeology accordingly became preponderatingly descriptive; effort was directed toward identification of ancient sites with modern tribes; research upon American prehistory, striking forward rather than back, upward rather than down, was left without foundations. And as under the prevailing dogma of our student days the Indian was considered a creature of yesterday, the problem of how he could so quickly have spread throughout these continents, attained astonishing linguistic diversity, and built up a very respectable and highly ramified civilization became so puzzling a riddle that many of us merely dodged the issue of origins and comforted ourselves by working in the satisfactory clear atmosphere of the late periods.

But now the Folsom discoveries have given us ample chronological elbowroom, even by Old World standards. This is a great relief to me personally, as I think it must be to many other believers in the essentially autochthonous growth of the higher American cultures. I plead guilty to a strong bias in that direction, but at the same time I recognize, as a result of a recent rather careful review of the history of American archaeology, how strongly fashions of thought can influence judgment. And I believe that all American archaeologists, the hundred-percenters perhaps even more than others, would agree that the question cannot be considered settled except on the basis of a great deal more factual information than is at present in our hands.

The obviously correct method is to start with what we actually know and work backward. Excellent beginnings have been made. The discoveries in the Valley of Mexico by Boas and Gamio of more ancient and simpler cultures underlying the Toltec and Aztec gave the first strong impetus to research upon the development of New World civilization. Those finds really opened the modern period of American archaeology. There followed the brilliant "Archaic" hypothesis of Spinden, the effect of which upon archaeological thought cannot be overemphasized. At about the same time recognition of the significance of the Basketmaker remains inaugurated the study of Southwestern beginnings. Vaillant's work in Mexico, Lothrop's in Salvador, the Ricketsons' at Uaxactun in Guatemala, Uhle's pioneer investigations in Peru, followed by Tello's and Kroeber's and, more recently, Bennett's in Bolivia, have all been potent factors in lengthening our historical perspective.

But our work to date has not, as a rule, been first-class. The methods of stratigraphic excavation have, it is true, been developed and refined; the surface survey, using potsherds as a criterion, has assiduously been practiced, particularly in the Southwest. But the study, classification, and published description of the artifacts and pottery, upon which our final conclusions must rest, are still, with far too few exceptions, both hasty and inadequate.[3] Important classificational and taxonomic advances have been made by Guthe and McKern in the East and by Gladwin and Roberts in the Southwest. But classifications and nomenclatures and the statistical analysis of stratigraphic data are useless unless the specimens concerned have undergone rigid typological study. There is no quick or easy road to success in research upon material culture.

Most of us have worked, I think, too much in restricted fields; and in those fields we have perhaps devoted ourselves too exclusively to site excavation. The comparative methods of ethnography might well be given greater consideration by archaeologists. Nordenskiöld's results, achieved on the basis of the scanty South American data, show how much can be accomplished by such means. Single lines of evidence should be followed over wide areas. We have been very remiss as regards this type of research. Studies do not exist, for example, of the typology and the distribution in the New World of such outstandingly important objects as metates, stone axes, spindle whorls, anthropomorphic clay figurines.

One could go on indefinitely pointing out valuable lines of investigation. But it needs no stressing that much more work is required before we can compare, trait by trait, the prehistoric cultures of the Americas with those of Europe and Asia, and so be able to draw sound conclusions regarding their relationship. It is also necessary to keep in mind the importance of ascertaining the actual as well as the relative chronology of cultural developments, not only in America, but also as between the New and Old Worlds. In America, however, we seem to come very soon to a dead end, for such authorities as Kroeber and Vaillant believe that the oldest remains so far discovered in Peru and Mexico are not older than the time of Christ.

But, while the estimates of Kroeber and Vaillant may be approximately correct, they are, after all, no more than well-considered guesses. What we need, for a chronological starting point, are ascertained facts. For these we must turn to southwestern United States, as there, thanks to Douglass and dendrochronology, we have the only accurate dates that have so far been made applicable to prehistoric American remains. The Maya time record must, however, also be taken into account, but with the reservation that its intrinsically reliable sequence of some seven centuries has not as yet been certainly correlated with Christian dating.

Let us take, then, the Southwest as our chronological and cultural datum. In the northern part of that area we find a succession of horizons whose relative ages have been established by stratigraphy, and which indicate a steady and seemingly almost wholly autochthonous growth from a non–pottery-making but already maize-growing stage (Basketmaker), through an early pottery-making, house-building stage (Modified Basketmaker), to increasingly higher achievements (Developmental Pueblo, Great Pueblo).[4] The actual age of all but the earliest part of this northern development has been determined by Douglass and his disciples. Basketmaker has not yet been dated, but by the latter part of the fifth century A.D. the Modified Basketmaker period was under way in the San Juan, to last, in that region, until about the beginning of the ninth century. Thereafter progress was extraordinarily rapid, the eleventh and twelfth centuries witnessing the highest achievements of the Great Pueblo period. In this we see confirmation of the generally held opinion that in the absence of outside stimulation progress of a nascent culture is slow, but that once it finds itself, so to speak, it can attain its peak in a relatively short time.

If Modified Basketmaker required four, or perhaps five, centuries to run its course and change into Developmental Pueblo, it might seem reasonable to postulate an even longer time for the preceding Basketmaker period. I once suggested, indeed, that Basketmaker beginnings might have been 1500 or even 2000 years before Christ. In the light of our present knowledge, this seems much too early a date and I now believe the San Juan Basketmaker to have been a relatively short period, extending back, perhaps, not more than a century or two before the opening of the Modified Basketmaker. I base this guess, for it is no better, to some extent upon the paucity of Basketmaker remains, but more upon a belief that the introduction of maize agriculture could not long have preceded pottery making. In other words, it seems to me that the Basketmaker was not a true developmental stage, but rather that it represents a short phase of transition during which an essentially nomadic population (and as such doubtless of very high antiquity in the plateau country) was assimilating, in maize, the most obviously and immediately useful trait from gradually expanding farming cultures to the south.

Until recently the actual source from which the Basketmakers derived knowledge of maize was a puzzle. No culture approaching the Basketmaker in antiquity was recognized anywhere north of the Valley of Mexico. The origin of Basketmaker pottery was also problematical. Nothing like it was known from more southerly regions. It even seemed that it might have been an independent invention, for, as Morris some years ago pointed out, all the steps in a logical growth from Basketmaker containers of unfired clay to the fired and later decorated pottery of Modified Basketmaker and Developmental Pueblo are found in the northern country. But in spite of this, and also in spite of the almost entirely self-contained evolution of Southwestern culture in the subsequent periods, the gross facts of the distribution of American civilization, with its highest and therefore theoretically its oldest manifestations in Middle and South America, and particularly the strong probability that maize was originally derived from a southern prototype, all make it appear that the Basketmaker-Pueblo development was peripheral to a southern nucleus.

The work of the Gladwins and their associates of Gila Pueblo has, of late, greatly strengthened the above hypothesis. These investigators have brought the hitherto neglected southern part of the Southwest into its own. They have established, on the firm basis of stratigraphy, the several periods of the important Hohokam culture of the Gila-Salt drainage and have linked those periods, through cross-finds of traded pottery, with the various stages of the Basketmaker-Pueblo series.[5] The results of their remarkable excavations of 1935 at Snaketown have not as yet been published, but I have the permission of Gila Pueblo to state that below the previously known Colonial Hohokam, which equates chronologically with late Modified Basketmaker and early Developmental Pueblo, they have discovered some five older phases. Although these have not been dated by dendrochronology, I would suppose that the first of them must run back to the time of Christ.

The finding of these pre-Colonial remains in Hohokam territory renders Anasazi development much more comprehensible by locating, on the road from Mexico, a culture probably as early as, or perhaps even earlier than, Basketmaker. It also strengthens the belief that Modified Basketmaker pottery was inspired by or perhaps actually copied from that of the pre-Colonials. Decision as to this point must await study and publication of the Snaketown ceramic material.

To sum up: We have a pottery-making culture (the Modified Basketmaker) in northern Arizona by at least A.D. 500. In the southern part of the state pottery making may well go back to the dawn of the Christian era.

From Arizona we are forced to jump clear to the Valley of Mexico before encountering known remains of even respectable antiquity. The vast intervening area is, from that point of view, a blank, and, as Mark Twain said of the weather, everybody complains but nobody does anything about it, save the Ibero-Americana group at the University of California. However, it seems certain that important early materials will eventually be found along the slopes of the Sierra Madre.

Vaillant, as has been said, believes that nothing he has yet found in the valley is older than A.D. 1. If this be so, and if the earliest pre-Colonial is of approximately the same age, the pre-Colonial must derive from still older, sub-"Archaic" cultures which still await discovery. And such cultures must have existed, for Vaillant's Arbolillo I is, as he has pointed out, very far from primitive. The question is whether they existed in Mexico.

Central Mexico, because it is within the range of *teocentli,* the supposed ancestor of corn; and also because "Archaic" remains are there found underlying volcanic deposits, was believed by Spinden to have been the breeding ground of American civilization. But Lothrop and Vaillant have shown that Spinden's "Archaic" is by no means the simple and fundamental sort of culture required by his hypothesis. We must have something more primitive, more uniform, and presumably much older. How much older should it be?

This brings us to consideration of our second New World chronology, that of the Maya. The Maya calendar was in full working order and monuments bearing Initial Series dates were being erected in 8.14.10.13.15 (Stela 9, Uaxactun), which corresponds to about A.D. 50 according to the Spinden correlation, to about A.D. 300 by the Goodman-Thompson-Martinez correlation, and to about A.D. 550 by a third correlation tentatively suggested by Thompson.

According to the hypothesis held by most students of Middle American history, Maya culture was derived from an antecedent highland culture akin to the "Archaic" of the Valley of Mexico. Traces, indeed, of such a culture have come to light in the Guatemala highlands at Arrevalo-Miraflores; and the theory is strengthened by the fact that these remains in some respects resemble materials from deposits of the prestela period at Uaxactun, itself the oldest dated Maya city. Were the Maya dates accurately correlatable with the Julian count we should have an exceedingly valuable datum for Middle American chronology. But while exact correlation is of the most vital importance for study of Maya history as well as for research upon the relations between the developed Maya and other advanced peoples of Middle and South America, it is of less significance for the present discussion of the ancient periods. The spread between the correlations amounts, after all, to only five centuries; and as the Goodman-Thompson reckoning splits the difference, and as it seems, at the moment, to be the one most acceptable to a majority of students, one may perhaps take it as a working basis.

Under the Goodman-Thompson correlation the Maya calendar was in full operation at A.D. 300, and Maya architecture and the other arts were apparently in full bloom. Cultural efflorescence can, it is true, be an almost explosively rapid phenomenon, as is proved by fifth- and sixth-century Greece and by what, on a more humble plane, happened in the Southwest between A.D. 900 and 1050. But such flowerings always seem to have required long periods of rooting, and in the very nature of the Maya calendar we have a strong indication of antiquity. Thompson believes that the time count must have reached its perfected form some four centuries before the erection of the earliest Uaxactun monument, namely, at about 100 B.C. And it is certain that no system so complex could have been devised save on the basis of astronomical data recorded over a long period, approximately how long, it may be remarked, calendarists should probably be able to calculate. Whether the necessary extent of such records was one or five centuries, the mere fact that they were kept implies a stability of residence and a freedom from turmoil which in turn argues for a relatively sedentary life and a secure, almost certainly agricultural, economy. We must accordingly postulate for the Maya, or for their cultural ancestors, a settled existence of, say, three centuries. This runs them back to 400 B.C., and, while we are speculating, it seems reasonable to allow several hundred years for the theoretically slow transition, in Middle America or elsewhere, from hunting to agriculture. So we now arrive, for the beginnings of American civilization, at a date somewhere around 1000 B.C., or approximately 2500 years before the Discovery. This seems to me an irreducible minimum. In the Old World a considerably longer time was apparently required to reach a comparable stage of advancement.

But where are the remains of the postulated cultural ancestors? Nothing that can be recognized as such has yet been found. Everything more primitive than the "Archaic" that has come to light is most reasonably to be interpreted as peripheral, as, for example, is the case with the Hohokam and Anasazi. One would suppose that traces of the basic culture should occur in the highlands of Middle America. Exploration has, of course, been very superficial, and there is a strong possibility that volcanic deposits, which cover so much of those regions, have buried the remains under lavas and tuffs, but if there was even a scanty agricultural, pottery-making population there during the postulated period of several centuries before the "Archaic," one would think that some sites or at least artifacts would have turned up. Intensive search, at any rate, is needed before we turn to other fields.

In the above guesses as to the time and location of basic New World culture, first consideration has been given to the Middle American highlands: because agriculture seems to be a prerequisite necessity for the development of such a culture; because maize was the New World staple; and because *teocentli,* currently believed to have played a part in the origin of maize, is apparently only to be found in those regions. Furthermore, the Maya was in many ways the most advanced of all American civilizations and on theoretical grounds one expects to find, as Nelson has pointed out, the early stages of a culture at or near the point where it reached its highest development.

The supposed role of Middle American *teocentli* in the ancestry of maize may, however, have confused us. Other possibilities must be considered. *Teocentli* may not have fathered maize; it may yet be found in South America. Some other plant ancestor, as yet undiscovered, perhaps even extinct as result of maize culture in the lands favorable to its growth, may exist, or have existed, in South America. These very problems, so crucial for New World history, are at present being attacked by Collins and Kempton as a joint project of the Bureau of Plant Industry and Carnegie Institution of Washington.

If maize should prove to derive from South America, the whole setup would in some respects be more comprehensible. According to Kempton, the great number of this plant's Andean varieties would indicate to a botanist, who knew nothing of *teocentli,* that maize originated in that area. And the number, size, richness, and diversity of the cultural remains in Bolivia and Peru give one the impression that they must root back to high antiquity. In later times South America seems to have contributed to the north the important trait of metalworking. The agricultural complex might similarly have spread north in the pre-"Archaic" period. The "Q-culture" of Lothrop and Vaillant has a southern tinge. Even if maize is of Middle American ancestry there is the possibility that sedentary life, with its attendant art of pottery making, might have been developed in South America on the basis of some other plant, and maize have been brought into cultivation in Middle America by northward-migrating people already familiar with horticultural processes. This, I admit, is clutching at a straw, but if no remains more primitive than the "Archaic" are ever found in Middle America we can only look to the southern continent for the foundations of New World civilization.

It will have become obvious that I am not a polygenist as regards American culture. I believe that it had a single point of origin, though this tenet, I grant, is illogical in view of my strong feeling that civilization sprang up independently in the Old and New Worlds. It is possible that there were both North and South American nuclei. But I nevertheless hold to Spinden's conception of an outflowing from one center; I merely feel that he mistook a latish branch for the root. And it may need a lot of digging to uncover it.

Gladwin, who has the invaluable habit of questioning everything which smacks of unproved dogma, and who, incidentally, is nowadays administering much-needed doses of intellectual salts to Southwestern archaeologists, has accused me, during our many discussions of the origin problem, of backing southward as successive failures to find really early remains first in Mexico and then in Guatemala, knock away one northern prop after another. He says that eventually I shall probably be pushed off the tip of Tierra del Fuego, and that it is a long jump to Antarctica. I shall come to a halt, however, in Central Chile. But not before all possibilities above that latitude have been exhausted, shall I begin looking overseas.

THE DEVIL'S GROTTO

Mody C. Boatright

Boatright's article, written from the viewpoint of the folklorist, preserves a ceremony that may well date from a very early period in the missionization of the La Junta area and one which almost certainly represents a blending of Christian elements with Indian concepts, basically Mesoamerican in origin, but undoubtedly present to some degree also in the culture of the prehistoric Indian occupants of the region. Boatright collected this story in 1925, and it was first published in 1927. One of the present editors (Kelley) visited the La Junta area many times between 1930 and 1950 and lived in Presidio in the summer of 1939 while conducting archaeological excavations nearby. During this period he twice visited the Devil's Grotto and the Catholic shrine built on the mountain shoulder nearby. The shrine itself was officially closed by edict of the Mexican government at that time and the ceremony described by Boatright was not currently practiced. Nevertheless, there were fresh offerings and testimonial papers in the shrine and the switchback trail that led up the mountain to it was well and freshly worn. Many of the local residents of both Ojinaga and Presidio, as well as of neighboring towns, had participated within easy memory in the ceremony and talked freely about it. In general their accounts paralleled that given by Boatright but included some variation on the basic myth and provided considerably more detail regarding the ceremony itself.

Thus, some informants said that the Devil took the form of a giant spider who wove a great web across the Rio Bravo (Rio Grande) or, alternatively, the Rio Conchos. In this web he trapped the persons (or the souls, in some accounts) of children and virgin young maidens and carried the hapless victims to the Devil's Grotto, where they met an unspeakable fate. Accounts of the ceremony also vary somewhat from Boatright's and these variations contain important elements. Thus, the Cross is taken from the Shrine where it normally rests (not at the cave mouth) four days before May 3. During the ensuing four days while it is paraded through Ojinaga and neighboring towns, the nights are times of fear, for the Devil is now free to leave his cave and wander at will. Doors and windows are kept tightly closed, candles are burned in household shrines, and no one goes outside at night. Then, on May 3, the local occupants gather, carrying with them drums

22

and horns and pots and pans, and raise a (veritably) holy din, "rounding up" the Devil. Led by the Cross, the worshippers, driving the Devil before them, climb the meandering trail to the shrine and with proper "Catholic" ceremonial the Evil One is ordered back into his cave. A ceremonial fire is then lit at the grotto mouth to restrain him within for another year.

The Devil's Grotto itself has a relatively small entrance room from the back of which a passage, probably an ancient gas or lava escape tube, drops at a steep angle into the depths of the mountain. Any sacrificial victim or more prosaic offering dropped into it would disappear from mortal ken. At the entrance of the cave are the remains of fires, but no other signs of occupation were noted. It probably was a pre-Christian shrine and so falls into the pattern, radiating out of Mesoamerica, of deities in caves. In many cases these deities became syncretized to the Christian trinity, the Virgin Mary, or to a saint—often with a vivid folktale of struggle in which the saint replaced the demon (see for example Hobgood's graphic account of the Chalma Shrine, Hobgood, n.d.). In the case of the Devil's Grotto another subpattern may have emerged in which, instead of replacing the original god or gods and thus purifying and Christianizing the Shrine, the Spanish missionaries chose to emphasize the negative aspects of the cave, making it essentially an accursed place, while constructing nearby on the mountain shoulder the new and highly visible Christian shrine, protected by the Holy Cross.

Clearly there are other Mesoamerican elements in the ritual and the myth. The four days of fear when the Devil roamed the world (five, counting the final day on which purification occurred) certainly represent the Mesoamerican five days of evil at the end of each calendar year. As in Mesoamerica, the relighting of the sacred fire by the priest (be he Catholic or pagan!) marked the beginning of the new year and at La Junta the literal imprisonment of the Devil for another year of calendrical and ceremonial order. Clearly the ceremony also carries implications of human sacrifice to the deity of the Grotto, another Mesoamerican element.

It is of special interest that such Mesoamerican elements are so well represented here. Archaeologists and ethnohistorians have established a sequence of agricultural village cultures in the La Junta area that range from circa A.D. 1200 to modern times without significant occupational break (Kelley, 1952a, 1952b, and 1953). The early occupation was essentially southwestern in cultural origins, but there were Mesoamerican elements present, especially in the later periods. Spaniards visited La Junta as early as 1581, with the Gallegos-Chamuscado *entrada,* while Spanish missions were first established in 1683, abandoned shortly thereafter, and reestablished in 1715. Shortly thereafter they were destroyed by Indian rebellion; efforts continued intermittently to establish more firmly the Holy Faith at La Junta, but these were not successful until after 1760 when a Presidio was established. Thereafter, Indian towns became Mexican towns through marriage between the soldiers of the Presidio and women of the towns (Kelley, 1950). Today Mestizo towns occupy the archaeological sites of Indian towns and in some instances bear the same names that they received as Indian towns in the contact period. In such a context it is not at all surprising that there should survive at La Junta de los Rios in the modern *mestizo* culture so many items of Mesoamerican origin. The soldiers stationed at the Presidio may well have been Tlaxcalans or other central Mexicans; certainly these Indians accompanied the various Spanish *entradas* into the area, providing still another source of Mesoamerican elements. The long fight to establish the Holy Faith in the area may be reenacted symbolically in the ceremony so well described in this article by Boatright.

For nearly two hundred miles as the crow flies—but not as the river runs—the Rio Grande flows southeast from Juarez and El Paso through a prison-like valley. Then between Ojinaga on the Mexican side and Presidio on the Texas side, the valley slightly widens to receive the Cibolo and Alamita creeks, which cut in from the north. For a hundred miles then the valley is pinched into the Grand Canyon of the Rio Grande. Twenty miles out from Presidio the Chinati Mountains in Texas rise to an apex of 7,000 feet above sea level; across in Mexico great palisades, pierced only by the Rio Conchos, tower thousands of feet and shut out the rain-bearing winds of the Pacific. The mountain slopes furnish the habitat of the creosote, the mesquite, the mimosa, and the various forms of cacti. The valley floor that supports the two little towns is the habitat of the *mestizo,* who fences his plat with stems of the barbed *ocotillo* and farms his cotton and corn very much as did his fathers in the days of the presidio system and the Chihuahua Trail.

In April the Great Spirit touches the heart of the desert, and the desert releases the beauty that for nine months has been dormant in the womb of the cactus. In an incredibly short time the yucca sends up its slender stalk; lateral buds appear, and then rich, waxy flowers, rivaled by those of the *sotol* and the *lechuguilla*. The dead, thorny stems of the *ocotillo* take-on a leafy liveness and tip themselves with crimson, like spears stained with blood. The cacti light their flames of white, of lavender, of rose, and of saffron.

The Great Spirit speaks also to the heart of man, and the simpleminded *mestizo* is aware of some great power outside of him and beyond him—something at once kind and sinister, something that makes his cotton and his corn to grow, or withholds the divine rain—something to be feared, worshiped, appeased, propitiated.

Thus I found the valley on May 3, 1925. I cannot vouch for its appearance in the late sixteenth century when explorers from Spain traversed the region, setting up at intervals on the mountain peaks huge wooden crosses, symbols of their conquests for their king and their God.[1] The *mestizos* in the valley will tell you that there have been topographical changes within comparatively recent times, and that these changes resulted from a titanic struggle in which a great priest confounded the devil and shut him up in a cave.

About three miles from Presidio a rugged mountain arises abruptly from the Mexican side of the river to a height of some thousand or more feet. This is the Mountain of the Holy Cross. Near the summit, at the west end, is a notch visible for miles. In this notch is a sort of shrine surmounted by a cross. Nearby is the Devil's Grotto, the mention of which is likely to cause shuddering among the older inhabitants of the region, as I found when I broached the subject in a Presidio barber shop.

"Does the devil live there?" I asked one.

"*Quien sabe?*"

"Is he thought to live there?"

"It is strange," he said: "strange things have been seen. Once some children were playing on the hillside, and they saw a burro coming down from the cave, and the burro didn't have any tail. The children laughed because they thought it funny to see a burrow without any tail, and they called their parents to look but the burro was gone. . . . *Quien sabe?*"

Other natives told of strange happenings near the cave, seen, not indeed by themselves, but by their grandparents and their great-grandparents. One grandmother, while gathering *mescal* on the hillside, saw a rabbit dancing on his hind feet, and then she saw that he didn't have any fore feet. She thought she could catch him, but when she reached for him, he was gone. She stuck a *lechuguilla* blade in her hand and suffered from an infection.

It was from Pedro that I secured the most complete version of the story. Pedro saw me and my companions wandering through the village, and with true hospitality he asked us to his house, where he entertained us with his antique harp of many strings. When we entered his *casita* of adobe we noticed two candles burning on an improvised altar in one end of the room. In the center of the altar, between the candles, was a chromo of the Son of Man on the cross. Above the Son was the Mother. Various saints had less conspicuous places. Paper and wax flowers in beer bottles were there in profusion, and by way of further decoration, two burnt-out electric light globes were suspended by strings from the low, beamed ceiling. This was Holy Cross day, and those who did not go over the river and take part in the processional would gather with their neighbors in their homes to render thanksgiving and prayer to the God and the good saint who, *muchos años pasados,* had wrought the deliverance of the valley.

This is substantially Pedro's version of the story:

Muchos años pasados—no living man knew how many—the valley had been prosperous and fertile. The rains came in the fall and in the spring; the Rio Grande flowed full and swift, and crude ditches were sufficient to lead its waters into the fields, where corn grew tall and cotton was never harmed by the pink bollworm. Cattle were fat on the hillside, and goats yielded milk and mohair. All the inhabitants of the valley were happy.

Then came all manner of distress. Crops withered; the bollworm came; cattle died of disease, and babies were born blind. At sunset when the people looked to the sky to implore a heavenly blessing, they would see a great rope stretched from Chinati Peak in Texas to the mountain in Mexico afterwards called Holy Cross. And upon this rope with many a weird grimace danced Satan, gloating over the mischief he had wrought and mocking those who tried to pray.

Now a saintly Spanish priest—Francisco, according to Pedro, but called Gomez by some—who was sojourning in the mountains, chanced one day to visit Presidio del Norte. Grieved to see the inhabitants thus prostrated by the evil one, the priest undertook their conversion. The cross, he said, was all-powerful, and to demonstrate the truth of his assertion, he asked that such an emblem be furnished him. When the devil made his customary appearance, this soldier of religion, armed with a crude wooden cross, advanced upon him. The devil's fiery breath might turn green hillsides into semi-deserts; it might cause the thorny cactus to spring up where the *alamo* had flourished; but behind the emblem of Christ, the priest was safe, and, thus protected, he advanced upon the enemy of man. The cable broke. The malignant one dropped into the valley. The priest pursued with renewed vigor. The devil resorted to his great physical strength, seizing great crags and hurling masses of rock and earth at the dauntless Francisco. But all in vain. The missiles were powerless. The devil was forced to retreat. He crossed the Rio Grande into what is now Mexico, fled up the mountainside, and finally took refuge in a cave, across the mouth of which Francisco placed the cross, effectively imprisoning his adversary. He then returned to the village and told the people of their redemption. He instructed them to make a shrine at the cave and to mount the cross near by. But once a year, he said, on the third of May, the anniversary of this victory, the cross might, with proper ceremony, be taken to the village that the people might be blessed with health, and to the farms that they might yield in abundance.

"Before the cross is removed," explained Pedro, "brush that has been blessed by the *padre* is placed around the cave and along the path to the river." This is lighted and kept burning while the cross is away. Pedro was not sure as to the exact purpose of the fire. He thought perhaps it was to keep the devil in confinement in the absence of the cross.

We left the home of Pedro, for we felt that to remain longer would be an intrusion. At dusk we looked toward the Mount of the Holy Cross. A tiny spark appeared at the notch; then sparks at intervals from the summit to the very river. Then flames shot up, and one imagined a great fiery serpent crawling out of the river and over the mountains. Then *mujeres* and *jovenes* began coming with birdlike step and entering the houses. From the street, we could catch a melody chanted in high nasal tones. A few words in the refrain came to us through the twilight; there were references to *"el diablo"* and *"la Santa Cruz."*

The cross itself is seldom brought across the river into Presidio these days; and since we did not visit Ojinaga, we did not see it. One respects the childlike faith of these simple people and does not intrude upon their worship.

The origin of the legend of the Devil's Grotto is fairly obvious. The early missionaries attempted to phrase the message of the church in terms which the Indians could comprehend. They did this to such an extent that one student of Mexican culture declares that in Mexico "the great mass of professing Catholics have retained in large part their primitive worship. . . . Mexico's patron saint, the Virgin of Guadalupe, owing its origin to an humble Indian who with difficulty persuaded the ecclesiastical authorities to accept the accounts of his 'vision,' is naught else but a slightly transformed Aztec deity, Tonantzin, patron of the local tribe of Totonaqui Indians, their goddess of earth and corn. Throughout, many native deities were similarly transmuted into Catholic saints."[2]

When we consider this further fact that the combat is supposed to have taken place on May 3, Holy Cross Day, it is not difficult to imagine some early missionary attempting to give content and significance to an occasion that without some such local legend would have meant little more than an empty ceremony.

Presidio now has an excellent highway. It hopes to have a railroad before a great while. It also has a high school in which United States history and the *Literary Digest* are studied. One wonders about the future of the custom. Already some of the youngsters doubt the truth of the legend; and one notices that the ceremonies are carried on largely by the old men and the women. To others the occasion is only a holiday. Will the Mexicans of the border forget the lore of their fathers, or will they learn a lesson from the Indians of the United States and perform their rites for the entertainment of the tourist and for the emolument of themselves?

4

THE PENITENT BROTHERS

Charles F. Lummis

This article, written by Charles F. Lummis in 1889, shows us something of the passion often attached to discussion of *Penitentes.* A subject surrounded with mystique and gross misunderstanding even today, the *Penitentes* evidently were, in fact, founded as an order by the Franciscans in Spain in the sixteenth century and transmitted to the New World by the Spaniards on their early incursions into Mexico. The "Third Order of the Franciscans" as the Brethren were once known, would never have recognized the aberration which the order became first in northwest Mexico and later in New Mexico. Originally dedicated to penance through fasting, prayer, and introspection, the Penitent Brothers were transmuted into what one might call the whipping boys of the Church in the Southwest. It is evident that the basic reason for the radical change in the Order's purpose arose out of a frontier situation where the extreme hardships lived on a day-to-day basis made the typical penances of fasting and prayer no penance indeed. Therefore, in response to the isolation felt in the early society of the Southwest, penance—of necessity—became more harsh, emulating the infamous autoflagellation craze which spread across Europe during the Middle Ages. The Church never condoned the extremes practiced by the *Penitentes* and, indeed, attempted to bring the practice to a halt—with little, if any, success until the latter part of the nineteenth century.

In this article and in other writings Lummis graphically and emotionally describes the practices of self-whipping, crucifixion, and other acts of autosacrifice. He was the first—at some danger to himself—ever to photograph any of the practices of the *Penitentes,* and certainly provides us with the keenest insight into the Brethren as they existed in the 1880s in New Mexico.

Lummis was overly optimistic when he stated that "the anachronism is fast dying out," for certainly the Order exists today, although in a greatly altered and softened form—especially since the *Penitentes'* reconciliation with the Church. The editors, however, have specific knowledge of scourging and other acts of auto-torture/penance being performed near Las Vegas, New Mexico, as late as the early 1950s. A form of crucifixion also purportedly still existed into the late 1950s in the same area, but we do not have any firsthand knowledge of the latter case. There can be little doubt, of course, that to one extent or another, in small and isolated areas and instances, the Penitent Brothers do, in fact, carry on the dramatic traditions of their faith.

"Until recent times the practice of self-flagellation (as a religious custom) continued to manifest itself intermittently in the south of France, and also in Italy and Spain; and so late as 1820 a procession of flagellants took place at Lisbon."

So the *Encyclopaedia Britannica* winds up what purports to be an outline of the history of self-whipping as a means of grace.

Aye, verily, venerable oracle! And so late as 1888 a procession of flagellants took place within the limits of the United States,—a procession in which voters of this Republic shredded their naked backs with savage whips, staggered under the weight of huge crosses, and hugged the maddening needles of the cactus; a procession which culminated in the flesh-and-blood crucifixion of an unworthy representative of the Redeemer!

The order of *Los Hermanos Penitentes* (The Penitent Brothers) was founded in Spain some three hundred years ago. It had nothing of the scourge in its original plan. Its members met for religious study and conversation, and were men of good morals and good sense, "according to their lights." The seeds of the order were brought to Mexico, and later to what is now New Mexico, by the Franciscan friars with the Spanish *conquistadores*.[1] Just when and how the devolution took place, how the flagellant branch was grafted upon the *Penitente* stem, I have been unable to learn; but it was probably after the order had taken root among the brave but ignorant and fanatic people who sprang from Spain's contribution to the New World. At all events, it is certain that for over a century there has been in New Mexico an order of *Penitentes* whose creed was founded upon the whip and the cross as instruments of penance. Up to within a decade the order in this Territory numbered several thousands, with fraternities in towns of every county. Their strongholds were in Taos, Mora, and Rio Arriba counties, where ten years ago they had respectively a membership of five hundred, three hundred, and one thousand. Los Griegos, a hamlet just below Albuquerque, was also a particular hotbed of them; and many dwelt in the fastnesses of the Sandia Mountains. In 1867, as I learn from church records, there were nine hundred *Penitentes*[2] within a radius of ten miles of the little town of Taos.

Each town had its independent fraternity, ruled by an *Hermano*

Mayor (Chief Brother), who was elected annually by his fellows. He had no superior, and was not even obliged to hold counsel with the neighboring *hermanos mayores*. In scores of lonely cañons throughout the Territory, the traveler may see to this day the deserted, low, stone houses, with huge, rude crosses leaning in slow decay against their walls—mute tokens of the bloody rites which the surrounding hills used to witness.

The order was too strong in early days to be excommunicated at one fell swoop; and the Catholic Church—to which all the *Penitentes* claim allegiance—went at the work with prudent deliberation, lopping off a head here and a head there in a leisurely way, which carried its full lesson without provoking rebellion. The policy has been a successful one. Town after town has abandoned its Holy Week "celebrations," fraternity after fraternity has melted away to nothingness. In the year 1888 but three villages in the Territory had *Penitente* processions; and only one—San Mateo, in the western end of Valencia County—enjoyed a crucifixion.

Lent is the sole season of *Penitente* activity. During the rest of the year their religion is allowed to lapse, and the Brothers placidly follow their various vocations as laborers, cowboys, or shepherds. With the beginning of the sacred forty days, however, they enter upon their sacrificial duties. Every Friday night in Lent, the belated wayfarer among the interior ranges is liable to be startled by the hideous *too-ootle-te-oo* of an unearthly whistle which shrills over and over one plaintive refrain.

As the midnight wind sweeps down the lonely cañon, that weird sound seems the wail of a tortured soul. I have known men of approved bravery to flee from that noise when they heard it for the first time. A simple air on a fife made of the *cerisos* seems a mild enough matter in the reading; but its wild shriek, which can be heard for miles, carries an indescribable and uncanny terror with it. The oldest inhabitant crosses himself and looks askance when that sound floats out to him from the mountain gorges.

If the hearer have the courage of his curiosity and will *explore* the sound, his eyes will share the astonishment and consternation of his ears. Let him cautiously stalk his game, and he may view a sight which might grace a niche in Dante's ghastly gallery. Ahead, a tall *pitero,* torturing that unearthly unharmony from his rude reed *pito,* and recognizable as the leading musician of a neighboring village: a few rods behind, two other natives bearing lanterns before the feet of the astounding figure which follows them—a head loosely hidden in a black bag like that which the hangman puts upon his victim; a body naked to the waist, and clothed below with no more than a pair of flapping linen drawers, now wet with red; bare feet, purple with the cruel cold of a New Mexican March, yet not too frozen to bleed in slow response to the frozen rocks; and arms swinging mechanically up at each step and bringing a broad, plaited whip down upon the macerated back with a heavy *swash!* A few rods more to the rear comes another man, in the same fantastic undress, but without the whip. He staggers under an enormous cross, its rear end crunching on the rocks and snow twenty feet or more behind, its weight five times that of its bearer. And slowly, painfully, with bleeding backs and feet and freezing bodies, the self-made martyrs with their solemn attendants file past the trembling watcher and disappear among the querulous pines, through whose arches the tootle of the fife floats fitfully back.

Each Friday night of Lent these strange specters flit through the loneliest mountain gorges, until Holy Week; and then the whipping goes on nightly—but still in privacy. It is not until Holy Thursday that the scattered knots of fanatics come together in some spot where they have a *morada* (brotherhood house), and do their penance by daylight, where the curious may see without danger to life or limb.

The hamlet of San Mateo—a straggling procession of brown adobes at the very foot of the mesa foundation of Mount Taylor, at an altitude of nearly eight thousand feet—contains four hundred people. It is perhaps the most unreclaimed Mexican village in New Mexico. Not half a dozen of its people speak the language of the United States. A little over a year ago a witch was stoned to death there, who had played the cynical trick of turning an estimable citizen into a woman for the space of three months! Numerous other inhabitants have suffered—though none else so severely—at the hands of witches; and several in the town have seen and held converse with his Satanic Majesty! Little wonder, then, that the dwindling *Penitentes* have still kept a foothold there, or that the population is in awed and active sympathy with their brutalities.

Half a mile along the crazy road which wanders up into the cañon, whose clear rivulet is the life of the people, stands the rude little log-built mill, its big, overshot wheel taking impulse from a monster spout of pine; its grumbling stones chewing the plump wheat into a brown, nutritous flour; its madonna-faced mistress divided between the falling grist and her toddling babe. Across the road a couple of hundred yards distant, backed up against a rocky bluff, the *morada*'s gloomy walls glower down upon the pretty scene. It is a low, rude hut of stone, some forty by fifteen feet in exterior dimensions, with one door, two small windows, and two rooms divided by a narrow hallway. The rough walls are unchinked, the floor is of earth. There are neither chairs, benches, tables, nor beds—nothing but two of the quaint New Mexico corner fireplaces; and a few pegs in the wall, from which depend the whips, stained and stiff with dry blood. Against the outer walls lean four rude crosses. The largest is twenty-five feet long, and weighs close upon eight hundred pounds; the smallest two hundred. A few hundred yards down the cañon, a sugar-loaf hillock, known as *El Calvario,* elbows the road. Upon its top stands another large cross—the scene of former crucifixions.

I had been watching feverishly for Holy Week to come. No photographer had ever caught the *Penitentes* with his sun-lasso, and I was assured of death in various unattractive forms at the first hint of an attempt. But when the ululation of the *pito* filled the ear at night, enthusiasm crowded prudence to the wall. The village air grew heavy with mysterious whisperings and solemn expectancy. Whatever they talked about, the people were evidently thinking of nothing else. I wandered through fields and arroyos at all hours of night, trying to trail that mysterious whistle whose echoes seemed to come from all points of the compass; but in vain. My utmost reward was a glimpse of three ghostly figures just disappearing inside Juanito's house on the hill.

But at last the 29th of March came around, and with it Holy Thursday. At nine A.M. the shrilling of the *pito* close at hand called us out of the house in haste; but already the three responsible *Penitentes* had vanished in the tall chaparral. We greased the rattling buckboard, and hurried over to the village. Every one was out, but they were no longer the friendly *paisanos* we had known. The sight of the camera box and tripod provoked ominous scowls and mutterings on every hand. Nine-tenths of the population were clustered in close, listless groups along a little wart of houses upon a hill which overhangs the *campo santo* (burying ground), at the upper end of town. Squatting with backs against the 'dobe walls, the men rolled cigarettes from corn-husks or brown paper, and talked intermittently. The women nursed their babes unconstrainedly, and rolled brown-paper or corn-husk cigarettes. I stowed the obnoxious instrument inside a friendly house, and waited. Waiting seems natural in a Mexican town. The minutes loafed into hours; and still the talking, the nursing, the smoking went on. Nobody thought of moving.

It was two P.M. when a stir in the crowd on the hill-top told us that it was coming at last; and the camera was straightway planted behind the adobe ramparts of the door-yard. In five minutes more a fifer came over the ridge, followed by five women singing hymns; and behind them a half-naked figure with bagged head, swinging his deliberate whip, whose *swish, thud! swish, thud!* we could hear plainly two hundred yards away, punctuating the weird music. In measured step the pilgrims paced along the reeling footpath and disappeared around a spur toward the *morada.* Half an hour later the fife again asserted itself up the cañon and soon reappeared with its persecutor, the singing women, and the lone self-torturer. As he passed on to the graveyard, we saw that little red rivulets were beginning to stain the white of his *calzoncillos.*

I hurried to the hill-top, to get near enough for a "shot"; but the mob, hitherto only scowling, was now openly hostile, and I would have fared ill but for the prompt action of Don Ireneo Chaves, whose reckless bravery—a proverb in all that country of brave men—none cared to provoke. With two stanch, well-armed friends, he held back the evil-faced mob, while the "forty" plates were being snapped at the strange scene below.

Suddenly another fifer came over the hill, followed by more women and seven *Penitentes.* Of the latter, four were whipping themselves, and three staggered under crosses of crushing weight. Slowly and solemnly they strode down the slope to the stone-walled graveyard, filed through the roofed entrance, whipped themselves throughout all the paths, knelt in prayer at each grave, kissed the foot of the central board cross, and filed out again. These services lasted twenty minutes. The foremost cross-carrier, after leaving the graveyard a few rods behind, fell face down under his fearful load, and lay there with the great cross-arm resting upon his neck. One of the *Hermanos de Luz* (Brothers of Light, who do not castigate themselves, but act as attendants upon those who do) took a whip and gave him fifty resounding blows on the bare back. Then two *ayudantes* lifted him to his feet, laid the great timbers upon his neck, and steadied the ends as he tottered onward. Once he was about to sink again, but they revived him with emphatic kicks. So the ghastly procession crept thrice from *morada* to *campo santo* and back.

At seven o'clock that night the fanatic band came marching down to the hospitable house of Col. Manuel Chaves, the most extraordinary Indian fighter New Mexico ever produced. A little family chapel stands a few rods from the house, behind two sturdy oaks, in whose never-forgotten shade Col. Chaves rested one awful day fifty-six years ago, when, sieved by seven Navajo arrows, he was crawling his bloody one hundred and fifty miles homeward to Ceballeta. Hither the procession turned. There were now five *Hermanos Disciplinantes,* but only one of them was using his whip—a short, youthful-seeming fellow of beautiful muscular development. Kneeling in turn and kissing the rude cross that leaned against one of the trees, each one waddled on his knees into the chapel and up to the altar, where all remained kneeling. Back of them were two-score women on their knees, while a dozen men stood reverently along the wall. The *Hermano Mayor,* José Salazar—a small, amiable-looking shrivel—raised his cracked voice in a hymn; and the audience followed, in the nasal drawl so dear to native New Mexican singers. It was an impressive sight—the little adobe room, whose flaring candles struggled vainly with the vagrant shadows; the altar bright with chromos of the saints, a plaster image of the Holy Mother dressed in tulle and wreaths of paper flowers; the black-capped, bare-backed five before the altar; and the awe-struck crowd behind—as they sang over and over, with intense feeling, if with scant harmony,

Las Columnas

En una columna atado
  Hallarás al Rey del Cielo,
Herido y ensangrentado
  Y arrastrado por el suelo.

En agriesta disciplina,
  Si lo quieres aliviar,
Llega, alma, á desagrabiar
  A la Paloma Divina.

Ay, Jesus! Ay, mi dulce dueño,
  Desagrabiar te queremos.
Recibe, poder amoroso,
  Las flores de este misterio.

Then, at a signal from the *Hermano Mayor,* the penitent five fell prone upon their faces, with arms stretched at full length beyond their heads; and thus they lay, motionless as death, for three-quarters of an hour, while the singing, with its fife accompaniment, still went on.

The services over, the *Penitentes* filed over to the house for supper—which dare not be refused them, even in that cultivated family. The *Hermanos de Luz* had already effectually blinded the windows; and the five active members, filing into the room, locked the door and plugged the keyhole before they dared remove their head-masks to eat.

This care to keep their identity secret is probably observed out of a fear for the Church, mingled with a desire to mystify the public. Still, the sympathizing villagers know pretty surely who each one is.

No one was allowed in the dining-room save the five self-whippers; and now came my golden opportunity. Metaphorically collaring the *Hermano Mayor,* the *Hermanos de Luz,* and the *pitero,* I dragged them to my room, overwhelmed them with cigars and other attentions, showed and gave them pictures of familiar scenes—a Mexican finds it hard to resist a picture—and cultivated their good graces in all conceivable ways. And when the Brothers of the Whip had supped, re-masked themselves and emerged, the Chief Brother and the Brothers of Light were mine.

On the morning of Good Friday, March 30, I was in the village bright and early; and so was every one else for twenty miles around. At ten o'clock the Mexican schoolmaster and another prominent citizen started up the cañon with me, helping to "pack" my *impedimenta.* Coming to a point in the road opposite the *morada,* they sat down, refusing to go nearer, and I had to carry the load alone to a hillock a couple of hundred feet southeast of the house, where I set up the camera.

Soon the procession hove in sight, coming from town. Ahead strode the fifer, proudly fingering his diabolical instrument; then came two *hermano*s with crosses, and another whipping himself, with half a dozen *Hermanos de Luz* attending them; then shriveled old Jesus Mirabal reading prayers aloud; and behind him fifty-one women and children, falling down on their knees in the dust-deep road at every fifty feet or so to pray, and singing hymns as they walked between prayers. They bore a large crucifix with the figure of the Redeemer—strange to say, dressed in a linen gown—a plaster image of the Holy Virgin, and numerous framed chromos of the saints. Tallest among the women was the Mexican wife of the Presbyterian missionary then stationed at San Mateo—a cynical commentary on our mission work.

Reaching the *morada* in their deliberate march, the *Penitentes* laid down their crosses and went inside; the women knelt on the ground before the door and kept up their singing and praying, while the Brothers of Light strode here and there with airs of great responsibility, until presently the procession was renewed and I marched beside it to dinner.

Now there were three Brothers using the lash and two carrying crosses; while two more strode unconcernedly along, each with a burro-load of *entraña* (buckhorn cactus) lashed upon his naked back. The *entraña* is one of the most depraved of all its diabolical family. Its spines are long, slenderer and sharper than the sharpest needle, yet firm enough to penetrate any ordinary boot. Get one *entraña* needle into the hide of a steer, and the maddened animal will gallop bellowing over the landscape till it falls from exhaustion. Yet these two fanatics wore huge bundles of it, held on by half-inch hempen ropes drawn so tightly about chest and arms and waist that they cut the skin and stopped the circulation; each must have had thousands of the thorns burrowing into his flesh, but he gave no sign. There was no sham about it. Don Ireneo cut a big *entraña* antler from beside the road, and threw it upon one of them as he passed. The cruel needles pierced his shoulder so deeply that the heavy branch *hung* there, yet he never winced nor turned his head! At the foot of Calvary the procession stopped, while the two men with crosses prostrated themselves in the dust—the crosses being placed upon their backs—and lay thus for ten minutes, the fife and the singers keeping up their discord the while. Every hour of the day these pilgrimages were made between the *campo santo* and the *morada*—a full third of a mile each way.

Shortly before two o'clock the women returned from town, "making the stations," and halted in front of the *morada*. Juan Baca brought forth the camera, and the *Hermano Mayor* marked a spot about one hundred feet from the door where I might stand. Then he called the Brothers from the house and formed the procession—the cross-bearers in front, then the Brothers of the Whip, and then the Brothers of Light and the women. " 'Sta bueno?" he asked through Juan; and when I replied that it was, he gave orders that no man should stir a finger until the pictures were taken. This ordeal over, the *Penitentes* retired again inside the *morada*; the women started on a fresh pilgrimage.

Meantime other *Hermanos de Luz* had burrowed out a deep hole some fifty feet in front of the *morada,* and laid the largest cross with its foot at the edge of the hole. The procession of women had returned and stood solemnly in front of the hundreds of spectators. And now the *Hermano Mayor* went inside with two of his assistants. In a few moments they emerged leading the allotted victim—a stalwart young fellow dressed only in his white drawers and black head-bag. As we learned later, it was Santiago Jaramillo—known also as "Santiago Jeems"—the cook at the house of Don Roman A. Baca, one of the sheep-kings of the Territory. In his right side was a gaping gash four inches long, from which the blood ran down in a steady stream to the ground. He walked firmly, however, to the prostrate cross and laid himself at full length upon it. A long, new, half-inch rope was brought, and the *Hermanos de Luz* began to lash him to the great timbers, placing the stiff hemp around his arms, trunk and legs in three or four loops each, and "cinching-up" the slack was roughly as they would upon a pack-mule. But now he was sobbing like a child. *"Hay! Que estoy deshonrado!* Not with a rope! Not with a rope! Nail me! Nail me!"

But the *Hermano Mayor* was obdurate. Always before, up to this very year, the victim had been spiked to the cross by great nails through hands and feet; and the death of a *Penitente* in process of crucifixion was by no means rare. In the single year of 1887, four young men perished thus in the *Penitente* settlements of southern Colorado. But the new *Hermano Mayor* refused nails, despite the appeals of the victim not to be dishonored by a lighter agony. He fared badly enough as it was. The stiff rope sank deep into his flesh, prohibiting the throbbing blood. In less than three minutes his legs and arms were black as a Hottentot's. A clean white sheet was now wound about him from head to foot, and tied there, leaving exposed only his purpling arms and muffled head. This was done, so one of the assistants explained to me, that no sharp-eyed bystander might recognize him by scars on his body. Now the rope was knotted to the arms of the cross, so that each end hung free and about thirty feet long. Two stalwart Brothers of Light grasped each rope; four others seized the cross; and heavily they lifted it so near to perpendicularity that the lower end dropped into the four-foot hole with an ugly *chug!* But its living burden made no sign. With shovels and hands the *ayudantes* filled in the hole with earth and rocks, and tamped it down, while Filomeno and Cisto steadied their respective guy-ropes.

A large rock was next placed some five feet from the foot of the cross; and another *Penitente* in cotton drawers and head-bag was led out, with a huge stack of cactus so tightly lashed upon his back that he could not move his arms at all, and scarcely his legs. He lay down with his feet against the foot of the cross and his head pillowed upon the stone, while the mass of *entraña* kept his back sixteen or eighteen inches above the ground. Even this was not a tight enough fit to suit him, and he had a large, flat stone brought and crowded under the cactus, so as to press it still more cruelly against his back.

Meantime, in gracious response to my request, the *Hermano Mayor* had paced off thirty feet from the foot of the cross and marked a spot to which I might advance in order to get a larger picture. And there we stood facing each other, the crucified and I—the one playing with the most wonderful toy of modern progress, the other racked by the most barbarious device of nineteen hundred years ago. What ambitious amateur ever dreamed of focusing on such a sight before?

For thirty-one minutes by the watch the poor wretch upon the cross and he upon the bed of thorns kept their places. A deathly hush was upon the crowd. Even the unwilling *pito* was still. The mill-stream split its music upon the rough old wheel, now locked and unresponsive. The fresh breeze rustled among the piñons on the steep mountainside, a few rods away. The undimmed afternoon sun flooded the rugged cañon with strange glory. Across the brook a chubby prairie dog, statuesquely perpendicular, watched the ghastly scene and barked his creaking disapprobation—the only animate sound that reach the ear.

Near the cross stood the old *Hermano Mayor,* and beside him Manuel, Juan, Filomeno, "Cuate," Cisto, Melito. Each had a narrow fillet of wild-rose branches bound tightly around his skull. Coming nearer, I saw that the claw-like thorns were forced deep into the skin, and that little crimson beads stood out upon each forehead.

At last the Chief Brother spoke a quiet word. The assistants scooped out the earth from the hole, lifted the cross from its socket, and laid it upon the ground again. The crucified was relieved of his lashings, was lifted to his feet and carried to the *morada*—a stout *paisano* under each shoulder, while his feet made feeble feint of moving. His brother victim was similarly taken in with his worse than Nessus robe; and the procession re-formed for its awful pilgrimages, which were kept up regularly until six o'clock, by which time their *calzoncillos* were wet behind with blood to the very ankles. An *Hermano de Luz* carried a tin pail containing a decoction of *romero;* and every two or three minutes dipped the ends of the "whips" in this, to give them an added sting.

These whips are about three and a half feet long, and weigh two or three pounds when thus wet. They are made of the tough fibers of the *palmilla,* or soapweed. The handle is braided; the lash, a couple of feet long and three to five inches across, is left to bristle like the tail of a horse. This is the "discipline of penance." To punish erring members they have the "discipline of castigation"—a hideous cat-o'-nine-tails made of wire, with the ends turned up claw-fashion, so that every blow ravishes from the back its tiny morsels of flesh.

As we passed Calvary again, a new horror was added. The *Hermano Mayor* came up behind each of the seven self-tortured, and with a flint-knife gashed their backs thrice across and then "cross-hatched" them thrice up and down. These were no mere scratches, but long, bleeding cuts—the yearly-renewed seal of the order.

At eight o'clock in the evening the procession came down again from the *morada*—this time marching the length of the town to hold *tinieblas* (dark services) in the little chapel next to the house of Don Lorenzo Sanchez. The *Penitentes* went inside and barred the door on the crowd. There were no lights within, and the windows were carefully masked. All that came to the shivering audience outside was the clanking of chains and muffled blows, and groans and shrieks. These services—which are designed to represent the arrival of the soul in Purgatory—lasted an hour. Then the *Penitentes* emerged, carrying one of their number in a blanket held by the corners. We learned afterward that for fifteen minutes he had hugged a stake wrapped with cactus, and had succumbed to this fresh torture. Around his unconscious form plodded seven women, weeping bitterly but low. Not one but feared it was her own husband, and not all that long night would her suspense be relieved. The poor wretch lay long at death's door, but finally recovered.

One short, stocky fellow who had been particularly zealous in his blows all day, and who had lain upon the thorns at the foot of the cross, attracted my particular attention; and walking back the third of a mile from the chapel to the plaza I kept at his side and counted the blows he gave himself—*two hundred and fifty-one!* During the day he had achieved over two thousand—and Heaven only knows how many before—but next day he was at work with his irrigating hoe! He is a young man, Antonito Montaño by name, and not easy of suppression. A mule once caved in his face, and a soldier in a drunken quarrel gave him grounds for being trepanned; but he is still keen to enjoy such tortures as the most brutal prize-fighter never dreamed of.

At midnight of Good Friday the *Penitentes* scattered from the *morada* toward their homes—in some cases forty miles away—to meet no more in a religious capacity until another Lent, or until the death of some Brother.

By their incredible self-torture one would naturally suppose them to be the most God-fearing and devout of men; but this would be a serious error. There are among them good though deluded men, like *Hermano Mayor* Salazar, and "Cuate"; but the majority of them, and particularly of the Brothers of the Whip, are of the lowest and most dangerous class—petty larcenists by nature, horse-thieves and assassins upon opportunity—who by their devotions in Lent think to expiate the sins of the whole year.

The brotherhood, though broken, still holds the balance of political power. No one likes—and few dare—to offend these fanatics; and there have been men of liberal education who have joined them to gain political influence. Indeed, priests of ripe experience here have avowed to me their belief that the order has long been kept alive merely to further the ends of scheming men.[3]

Until very recently there were also female *Penitentes;* and only three years ago there dwelt in San Mateo fully ten women who whipped their bare backs, wore cactus thorns in their loose shoes, and wound their legs with rope and wire till the blood stopped—practices which still obtain among the men. Other common forms of penance are to lie down in front of the church door and request worshipers to trample upon them and kick them; or to crawl on hands and knees along a path paved with cactus.

The *Penitentes* have a book of rules, but it is impossible for an outsider to get hold of a copy. Some of their laws are well known, however. One of their most curious customs is that regarding burial. When a Brother falls sick, he is removed to the *morada* and cared for by members appointed by the *Hermano Mayor,* no one else being permitted to see him. If he dies, the Brothers wrap him naked in a blanket and secretly bury him an hour after midnight, feet downward, in a hole in some secluded spot. His clothes are then left at his home—the first and final token his family has of his decease, and perhaps even of his sickness. No married man, by the way, is allowed to join the order without the consent of his wife.

5

ALVAR NUÑEZ CABEZA DE VACA

The First Overland Traveler of European Descent, and His Journey from Florida to the Pacific Coast—1528–1536

Adolph F. Bandelier

In the 1880s the great natural historian Adolph F. Bandelier published several papers on the early Spanish penetration into the Southwest. Bandelier had become interested in the initial Spanish exploration of New Mexico and Arizona as early as 1880 (Lange and Riley, 1966, pp. 23–26) and a visit to Frank Cushing at Zuñi in 1884 added greatly to his interest, especially in the Coronado group—Marcos de Niza and the black adventurer, Esteban (Lange and Riley, 1970, pp. 47, 50).

Bandelier was by the mid-1880s deeply involved in writing up the results of his archival studies and in-person investigations of Southwestern Indians and archaeological sites. This field and archival work would mainly appear in the two-volume *Final Report* (1890 and 1892) and in the manuscript "Histoire de la Colonisation et de missions de Sonora, Chihuahua, Nouveau-Mexique et Arizona jusqu'á l'année 1700" sent to the Vatican in 1887 and lost for many years. Father Ernest J. Burrus discovered the "Histoire" manuscript in 1964 and, parenthetically, began publication of it in an English translation in 1969. The short articles and the longer *Outline of the Documentary History of the Zuni Tribe,* should all be viewed in the larger context of these major works.

Adolph Bandelier's paper on Cabeza de Vaca, published in 1886, shows Bandelier at his scholarly best. Drawing on a variety of sources and especially utilizing the Oviedo account as well as the surviving Vaca *Naufragios,* Bandelier makes a good case for the Vaca party swinging south of both New Mexico and Arizona. Although later work by Sauer (1932) and especially by Hallenbeck (1939) made an opposite case, putting the route of the party far to the north, scholarly opinion, though still divided, seems to be swinging back to a belief in the more southerly route. Bandelier makes the case for this with great restraint and caution and his arguments hold up well today.

One question about Vaca's later life asked by Bandelier can be answered today. It now seems clear that Vaca's imprisonment in Paraguay was indeed unjust and rose from his attempts to protect the Indians of that area from exploitation by the Spanish settlers.

A biography of Cabeza de Vaca is easily condensed into a few paragraphs. I have been unable to find the year of his birth and equally unsuccessful in tracing the date of his demise. The latter, however, took place after 1565, and possibly at Sevilla in Spain.[1] The original name of his family was Alhaja, but was changed to Cabeza de Vaca in A.D. 1212. The family belonged to the Andalusian nobility (conferred upon them after the battle of las Navas de Tolosa—twelfth of June, 1212), and lived at Xerez.[2] He went to the Indies as treasurer and alguazil major of the expedition of Panfilo de Narvaez, of which ill-fated body he, two other Spaniards, and a Negro were sole survivors. With these associates, he performed the almost incredible feat of crossing from Florida to the state of Sonora in Mexico. After his return to Spain in 1837, he was made governor of Paraguay, or rather *Adelantado* (commander of an expedition for conquest and settlement), and remained in South America until 1544, when he was arrested and brought to Spain as a prisoner. Thereafter Cabeza de Vaca disappears from history; it is impossible to determine whether his arrest and imprisonment were just or not.

That remarkable overland trip, executed on foot and under the most distressing circumstances, forms the subject of this sketch. Cabeza de Vaca is commonly credited with having discovered New Mexico, but this is an error, though a widely circulated one.

The sad tale of Narvaez's disasters has often been told. Misfortunes befell him from the day he left San Lucar de Barrameda in Spain (17–29 June 1527).[3] They culminated in the destruction of his fleet, in his own death, in the gradual extermination of his men, except four, Alvar Nuñez Cabeza de Vaca, Alonso del Castillo Maldonado of Salamanca, Andrés Dorantes of Béjar, and Estevanico, an Arabian Negro of Azamor. These four men, after six years of separation, met on the coast of eastern Texas.[4] They had been prisoners of various roving tribes, by whom they had been dragged hither and thither, sometimes inland, sometimes along the coast. Their captors rarely showed any consideration; on the contrary, they ill-treated the wretched Spaniards until Cabeza de Vaca, having observed the methods employed by Indians for healing and curing, and urged by the same Indians to become a medicine-man, began to apply his scanty knowledge of medicine and surgery with considerable success. He also became a peddler, penetrating into the interior and along the coast as far as one hundred to one hundred and fifty miles, exchanging shells and shell beads for skins, red earth, flint flakes and other products of northern countries. He reached the vicinity of Red River, south of Shreveport, but always returned to the coast again in hopes of meeting some companions of misfortune.[5]

When the four unfortunates at last came together, they were naked like their Indian masters, their bodies were emaciated, bruised and torn. But they had acquired a great store of practical knowledge about the country and its inhabitants, and the practice of medicine seemed—for one of them at least—unusual prestige among the natives. Communicating to each other what they had seen and learned, they reached the conclusion that, in order to extricate themselves from their forlorn condition, it was best to improve the hold which success in healing and curing furnished, and thus induce the Indians to gradually lead them where people of their own race might be met with. To the stormy waters of the Gulf, which had swallowed their ships as well as the frail boats and rafts hastily constructed on the coast of Florida, they did not dare to entrust themselves. Besides, the Indians would not have suffered them to escape in that direction. Their only hope, therefore, lay in the west. They knew that expeditions from Mexico reached the Rio Panuco and the Pacific coast. By shifting slowly from one Indian tribe to another, always proceeding in a westerly direction as much as possible, countries might at last be reached into which other Spaniards penetrated, or whose inhabitants had knowledge of Spanish settlements.

In the course of ten months[6] this adventurous plan was carried out, and on the 1–12 of May, 1536, Cabeza de Vaca and associates reached San Miguel de Culiacan, in Sinaloa.[7] They had traveled as successful medicine men from tribe to tribe. Their cures were attributed by themselves to miracle, since they accompanied them with prayers, and made the sign of the cross over invalids. Whatever may be thought of this explanation, it is given sincerely by the wanderers. Unacquainted with the art of healing, driven to practice it by urgings, threats, and even violence of savages who controlled their lives, the Spaniards had consented with fear and trembling, and when, against their own hopes, success attended the first cases, it was but natural to attribute such unexpected results to miraculous intervention of divine power. What sort of treatment they adopted can be inferred from what knowledge they confess to of the practices of medicine-men among Indians, consequently of curative herbs also. To this they added Catholic prayers and empirical facts, such as any person at the age of reason is likely to possess. Armed with the Indian sorcerer's favorite rattle, performing the sign of the cross and orations in Latin, they represented a grotesque compound of the medicine-man and of the missionary.[8] But their success was such that they acquired full ascendancy over the savages, and they improved it, not for purposes of lust and greed, but in order to prevail upon the natives to guide them as swiftly as possible and as directly as possible "toward sunset."

It is not the wanderer's sufferings and woes, neither is it the adventurous cast of the whole journey which attracts our attention here; it is the small cluster of facts, topographical, botanical, zoological, and ethnographical, gathered, and subsequently recorded, by Cabeza de Vaca and his friends. These data are necessarily meagre, still they enable us to trace the line of march which the travelers must have followed. That line of march led them, not as has commonly been admitted, through any part of New Mexico, but considerably south of it through southern Texas and central Chihuahua into Sonora; thence south into Sinaloa.

Until now, investigations of the trip of Cabeza de Vaca have been founded upon his book, published at Valladolid in 1555, under the title of *Naufragios, y Relación de la Jornada que hizo à la Florida*.[9] Accessory information was gathered from the contemporary work of Gomara and from Herrera's great and reliable compilation. Another contemporary of Cabeza de Vaca, and one who was personally acquainted with him, has, in the meantime, been overlooked. This is Gonzalo Fernandez de Oviedo y Valdés. His voluminous *Historia general y natural de Indias* contains an almost literal copy of a report which Cabeza de Vaca, Castillo, and Dorantes jointly made to the Royal Audiencia of Santo Domingo, besides notice of an interview which Oviedo had with the first one at Madrid, and a critical comparison of the two writings.[10] It appears that the joint report was never printed, although this, and not the *Naufragios* is the proper official document. Still there is little discrepancy between the two. They corroborate each other in all important topics, and differ merely in subordinate matters.

While Narvaez evidently landed on the western coast of Florida, and the majority of his men perished around the Mississippi Delta at sea, or on the shores west of it, only the mouths of the great rivers are mentioned.[11] Their most unhappy days were spent in a quadrangle, bounded by the Gulf on the south, the Mississippi on the east, Red River on the north, and Trinity River on the west. West of Sabine River they started on their long peregrination in August, 1535,[12] heading as directly as possible for the west.

They had acquired such influence over the Indians that the latter, even sometimes against their own inclinations, guided the Christians almost constantly toward *sunset*.[13] Still they kept at no great distance from the coast, though with the intention of removing from it.[14] They traveled five days, crossing a river "wider than Guadalquivir at Sevilla," and quite deep.[15] This river was the Trinity. Three days' march west of this river they began to see mountains, one range of which seemed to sweep directly northward. One day further, or "five leagues further on," they reached another river, "at the foot of the point where the said mountains commenced."[16] That river was the Brazos and by "mountains" the hills of central Texas must be understood. Cabeza de Vaca says he estimated the distance of these "mountains" from the sea to be fifteen leagues (forty miles about). People from the coast came in one day to visit them.[17]

Here they changed their direction, and moved northwards along the base of a "mountain chain," and partly away from water-courses, eighty leagues according to the joint report—fifty according to Cabeza de Vaca. The last estimate is more likely, for the journey was painful and slow, and they experienced great scarcity of food as well as of water.[18] In this manner they reached the vicinity of Fort Graham. Here they changed their route, making towards sunset again.

Including lengthy stays among Indian hordes, our Spaniards consumed nearly two months in these wanderings, so that it was November when they began to move westward again. Guided by sunset and sunrise, they consequently followed a line *south* of west, it being now late in the fall. The further they advanced, the greater became that southerly deflection. They crossed the Colorado and finally struck a large river, to which they gave the name "Rio de las Vacas"[19] or, river of the cows, since the buffalo herds were said to roam more than fifty leagues up the river.[20] This is the last stream mentioned in either of the "relations." It was evidently the Rio Grande.

Here both reports become extraordinarily diffuse, although the joint narrative is less so than Cabeza de Vaca's book. Still, it is easily discernible that the Spaniards struck the Rio Grande *without crossing the Pecos,* therefore below or very near the latter's mouth. Refusing to go due north where the "cows" were, they followed the eastern bank for fifteen (the *Naufragios* have seventeen) days.[21] The mountains were to the north, and during this tramp they suffered much from hunger. At the end of fifteen, or of seventeen, days they crossed the river to the west. The distance from the mouth of the Pecos to Presidio del Norte (where the Rio Conchos empties into the Rio Grande) is about two hundred and fifty miles, a reasonable stretch for fifteen days of wearisome and difficult foot travel. I conclude, therefore, that they crossed the latter river about Fort Seaton. Thereafter their route lay towards sunset again, and no more water courses are mentioned.

At the end of seventeen days (says Cabeza de Vaca) they entered high mountains, and found people who lived in houses of sod and clay, as well as in huts of boughs and palm leaves.[22]

In a straight line, the eastern flank of the Sierra Madre of Chihuahua is scarcely two hundred miles from the mouth of Conchos. This distance increases if we take a more southerly deflection. At all events, it was easy for the four adventurers to reach the mountain-chain in the time specified. They traversed it for upwards of eighty leagues (two hundred and sixteen miles), and at last reached a valley which, owing to the fact that its inhabitants fed them on hearts of deer, was called by them *Valle de los Corazones* (Valley of the Hearts),[23] a name which, for some time thereafter, has been quite prominent in the history of colonization of the Pacific coast.

The valley of the *Corazones* lays south of Batuco, in the present state of Sonora. It was also north of the Yaqui River.[24] Consequently it belonged to what is called the lower Pimeria, and its inhabitants were Pima Indians. It was in a straight line, south of west of Presidio del Norte (or in the proper direction of sunset) and the distance, allowing for circuits and turns, which a very difficult mountain region would cause, agrees perfectly with the itinerary of Cabeza de Vaca and his followers. Here they found the first traces of Spanish intercourse, and henceforth turned to the south, almost reaching the Pacific coast. They kept at a distance of about thirty miles from it.[25] Near the confines of Sonora and Sinaloa, between the Yaqui and Mayo rivers, the wanderers at last met their first countrymen—Làzaro Cebreros and four soldiers.[26] Still their troubles did not end here, for Cebreros, as well as the Captain Diego Alcàraz, ill-treated them for a time, and it was only at Culiacan (where they arrived on the twelfth of May, 1536) that Melchior Diaz extended to the sufferers a hearty welcome, and bestowed upon them every attention which their long misfortune demanded.

If, now, we retrace our steps from the well-ascertained point of Culiacan, following the trail of Cabeza de Vaca as laid down by himself and his associates, we have to look for the valley of the "Hearts," one hundred leagues at least (two hundred and seventy miles) north of our point of departure. That distance leaves us north of the Rio Yaqui and south of Batuco, latitude twenty-eight degrees thirty minutes about, in Sonora. The first great river east of Sonora is the Rio Grande, next comes the Colorado in Texas, finally the Brazos. Cabeza de Vaca and his friends, traveling from east to west, crossed all the streams mentioned by them. Consequently, those streams ran from north to south on an average. Such a system of drainage flowing to the Gulf, west of the Mississippi, is found only in southern Texas. Therefore the Spanish adventurers remained in southern Texas until they reached the Rio Grande, and never entered the territory of New Mexico.

Once across the Rio Grande, they moved uniformly towards sunset, that is south of west. That course, instead of approaching New Mexico, carried them away from its southern borders.

The itineraries of the castaways contain references to plants of the regions traversed, and these references bear upon the route followed, inasmuch as they characterize vegetation. In the earlier part of the narratives, those which treat of the eastern sections, the coast and the swamp flora of Louisiana is sufficiently indicated.[27] Further on, on their westward journey, three of the most characteristic nutritive plants of the southwest are mentioned on various occasions. These are the Tuna, or prickly pear (*Opuntia*), the Mezquite (*Algarrobia glandulosa*), and in the hilly or mountainous districts of Texas, the Piñon (*Pinus edulis*).[28] West of central Texas, however, and along the Rio Grande, stress is laid in the fact that vegetation becomes scant and devoid of alimentary species. In the Sierra Madre palms are alluded to.[29] All these data corroborate the route which I have determined.

It is equally noteworthy that nowhere any mention is made of the great plain now called *Llano estacado,* which occupies southeastern New Mexico as well as northern Texas. Its extent, peculiar vegetation and great aridity could not fail to attract the attention of the travelers. Their Indian guides, however, kept far south of the desert, thus tracing a line of march through southern Texas at least one degree of latitude below the New Mexican boundary.

Had the adventurous Spaniards ever trod the soil of eastern or southern New Mexico, they would have come in contact with immense herds of buffaloes. They saw the great quadruped several times during the first six or seven years of their adventurous career. Cabeza de Vaca states that it occasionally reached the Gulf coast in Florida[30]—but so soon as they began to travel westward, the buffalo country remained always to the *north* of them, and at some distance.[31] Once across the river and in Chihuahua, they did not hear any more of the "hunchbacked cows."[32] To leave the buffalo grounds steadily in the north while traveling to the west meant striking across southern Texas exclusively, and to reach the Rio Grande at or below the mouth of the Pecos River.

Lastly, the narratives fairly teem with diffuse information about the inhabitants of the country. Unfortunately the names used in order to designate tribes and bands are such that we cannot determine anything from them. Out of eighteen or twenty names of "languages," not one can be identified as yet.[33] It is different, however, with the picture presented of the degree of culture and mode of life. This picture shows roving tribes without fixed abode, subsisting from fishing along the coast at certain periods of the year, scattering toward the interior during the seasons when certain wild fruits ripened. The weapons of these natives consisted of bows and of arrows tipped with fish bones, shell fragments, and with flint brought from the interior by exchange. Further westward the mode of life became less transitory, and as they approached the Rio Grande, while the population was more numerous, their excursions seemed to be confined to buffalo ranges, which invariably lay further north.[34] Beyond Texas in Chihuahua, Indians were as wild as east of it. It was only among the "high mountains," which I have identified as the Sierra Madre, that tribes were found who enjoyed more permanent abodes.

There, too, the Spaniards met with the first fields of maize or Indian corn;[35] neither in Louisiana nor in Texas, nor in Chihuahua, had they found any tribe which cultivated that great American staple. Beans were raised on the Rio Grande; otherwise vegetable food consisted of wild fruits, leaves, and roots exclusively.[36]

Neither did the inhabitants of the country use or make any *pottery*. Gourds supplied the want of ceramic utensils.[37] Had, now, Cabeza de Vaca and his companions touched any part of New Mexico, they could not have failed to meet corn-tilling and pottery-making aborigines, or to hear of them in a very definite manner, as also of the permanent abodes of the so-called Pueblos. Nothing of the sort is told or intimated. In central Texas, between the Brazos and Colorado, a copper rattle was given to them which, the Indians claimed, had been brought from the west, together with some cotton cloth.[38] The most southerly villages of New Mexican natives existed in the sixteenth century about San Marcial,[39] at least three hundred and fifty miles north-northwest of Presidio del Norte. Intercourse was difficult and slow; the tribes of central Texas seldom, if ever, came in contact with the Pueblos, and then only on buffalo hunts. It is not surprising, therefore, that the travelers heard nothing of countries and people so far distant, and it is certain that they never set their foot on New Mexican soil, as far as the territory is understood to extend at the present time.

The first houses of earth or sod which they saw were those in the Sierra Madre of Chihuahua. The locality or region is established by the statement that the people of these villages had parrot's feathers in such quantities that they traded them off further north in exchange for turquoises.[40] The green parrot is no inhabitant of either New Mexico or

Arizona. It dwells in the pine forests of the Sierra Madre; therefore south of the Mexican boundary. The Indians who inhabited these buildings belonged, evidently, to the Jovas, a linguistical branch of the Pimas of Sonora.[41] Like their congeners they had houses of sod or of large, coarse "adobes," as an exception, the *rule* being for them to live in huts of canes and palm leaves.[42] Such is also the description furnished by Cabeza de Vaca and his friends. Their joint narrative says: "And those Indians had a few small houses of earth, made of sod, with their flat roofs."[43] This style of architecture is widely different from the compact, many-storied Pueblo villages.

The people of these settlements informed Cabeza de Vaca that the parrot plumes which they owned were traded by them with tribes who, in the north, lived among high mountains.[44] This may be an allusion to the New Mexican village Indians, although it is not absolutely certain. Large houses of clay (and rubble) were inhabited by the Opatas also, in the northern Sierra Madre, and the many-storied *casa grande, casa blanca,* on the banks of the Gila River in Arizona were formerly Pima villages.[45]

Even if the information thus picked up and transmitted by Cabeza de Vaca should relate to New Mexico, it does not entitle him to the credit of being the discoverer of that country. Neither was his trip necessary for directing the attention of the Spaniards to the north. But it increased their desire to penetrate in that direction, and furnished a daring, although injudicious guide, in the person of the Negro Estevanico, to the subsequent discoverer of New Mexico and of the Pueblo Indians—Fray Marcos of Nizza.

6

FRAY JUAN DE PADILLA
The First Catholic Missionary and Martyr in Eastern Kansas. 1542.
Adolph F. Bandelier

The martyred Franciscan priest, Juan de Padilla, obviously caught the imagination of Adolph Bandelier who himself became a Catholic convert in 1881 (White and Bernal, 1960, pp. 248–49; Lange and Riley, 1970, p. 4).

Although this account of Padilla and the other friars with Coronado (published in 1890) is a valuable source document, there are certain modifications that are necessitated by subsequent research. From the careful reconstruction of Father Angelico Chavez (1968, pp. 64–81) it now seems clear that Coronado's missionaries (besides Father Marcos de Niza [Nizza] who left Zuñi in the fall of 1540) included Father Juan de la Cruz and lay brother Daniel the Italian who returned to Mexico with Marcos in the fall of 1540, two other priests, Antonio de Castilblanco and Juan de Padilla, and the lay brother Luis de Ubeda. The fate of Ubeda has never been proven: Bandelier's assumption that he was martyred is, in fact, not supported by evidence, and Juan de la Cruz, as stated above, did not remain in New Mexico at all.

Bandelier sheds a romantic haze over the life and death of Father Juan de Padilla, but in fact, as Chavez (1968, pp. 68, 72) has so cogently pointed out, the Father seems to have been somewhat indifferent to Indians and with something like madness was searching for the *European* Kingdom of Antilla (see also Riley, 1971).

Lest we sound too critical of Bandelier, it must be said that the question of which ecclesiastics actually went with Coronado had become extremely confused by the later sixteenth century and had remained so into modern times. Only the recent keen scholarship of Chavez has given us reasonably certain information about the friars involved.

When Coronado made his unsuccessful attempt to colonize New Mexico in 1540, he was accompanied by four Franciscans: Fray Marcos, surnamed "of Nizza," then Provincial of the Order in Mexico; Fray Juan de la Cruz; Fray Juan de Padilla; Fray Luis, a lay brother. The latter is called Fray Luis Descalona by Castañeda; de Ubeda, by Mota-Padilla.[1]

Fray Marcos did not remain long. He accompanied the expedition to Zuñi-Cibola only, and returned thence in the fall of 1540. Castañeda attributed his speedy return to fear, caused by the hostile attitude of the soldiery toward the priest, who, he claims, had deceived them by his exaggerated reports of the wealth and beauties of New Mexico. We have disposed of the calumnies of Castañeda elsewhere. The obvious reason of the friar's return was his feeble health. Hardships and physical suffering had nearly paralyzed the body of the already aged man. He never recovered his vigor, and died at Mexico, after having in vain sought relief in the delightful climate of Jalapa, in the year 1558.[2]

Fray Juan de la Cruz was already of advanced age when he joined the expedition. He was a Frenchman by birth, of the province of Gascony (Aquitania), and had worked as missionary in the district of Jalisco. Of him it is said that Coronado held him in such high esteem as to give orders that every soldier should touch his hat or helmet whenever his name was mentioned.[3] When Coronado evacuated New Mexico in the spring of 1542, Fray Juan de la Cruz asked to be left behind, among the Tiguas of the present site of Bernalillo, on the Rio Grande. His request was granted, although everybody felt that sure death awaited the old man as soon as the Spanish arms would withdraw. The Tiguas had, after the protracted hostilities with the Spaniards in the winter of 1540–41, maintained a hostile attitude. The monk still hoped to succeed as soon as the military would have left the country. So he remained alone on the banks of the great water artery which divides New Mexico into a western and an eastern half. He disappeared there. It is quite likely that the Indians murdered him, but as yet no positive statement in regard to his fate has been discovered. From the martyrologies we should conclude that his death occurred on the 25th of November, 1542. Gonzaga, who has written a short notice of Fray Juan de la Cruz, calls him an old man and a chorister.[4]

Fray Luis Descalona, probably a native of Ubeda, in Spain, also remained in New Mexico after Coronado's departure. Although loaded with years, he was but a lay brother. He selected for his abode the great village or pueblo of Tshi-Quite, or Pecos (the Ciquique or Cicuye of Coronado's chroniclers). Thither he went, taking with him the remnant of the sheep which the Spaniards had brought to New Mexico and which Coronado had presented to him. Fray Luis built himself a little hut outside of the great pueblo and was living there shortly before the departure of Coronado. He told the Spaniards who came to bid him good-bye that the Pecos Indians were usually kind to him, but that, nevertheless, he expected to be killed by them. For, though the bulk of the tribe liked him, the wizards were bitterly opposed to his stay, and they would certainly put him out of the way sooner or later. Nothing was heard of him or of Fray Juan de la Cruz thereafter.[5] Nor have we, as yet, been able to secure any tradition from the Indians touching their fate. Judging by subsequent events, it appears more than likely that they suffered martyrdom at the places which they had selected for their field of work. Of the sheep which Fray Luis brought to Pecos, all traces had disappeared when Espejo passed near the place forty years later. The Pueblo Indian, abandoned to himself, is careless with animals and cruel to them through neglect. This was still more the case in the sixteenth century than it is today. It is likely that the Pecos ate the sheep after killing the lay brother.[6]

As yet no relics of any kind have been discovered in New Mexico that might be safely attributed to any of the missionaries here mentioned. Nor do the official ecclesiastic or other sources from the seventeenth century make mention of any such discovery. Of all the Pueblos, the Zuñis and the Pecos have probably the most definite recollections of what they call the "First Conquest." Still, in regard to the latter, it remains undecided as yet whether their traditions apply to the time of Coronado or whether they concern events of the permanent occupation of New Mexico by Juan de Oñate in 1593.[7]

Fray Juan de Padilla was a native of Andalusia, in Spain, and comparatively a young and vigorous man when he joined Coronado's corps, or rather his Provincial Fray Marcos of Nizza. Yet he had already occupied important positions in Mexico. Thus he was the first guardian of Tullant Zinco, whence he passed over to the province of Michuacan, where he became Guardian of the Convent of Tzapotlan, in Jalisco.[8] He gave up that honorable position to become a missionary in the unknown north. How many of his brethren have made similar and even greater sacrifices! How many of them have refused important and influential offices in order to seek and find death among savages! No sacrifice was too great for the missionaries, no danger too imminent. When the duty of converting and educating the aborigines called for them, they were always ready and glad to undertake the humblest mission, the most trying task.

It would appear that Fray Padilla was as strict as he was full of energy. In Coronado's camp he watched the conduct of the men and used to reprehend and punish severely all evil-doers.[9] A vigorous constitution admirably assisted a fiery, nay, an impetuous soul. It is known that Coronado preceded the bulk of his army to Cibola-Zuñi, and that all the ecclesiastics accompanied him. As soon as he was established among the Zuñis he sent an exploring party to the Moquis, at Tusayan.[10] Father Padilla accompanied the detachment of twenty men which Don Pedro de Tobar commanded. The Moquis (probably of the now ruined village of Ahuatuyba) refused to receive the foreigners and met them in arms. Seeing that all endeavors to pacify the Indians were unavailing and only increased their hostile demonstrations, also that retreat was practically impossible, Fray Padilla remarked to the commander, "Verily, I do not know what we have come here for." The soldiers heard this remark and immediately charged, dispersing the Indians. This opened the way to the Moqui Pueblos, who thereafter showed the most cordial dispositions.[11] Upon the return of this party Coronado sent another body of twenty men under the orders of Hernando de Alvarado to the east and F. Padilla accompanied it. It was on this journey that the Spaniards saw Acoma, the famous rock (Acuco), the Rio Grande at Bernalillo (Tiguex), Pecos (Cicuye, or Ciquique), and that they heard for the first time of Quivira.[12] Whether Fray Juan returned to Zuñi from Tiguex, or whether he remained with Alvarado at Bernalillo, we are unable to determine. After the whole of the little army had been gathered in winter quarters on the Rio Grande, and when the unjust and bloody war with the Tiguas was over, preparations began for the memorable journey to Quivira, in which Father Padilla, of course, participated.

We need hardly recall here that the incentive to that adventurous enterprise was furnished by the statements of a captive Indian, a prisoner among those of Pecos, and who claimed to have been born on the eastern confines of the great plains. He gave the Spaniards to understand that far away in the East there was a country or tribe called Quivira, which was rich in gold, silver, and other elements of wealth. This individual was surnamed by the Spaniards "the Turk," on account of the manner in which he carried his head closely shaven with only a tuft of hair growing on the top of the skull. This kind of headdress is neither Pueblo nor Apache, nor Navajo. It would rather indicate that the Turk belonged to some branch of the Pawnees. However this may be, it is certain that the representations of the Turk made a great impression upon the minds of officers and men, and that they finally believed them. Everything seems to indicate that in the intercourse between the Spaniards and the Indian captive there was considerable mutual misunderstanding at the outset, but that also—after the latter saw that the white men placed upon his statements and signs an importance which to himself must have been a matter of surprise—he improved the opportunity to obtain a way of returning to his native tribe, and lastly, that there grew out of it a connivance between him and the Pueblo Indians for the purpose of getting rid of the Spaniards by sending them on a wild goose chase into the steppes where they were expected to perish. In short, Coronado was grossly betrayed. That the representations of the Turk about gold and silver rested on misconceptions is evident, for he could not judge of the chemical properties of metals; he had no idea of the difference between gold, brass, or yellow mica-particles giving a glistening appearance to rocks, except from external appearance. No tribe north of Mexico was ever found in possession of gold, with any definite conception of its value as a metal, still less as a medium of exchange. But neither were the Spaniards prepared to guard against such a misunderstanding. They had found gold in use at Mexico as an ornament. They were still under the impression of the reports from Peru and New Granada.[13] When therefore the Turk pointed to gold as a substance which he seemed to recognize they could not suspect that he was mistaken himself. So both parties were honestly deceived at first. But, after the Turk saw the importance placed by his white interlocutors upon the yellow stuff which they showed him and about which they inquired, he came to the conclusion that the opportunity was really a golden one for him to escape from a country where he had rendered himself unpopular, or which was unsympathetic to his tastes. He fomented troubles with the natives. When he saw that the Spaniards remained masters of the situation, he further exaggerated the wealth of Quivira; and when the Pueblos noticed that the unwelcome guests made preparations to leave, they naturally sought to induce the Turk (whose importance had grown in their eyes) to favor them also by misguiding the strangers as much as possible and leading them to destruction.[14]

We have already mentioned that the Tiguas of Bernalillo had not become reconciled with the Spaniards. The Pecos also had some trouble caused by the slanders of the Turk. But these had been adjusted, and when Coronado left Tiguex on the 3d of May 1541, he marched directly upon Pecos, where he was received with open arms. Nine days after his departure from the Rio Grande he reached the great plains northeast of Pecos.[15]

The particulars of this eventful expedition need be but briefly stated here. Coronado had not a single hostile meeting with the Indians. He lost one or two men, but through accident, not at the hands of the natives, who everywhere received him well and whom he in return treated fairly. He left the main body at the eastern edge of the great plains and went to Quivira with only twenty-nine horsemen, and probably Father Padilla. The main body returned to Bernalillo on the Rio Grande in advance of him. He reached there safely in August, but with empty hands. The march had resulted in a disappointment. Only a fertile country, much more fertile than any part of New Mexico, but thinly inhabited by roaming Indians, had been found. Discouragement followed upon disappointment. A severe contusion, resulting from a fall from his horse, gave to the commander a welcome pretext for abandoning New Mexico in the following year.[16]

For the purpose of this paper a careful examination of the route taken by the Spaniards on their trip to and from Quivira, and identifications of the localities and of the tribes met, are indispensable. Quivira was the place where, subsequently, Father Padilla sacrificed his life as a missionary. We must therefore ascertain where Quivira was, what it was, and what people were its inhabitants. The data at our command, while comparatively meager, yet are still, perhaps, more complete than any yet brought to bear upon the subject, and we therefore don't hesitate in undertaking the task. Should subsequent investigations alter our conclusions or confirm them, we shall feel only too happy.

It is unimportant to determine the route followed by Coronado from Bernalillo to Pecos. From Pecos he marched to the northeast, and, after crossing a deep river, found himself on the plains on the 12th of May. The deep river was the Canadian. Between it and the Pecos village he had, according to the eye-witness, Jaramillo, crossed two creeks; one of these was the Rio Pecos, the other the Gallinas. To cross the Canadian it was necessary to build a bridge. No other river, four days' march northeast of Pecos, is wide and deep enough to require such preparations for its crossing.[17]

Beyond the Canadian the plains were reached, and ten days after the crossing had been effected the first Indians of the plains, the Querechos or Apaches (subsequently called Vaqueros), were met. Here the Spaniards changed their course from northeast to toward the rising sun, that is, almost due east. Very soon they met enormous herds of American bison or buffalo.[18]

It is well to note this change in direction; it is also well to observe that soon the Spaniards found out that their Indian guides had lost their reckoning. It is a constant fact that any one lost on the plains inclines to the right and finally describes a circle. After thirty-seven days of march the Spanish army halted on the banks of a stream which flowed at the bottom of a broad and deep ravine. For several days past the

appearance of the country had begun to change; a more exuberant vegetation had made its appearance, and Indian villages were met with
whose inhabitants were clothed. There was in the Spanish troop one
man especially charged with counting the steps in order to approximate
the distances. According to his reckoning they were then, at the end
of thirty-seven days, two hundred and fifty leagues or six hundred and
seventy-five miles from Bernalillo. But this distance cannot be taken
as an air-line. Coronado had marched to the northeast for seventeen
days, thence first east, afterwards slightly south of east. We must also
note that no other river had been met with since the crossing of the
Canadian, except a small one at the bottom of a deep ravine, and which
had been struck a few days previous. Owing to the direction and manner
in which Coronado advanced, after crossing the Canadian, the only
watercourse which he could have met at that distance was the Canadian
again. The first stream was probably the north fork of that river, and
the second, where the army came to a halt, was the main branch below
the junction in the eastern part of the Indian Territory.[19]

The place was occupied or roamed over by an Indian tribe which
is called the Teyas. Who these Indians were we cannot attempt to de-
cide. They tattooed themselves, either with paint or by incisions. This
custom would tell in favor of their being the Jumanos, a semi-sedentary
tribe shifting to and fro across the eastern part of New Mexico at the
time. Leaving this matter undecided, we must remark that the Teyas
signified to Coronado that his guides had led him completely astray,
the Quiviras being far to the north of the place. Castañeda adds that
those guides had led Coronado in too southerly a direction: "Too near
to Florida." This is a further confirmation of what we have said, namely,
that the Spaniards marched like people losing their reckoning on the
plains, in a circle or arc of a circle, first northeast, then east, afterwards
even south of east.[20]

At this place Coronado left the main body, and with twenty-nine
horsemen, and probably Father Padilla, struck out for Quivira. He
moved northward, and at the end of about forty days (the number is
variously given) a large river was reached, which he crossed to its north
bank and followed its course to the northeast for upwards of twenty
days. Finally turning to the north inland, he reached, after sixty-seven
days of short marches and occasional delays, the region called Quivira.
The great river north of the Canadian can only have been the Arkansas,
and they struck it at some point below Fort Dodge, whence the river
flows to the northeast. It is noteworthy also that Jaramillo states, while
going in that direction, they descended the course of the stream.[21]

It is, therefore, in northeastern Kansas, perhaps not far from the boundary of Nebraska, that we must look for the homes of the Quiviras in the years 1541 to 1543. The descriptions of the country furnished by Coronado himself, by his Lieutenant, Jaramillo, and (from hearsay) by Castañeda, agree very well with the appearance of that country. As long as they remained south of the Arkansas the land was one great plain without timber and very little water;[22] north of the Arkansas its aspect changed. Coronado says: "The province of Quivira is situated nine hundred and fifty leagues from Mexico, where I came from, and in forty degrees; the soil is the best that can be found for all kinds of products of Spain; for in addition to being strong and black, it is well irrigated by brooks, by springs, and by rivers; I found prunes like those of Spain, nuts, excellent grapes, and mulberries."[23]

Jaramillo says:

> This country has a superb appearance, such as I have not seen any better in all Spain, neither in Italy or France, or in any other country where I have served your majesty. It is not mountainous; there are only hills, plains, and brooks with very good water. I am completely satisfied with it. I presume it must be very fertile, and favorable for the raising of all kinds of fruit. As for cattle (herds) experience proved that it is very convenient; considering the multitudes of animals that are met with, and which is so great it can only be imagined. We found prunes of Spain of a kind that is not completely red, but similar to red prunes; there are also black and green ones; it is certain that the tree and the fruit are the same as those of Spain. Their taste is excellent. We found, in the country of the cows, flax, which grows wild in small tufts isolated from each other, and as the wild cattle don't eat it, the stems and blue flowers are visible; although small, it is good. On some brooks sumac is found similar to that of Spain; and grapes of fair taste, although wild.[24]

Castañeda says: "The plants and fruit resemble those of Spain; there are prunes, grapes, mulberries, etc., etc."[25]

We forbear further quotations, and only call attention to the great similarity of the vegetation as described with the wild plants of northeastern and eastern Kansas. The appearance of the Indians, however, was not in accordance with the richness of the soil and of its vegetable products.

Castañeda: "The natives do not cultivate them [the plants which he enumerated], because they ignore their properties. Their customs are the same as those of the Teyas, and their villages resemble those of New Spain. The houses are round, have no halls; the stories resemble lofts. The people sleep under the roofs, where they also preserve what they have; these roofs are of straw." In another place he remarks: "The Indians of that country had neither gold nor silver, and knew nothing of such metals. The chief wore on his breast a copper plate, which he prized very much."[26]

Coronado:

> I had been told that the houses were of stone and with many stories. Not only are they of straw, but the inhabitants are as wild as any of those I had seen until then. They have no mantles, nor cotton to make them with. They merely tan the hides of the cows which they hunt and which are dispersed about their village, near a large river. They eat the flesh raw like the Querechos and the Teyas; they are at war with each other. All these people resemble one another. The inhabitants of Quivira are the best hunters. They grow maize. . . . In all the provinces and all the country I have gone over, I have not seen, nor have there been mentioned to me, more than twenty-five villages, the houses of which are all of straw. . . . The natives are tall; some of them above average size. I found some of them as high as ten spans (palms) in height. The women are well formed. Their features have a Moorish rather than an Indian cast. The natives gave me a piece of copper which one of their chiefs wore suspended to his neck. It is the only (piece of) metal which I saw in that country. [Further on:] What I have been able to find out is, that in all this country neither gold nor any other metal is found. I was only informed of small villages, the inhabitants of which, for the greatest part, do not till the land. They have only huts of hides and of reeds, and change their abodes with the cows.[27]

Jaramillo: "The houses of these Indians were of straw, many of them circular, the straw descending to the ground like walls. They do not at all look like ours. Outside and on the top there is a kind of chapel or loft, with an entrance, where the Indians could be seen seated or lying down."[28]

All this proves that the Quiviras were Indians of the plains, living chiefly from the buffalo and from very limited agriculture, changing the sites of their hamlets as the bison moved to and fro. Neither do they appear to have all been of one stock. Says Coronado: "The diversity of languages spoken in this country is extraordinary; every village has its own. We suffered greatly from the want of interpreters, for I was compelled to send officers and horsemen in every direction to find out if anything could be done in your majesty's interests. Although the most diligent search was made, no other inhabited country could be discovered but this one, which amounts to but very little."[29]

And yet, notwithstanding these and other very positive statements,

Quivira became fifty years later a golden phantom, a delusive specter, important in the end for the increase of geographical knowledge, fatal to all who undertook to grasp it. What we have had occasion to say of it elsewhere we repeat here: It is for the North American Southwest what the myth of El Dorado proved to be in South America.[30]

It is not the place here to follow this digression, but we may, having located the Quiviras at the time of Coronado, ask to what tribe the Indians thus called, belonged? The name Quivira was probably not the one they gave to themselves. Outside of New Mexico, that is, among the numerous tribes of Indians west of the Mississippi, it seems to have been unknown. Still we find, in 1725, on the upper Red River, the Quirireches, a village of the Canceys or Kansas.[31] The general drift of all the Indian tribes ranging between the Mississippi Valley and the mountain region of New Mexico has been, within the past three centuries, from north to south. Many have disappeared, and the Quiviras seem to have shared that fate. In the beginning of the seventeenth century, we find them in southern Colorado.[32] Thirty years later in eastern New Mexico, still later in northeastern Texas.[33] After 1700 they faded out of sight. But while the Quiviras were still roaming over southern Colorado and western Kansas, Spanish writers bring them in connection with the Tindanes. The word *Tindan* recalls a Spanish form of the word *Thinthon* or *Thinthontha,* used in the latter half of the seventeenth and in the eighteenth centuries to designate the extreme southerly branch of the Dah-co-tas or Sioux; the Teton-Sioux; also called *Gens des Prairies.*[34] That the Quiviras were a northern stock is quite likely. That they were not a numerous band seems proven. The suggestion is, therefore, not out of place, that they may have been an outlying band of the great Dahcota stock who, gradually drifting further south in the course of little less than two centuries, finally merged into one or the other of the tribes, either of Texas or of the Mississippi Valley. The exaggerated accounts of their numbers and wealth are thus disposed of by Fray Alonzo de Posadas in 1586:

> Many pretend to say that the Quiviras consists of many cities; that the one particularly so called is one of them, and that all are rich in gold and silver. On this point it seems that the information is more liberal than truthful, since neither our Spaniards nor any of the Indians who border upon that nation affirm to have seen any metal that came from that country. . . . And as for the cities which they represent as being so populous, and some of them so extensive as to cover leagues, while it is certain that there are many people, they are settled in the manner following: Every Indian has his dwelling, and adjacent to it his garden plot and field, on which he raises and

harvests his crops. Thus the settled expanses appear very large, without containing, however, the population attributed to them.[35]

Having located the Quiviras in 1541, and suggested at least what they probably were, I return to Fray Juan de Padilla. It is not unlikely that he accompanied Coronado on his trip thither. Jaramillo says, at least, that he "wished to return." The "Relacion Postrera de Sivola" positively states he went with Coronado, and that document was written by one (possibly by a priest) who was in New Mexico at the time.[36] At all events, when the Spanish corps, discouraged, disgusted with New Mexico, and dissatisfied with its commander, left the banks of the Rio Grande, Fray Juan de Padilla remained behind with Fray Juan de la Cruz, one Portuguese soldier named Andres Docampo, two "Donados" from Michuacan, called respectively Lucas and Sebastian, and some Mexican Indians. It is positive that no other Spaniard or soldier, except the three priests and Andres, remained in New Mexico in company with the Portuguese, the two Donados and two Indians from Mexico, also with a Mestizo boy. Father Padilla left the site of Bernalillo for Quivira. He took along the most necessary equipments for saying Mass; probably a few provisions, and at least one horse. The date of his departure we cannot find, but it must have been in the summer or fall of 1542.[37] Of the route taken by the little band, we only know that they passed through Pecos, where Fray Luis was already established; but we can surmise that they did not follow the trail of Coronado and of the main body. Coronado himself tells us that he effected his return from Quivira in thirty days, and that he brought with him Indians who served as guides. It is probable, therefore, that the latter led him, Indian fashion, in a line as straight as possible; that is, from northeastern Kansas to the southwest, through that state, and possibly through the southeastern corner of Colorado into New Mexico.[38] It is likely that Fray Padilla took the same route, even if he was not guided by Quivira Indians, a point which I do not venture to affirm or deny.[39] Certain it is that they reached the Quiviras without hindrance, and that they were well received. Coronado had caused a large cross to be erected in or near one of their villages or hamlets.[40] This cross was, for the missionary, a starting point for his labors.

All went on well for a time until the priest decided upon leaving the tribe and laboring temporarily, perhaps, among another group of natives.[41] This was highly imprudent on his part. His intentions were of the best, but he was not sufficiently conversant with Indian nature. A missionary who has been well treated by one tribe cannot leave that tribe without exposing himself to suspicion and jealousy. The Indians looked upon the priests as upon powerful wizards. They looked upon ceremonies of the Church as magic performances, from which they expected the same and greater material benefits than those which they derived or believed they derived from their own practices of sorcery. The more popular a missionary became, the more dangerous it was for him to change his field of work. Such was the case at Quivira, and the danger was still greater from the fact that, as Coronado tells us, the people were often at loggerheads with each other. By leaving his first place of abode Fray Juan de Padilla exposed himself to the double danger of being looked upon by his first acquaintances as a traitor who abandoned them in order to impart to others the benefits of his wisdom, and, by those to whom he went, as an enemy coming from people with whom they were at war.

Castañeda says that the friar intended to go to the Guyas, a tribe with whom the Quiviras were at war, and that the latter therefore killed him.[42] Jaramillo gives no such account. He attributes his death to the cupidity of the Quiviras, and states, besides, that Indians from Tiguex (Tiguas) had instructed them how to perform the deed.[43] The most detailed account of the event so far found is in Mota-Padilla, who, although an author of the eighteenth century, still deserves consideration from the fact that he examined original sources yet unknown to us. He states:

> The Friar left Quivira with a small escort, against the will of the Indians of that village, who loved him as their father. But at one day's journey he was met by Indians on the warpath, and, knowing their evil intentions, he requested the Portuguese to flee, since the latter was on horseback, and to take with him the Donados and the boys, who, being young, were able to run and save themselves. Being defenseless, they all fled as he desired, and the blessed father, kneeling down, offered up his life, which he sacrificed for the good of the souls of others. He thus realized his most ardent desire—the felicity of martyrdom by the arrows of these barbarians, who afterward threw his body into a pit and covered it with innumerable rocks. The Portuguese and the Indians, returning to Quivira, gave notice there of what had happened, and the natives felt it deeply on account of the love which they had for their Father. They would have regretted it still more had they been able to appreciate the extent of their loss. The day of his death is not known, although it is regarded as certain that it occurred in the year 1542. Don Pedro de Tobar, in some papers which he wrote and left at the town of Culiacan, states that the Indians had gone out to kill this blessed Father in order to obtain his ornaments, and that there was a tradition of miraculous signs connected with his death, such as inundations, comets, balls of fire and the sun becoming darkened.[44]

Vetancurt, in his *Menologia,* places the death of Father Padilla in 1544, and on the 30th of November. We prefer to follow Mota-Padilla as to the year, for he is more in accordance with the two contemporaries, Jaramillo and Castañeda,[45]

The news of the fate of Fray Juan Padilla was brought to Mexico many years afterwards, though certainly previous to 1552, by the Portuguese, Andres Docampo, and the two Donados, Lucas and Sebastian.[46] The return of these three men—unarmed, destitute and unaccompanied by anyone—from northeastern Kansas to Tampico, on the Mexican Gulf, finds a parallel only in the wonderful journey of Cabeza de Vaca and his three companions from eastern Texas to the Pacific coast. Were the fact not established beyond a doubt, it might be looked upon as a fairy tale of old. But it is indisputably proved by official testimony. As to the details of their remarkable journey, none of the sources at our command have much to say. Both Herrera and Gomara state that the Portuguese and his companions were captured by the Indians and remained in the power of their captors for ten months, after which time they fled. It is also stated that a dog accompanied them.[47]

Of the two Donados, Sebastian died very soon after his arrival at Culiacan. The other became a missionary among the tribes of Zacatecas, where he died at an advanced age.[48] Of Andres Docampo nothing further is as yet known.

May we be permitted to transcribe here what, on another occasion, we have written on the deaths of the three Franciscans, whose sad and at the same time glorious end the above pages have related?

They were never heard from again. Such is the funeral oration—simple, but pathetic from its very simplicity. Of these, the two old monks, Fray Juan de la Cruz and Fray Luis, remaining alone in the newly-discovered land, happy to conclude their days there in whichever way it might be, provided it was in the service of their Lord and Master and for the honor and glory of his name.

The end of Fray Juan de Padilla was different. As his life had been of a more vigorous cast, so his martyrdom sounded high through the land. His sepulchre in Kansas has never been found, but it is noteworthy that from Mexico, as well as in later years from New Mexico, all attempts on the part of the Spaniards to penetrate beyond the region where his death occurred have signally failed. That region is the same where the hardiest pioneers of Catholic civilization coming from the south met, figuratively speaking, the pioneers of Catholic civilization from Canada. The tomb of Fray Juan de Padilla, therefore, marks not a *ne plus ultra,* but the point where the two standard-bearers of Catholicism came together to join both ends of the advance of Catholic faith across the North American continent.[49]

7

THE FEATHER SYMBOL IN ANCIENT HOPI DESIGNS

J. Walter Fewkes

During the last decade or so of the nineteenth century and continuing for a number of years into the twentieth century, the ethnologist-archaeologist J. Walter Fewkes worked in a number of Southwestern areas. He directed major excavations (Mesa Verde, for example) and did a considerable amount of field ethnology, particularly among the Hopi. In the trend of those times Fewkes, like his contemporaries Bandelier and Cushing, was especially interested in interpreting the archaeology of Southwestern peoples in light of their historic and contemporary cultures.

In this article written in 1898, J. Walter Fewkes makes an elaborate study of ancient Hopi feather designs as exemplified in prehistoric pottery decorations. Fewkes recognized the possibility of having these designs interpreted by living elders and priests of the Hopi, a technique later used by Dutton (1963) in her analysis of the K'uaua kiva materials. Fewkes believed, however, that there was considerable discrepancy between historic and prehistoric designs and felt that the feather symbolism changed and evolved over time.

After the long years of rather particularistic studies of Southwestern cultures we are, today, turning once again to the broad implications of continuities in time and the meaning (and organization) of contacts within the Southwest and between the Southwest and other areas, particularly Mesoamerica. For the modern scholar, Fewkes's article may be more valuable as a base for comparing the feather designs of Hopi with those of peoples and cultures on the same general time horizons further south. Fewkes's work also points up the vast and many-faceted involvement with feathers in art and religion that is so basic to the great Mesoamerican-Southwestern *oikomene*.

Although the prehistoric Indians of Tusayan have left no written records in the forms of books, documents, or codices, there survives from their time a most elaborate paleography which has been preserved on imperishable material in the dry soil of Arizona for several centuries. This paleography is a picture writing, often highly symbolic and complicated, but from it the student can obtain an idea of Hopi thought and its expression at that remote time. It reveals phases of ancient life which have been modified or lost in the subsequent development of the race.

The most abundant of all objects found in the ruins scattered over the Southwest are fragments of pottery, and if the cemeteries of these ancient habitations are excavated large collections of decorated bowls, vases, and jars may be had from any ruin of considerable size. The majority of these fragments of pottery from Tusayan are richly decorated with designs, some of which are very complicated. The figures represented in this ornamentation are often realistic, but many are highly symbolic and conventionalized. It is an object of the present article to discuss one symbol of the latter group, and for this purpose I have chosen the feather, which, through its metamorphosis in form, is one of the more difficult to recognize.

Before passing to a consideration of the feather in ancient Hopi symbolism, it may be interesting to note that very few of the figures with which pottery from pueblo ruins is decorated have been interpreted, and we may say that the study is as yet in its infancy. The ancient Tusayan ware bears several designs of a simple, geometric shape, which are widely distributed over the whole Pueblo area of the Southwest. So far, however, as my knowledge of ancient Pueblo paleography goes, the symbols of the feather as here indicated are confined to ruins of villages which are purely Hopi in origin, although they may later be found elsewhere in Arizona or New Mexico.

I have shown in several previous publications on the ceremonials of the Hopi ritual the significant part which the figure of the feather plays in the decoration of altars and ceremonial paraphernalia, but I am unaware that any one has yet called attention to the very important use of the feather symbols in the decoration of ancient Hopi ceramics. A pottery ornamentation has a religious intent, and, since from its presence as a decorative element there is every reason to believe that the feather in ancient times held much the same position in the ritual as at present, it is instructive to trace its many variations as a symbol.

While what is here written is drawn more especially from the paleography of Sikyatki,[1] it is true, likewise, of that represented in all the Tusayan ruins where yellow ware is abundant. I might instance examples from old Cuñopavi, Kisakobi or Old Walpi, and Old Micñinovi. It does not, however, hold in all particulars when we study the red ware characteristic of the ruins along the Little Colorado river, where the feather takes another symbolic form not fully discussed in the present article. It applies to representations of the feather as depicted on altars now in use in Tusayan, symbols of feathers on dolls and ceremonial paraphernalia used by people who are lineal descendants of the inhabitants of the ruined pueblos mentioned above. The ruins of Sikyatki lie about three miles east of Walpi, and the pueblo of which they are the remains was destroyed previously to the middle of the sixteenth century.

I have grouped all the striking modifications in bird and feather symbols in close approximation in an installation of the more instructive pieces of pottery from Sikyatki in the National Museum, at Washington, and the reader may there find a larger series illustrating ancient Hopi paleography than has ever before been displayed. A forthcoming report[2] of the Bureau of American Ethnology, under the auspices of which institution these objects were collected, will describe these variations in detail, and as this report is elaborately illustrated, the reader will soon have abundant published material from which to study modifications of the feather symbol in ancient Tusayan.

We have no difficulty in recognizing among the many figures of animals which the ancient Hopi potter depicted on her wares the great group to which any one belongs. Four-legged animals of two kinds, frogs and lizards, are readily separated from mammals; apodal reptiles or snakes are easily distinguished from both, and there is no difficulty in separating the moth or butterfly from the spider or dragonfly. The great group to which the animal depicted belongs is not difficult to discover, and from a large series of related designs one may trace quite readily the changes in form which have resulted in highly conventionalized modifications.

The most constant group of animals chosen for realistic or symbolic representation on ancient Tusayan ceramic ware is that of birds. More than two-thirds of all the pictographs on ancient pottery where animals are intended represent avian forms. The modifications which these figures pass through as they become conventionalized likewise exceed in number and variety those of any other animals, and a comprehensive study of the different symbols representing birds would be a most interesting and instructive one. This study is important as a groundwork for the following conclusions, for in no other way can we identify as feathers some of the highly modified symbols which are here considered. An adequate discussion of different forms of birds in ancient designs would necessitate more pages of text and illustrations than could here be devoted to it. If my conclusions seem hasty, I must ask the reader not to reject them without examining collateral evidences which I have elsewhere presented.

The ancient Hopi decorator not only represented birds in many more different shapes than she did other animals, but even decorated other animals with feathers in accordance with ancient traditions. Nor did she stop with animals; symbolic figures of the sun or the lightning or the rainbow have symbols of feathers attached to them, and this, to us incongruous, association is often essential to indicate the symbol. This predominance in the number of pictures of feathered gods is a faithful reproduction of denizens of their ancient Pantheon. The majority of the gods were avian in character, even when anthropomorphic.[3] Several animals, as mythic lizards, snakes, and even mammalian forms, are represented in ancient pictography, furnished with crests of feathers on their heads. These are drawn in this way in conformance with ancient legends, and, with traditions to guide us, we have little difficulty in determining some of the symbolic forms which the feather takes in pictography. This method is used by me as corroboratory evidence in determining the prescribed symbols of feathers which have been previously identified by their relative positions on the bodies of birds.

It is plain, I think, that having determined from an avian figure the form of the organs and appendages of the bird in their different modifications, due to conventionalism, we are able to recognize the symbolic forms adopted by ancient artists to represent the feathers of wing, tail, or body. If figures of feathers were so well drawn that we could identify them as such, we would have no difficulty in recognizing a feather when drawn on a fragment of pottery, where no other part of a bird was represented. An accurately drawn feather in such case would be easily recognized; but the feathers made by the ancient Hopi decorators of pottery were not accurate representations—they were symbolic. The only way we can identify them is by association. Having determined the head, body, legs, tail, and wings of an animal which must be a bird, we examine the separate components which form the tail and conclude what part represents a tail feather. We use, in other words, the morphological method of determining the homologies of organs and appendages which we borrow from naturalists and apply to pictographs.

Having thus determined the symbol of a tail or wing feather from its position in representations of birds and fixing in the mind its form, we are able to recognize it where it reappears, isolated, or in new combinations. While this way of determining the feather symbol was the method adopted, there was brought to its aid likewise the testimony of living priests, among whom knowledge of some of the ancient symbols still survives. This latter aid to a comprehension of the symbols of ancient paleography is valuable, so far as it goes, but it does not take one long to discover that it is limited in its application. Many ancient designs are incomprehensible to living Hopi priests, and their interpretations are in some cases simply conjectural. The decay in knowledge of the meanings of old symbols is due to the fact that most of the ancient symbolism has been replaced by the modern.

In their drawings of animals the ancient Hopi artists were often far from realistic. They violated many fundamental rules in perspective. This is well illustrated in profile figures. It often happens, for instance, in delineating the head of an animal as seen from one side, that both eyes are represented. The feathers of a bird's tail, normally on a horizontal plane, are brought into a vertical. Internal organs which are hidden from sight are sometimes represented—a characteristic of modern Pueblo art, where, as in pictures of antelopes, it is not uncommon to find the heart and oesophagus, or even the intestinal tract, drawn as if the animal were transparent. In a figure of a bird shown on plate 59 in my preliminary account of Sikyatki [Smithsonian Report, 1896], where the artist apparently had no available space in which to represent the extremity of the tail, it is bent upward, and the tips of three feathers conventionalized into three triangles, one of the symbols of wing feathers, as elsewhere shown.

In their simplest forms figures of birds are crudely represented, consisting of a head with curved beak and elongated body, which is continued backward into three or four parallel lines, representing tail feathers.

It is an instructive fact that *three* seems to be the predominating number of tail feathers in pictures of birds, as seen in the clusters of symbolic feathers, f,[4] in the richly decorated vase a part of which is depicted in figure 5. This number, however, is not universal, for there are many well-drawn figures of birds with more than three tail-feathers, and in some of the simpler forms there are but two. Certain jars in the form of birds have the wing and tail feathers represented by parallel lines, and the same bands are often employed on the bodies of dolls to represent a feathered garment which some mythological personages are reputed to have worn.

One of the common forms of the feather symbol is shown in figure 1, which represents the tail of a bird as pictured on a beautiful food basin from Sikyatki. In this figure five feathers are represented, and the characteristic marking of each feather is a division into a black and red zone by a diagonal line. The upper part of the figure represents the body and the two lateral appendages the wings, which in the original figure are well represented. A figure of feathers with the same outline, but destitute of the characteristic markings of figure 1, may be seen in figure 2, where three feather symbols are represented.

Figure 2[5] represents a crest composed of three feathers copied from a design on the head of a reptilian figure depicted on the interior of a food basin from Sikyatki. There are other figures of animals which bear this symbolic form of feather on the head, and its occurrence as a decorative design on the exterior of food basins, where there is no other suggestion of a bird, is common.

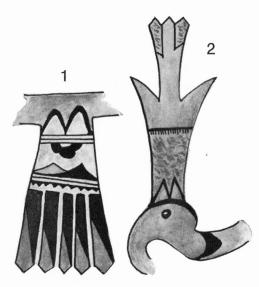

The same form of the feather symbol appears in figure 3, where we have the triangular tips differently marked from any of the previous symbols. There are in the Sikyatki collection designs representing birds where the feathers of the tail are identical in shape and markings with these, and it is reasonable to suppose that in this figure they represent the same parts as when attached to a picture of a bird.

The fragment shown in figure 3 represents a portion of the upper surface of a vase, of which the dotted line is the border of the orifice.

Having determined from its position on a bird that the main design in figure 3 is a conventionalized feather, let us see if there is corroborative evidence from other sources telling the same story.

In modern Hopi ceremonials the priests use a small gourd receptacle for sacred water, specimens of which have been figured elsewhere.[6] It sometimes happens that an earthen vase is used for the same purpose. This water gourd is covered by a cotton net, and feathers are tied to that part of the net which surrounds the orifice. When an earthen vase is used, a cotton string is tied around the neck of the vase, and to this string feathers are attached. Apparently we have a deep-seated and significant connection between the ancient vase and the modern ceremonial counterpart with appended feathers. The ancient form had symbols of feathers painted on the upper surface about the orifice, the modern has the feather itself tied in the same position.

In the design represented in figure 3 we have, therefore, symbols of feathers represented as tied around the neck of an ancient Sikyatki vase. The figure represents only a portion of the top of this vessel, but gives enough to show the general character of this form of feather symbol. If we compare this symbol with those on the head of the picture of Tuñwup[7] on the upright slats of the Katcina altars of modern times we will find an exact correspondence. They are also the same in shape and markings as the painted wooden sticks representing feathers on the heads of several dolls.[8]

The symbolic picture of the feather has still other modifications in its markings from the preceding, although preserving the same shape. One of the most highly conventionalized symbolic figures of the feather is a triangle in which there are two parallel lines on one side. This form of the feather symbol is said to be the feather of the wild turkey, and the double marking recalls that of a tail feather.

We find this symbol on the angles of the lightning snakes of the sand-picture of the Antelope altar at Cuñopavi,[9] on wooden slats of the Flute altars,[10] and elsewhere. I have ceramic objects from the ruins of Homolobi and Chevlon which bear this form of feather symbol, and it appears to have been used as far south as Pinedale, on the northern edge of the Apache reservation.

One of the most beautiful vessels from the cemetery of Sikyatki is the "butterfly vase," the complicated design on which I have figured in plate 60 of the Smithsonian Report for 1895. I have represented a sector of this design in figure 5 in order to point out the feather decorations which form an important element in the ornamentation. The other sectors closely resemble that figured, with the exception that the butterflies in alternating sections have different markings on their heads, indicative of the sex. The butterfly here represented is female, and it is interesting to note the fact that the symbol of the female was the same when this vase was made as that now used in Hopi ceremonials.[11] There are three clusters of feathers (*f*) in this section, and each cluster is composed of three members. One of these clusters corresponds with those from the head of the reptile, figure 2.

The three feathers shown in the cut below the butterfly, and peripherally placed on the surface of the vase, are likewise feather symbols, but as they have different markings from the others are probably from a different genera of birds. This form of feather symbol is a common one on ancient Sikyatki ware. One of the best illustrations may be seen in the wing of the bird which is figured on plate 60 of my preliminary report on Sikyatki. That portion of the wing which reproduces the wing feathers is shown in figure 4, and its resemblance to the feathers on figure 5 will, I think, be evident at a glance.[12]

On several of the food basins from Sikyatki we find two or more feathers of this kind represented as hanging from a ring-shaped or crescentic figure. One of the former is represented in plate 61 of the Smithsonian Report for 1895. The latter symbol has come down to modern times, and the figure painted on a shield of the Soyaluña ceremony, represented in color on plate 104 of my article on Tusayan Katcinas,[13] is almost an exact reproduction of the design on a Sikyatki

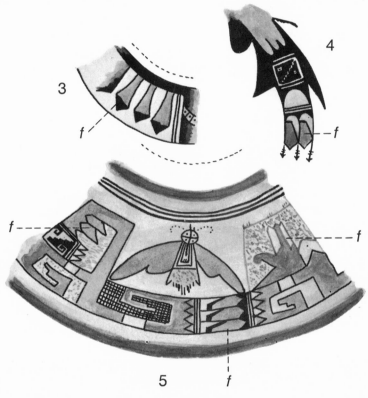

food basin. This is one of several symbols on modern ceremonial paraphernalia which we can trace back over three hundred years by the aid of archeology.

The feather may lose all semblance to the preceding forms and become a simple triangle. This is the case in figures 6 and 7 from a vase and food basin from Sikyatki. If the whole design, of which figure 6 is one wing, were represented we should have no hesitancy in regarding it a figure of a bird. From their position on this figure, then, we conclude that their triangular designs are wing feathers. If we seek to apply the conclusion that the triangular figure represents a feather to the jar, a portion of which is shown in figure 7, we find that the seven triangular designs in this figure bear the same relation to the orifice of the jar as the symbols of feathers in figure 3. This relationship, as will readily be seen, is confirmatory of the conclusion that the feather symbol is sometimes reduced to a simple triangle; or, looking for corroborative evidence, we approach the subject in another way.

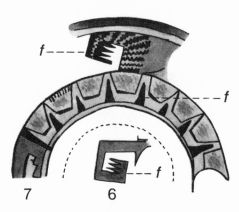

The conception of a serpent with a plumed head is common in modern Tusayan, and we find several serpents represented on ancient food basins from Sikyatki. Two of these figures have triangular appendages on top of the head, and, as there are no other designs on that organ that can be referred to [as] feathers, we conclude that the triangular symbols represent the feathered crest of the Great Plumed Serpent. Evidently not all triangular figures represent feathers, for some may be simply ornamental geometric designs; but that many figures of this shape are symbols of feathers there can hardly be a reasonable doubt, from the evidence adduced above.

From our studies of the triangle as a wing feather we are able to interpret many designs where all semblance to the feather or wing is lost. Thus in the upper part of figure 7 we have one of the most common designs on ancient Hopi ceramics. There is nothing in it to suggest a bird's wing, but if we compare it with the wing on the undoubted figure of a bird (figure 6) we find a perfect homology.

The presence of eagle feathers on ancient Hopi disks, symbolic of the sun, is frequent, and feathers are still inserted in a cornhusk border on the margin of hoops covered with painted buckskin representing the sun in modern Tusayan ceremonies.[14] In the old forms of sun pictographs the disk is represented by a circle, and the symbolic feathers are arranged in four clusters on the margin. In some instances each of these clusters of feathers is accompanied by a curved horn similar to that near the right-hand cluster of feathers in figure 5. The significance of this curved addition is unknown to me, but there are a large number of specimens in which a similar design is associated with two or more feathers.

In figure *9* we have a symbolic form of feather which is very common in ancient Hopi decorations. The whole design from which this was taken represents a bird in which the part lettered *w* is the wing and *b* the body. It will be noticed that this feather is attached to the body

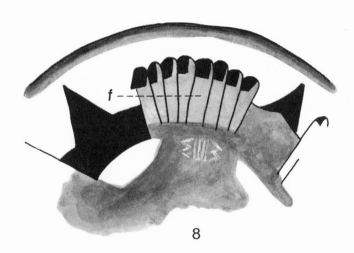

8

directly under the wing, and as feathers found on the breast of birds are at present given an especial signification in ceremonials, it is supposed that the symbol in this design has a similar meaning. This symbol is therefore identified as the breast feather.

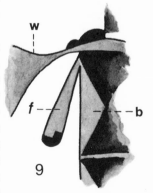

9

In looking over the variety of designs in which this form of the feather symbol occurs, one of the most instructive is shown in figure *8*, from a food basin obtained at Sikyatki by Dr. Miller of Prescott, Arizona, after my excavations at that ruin were abandoned. The complete design on this bowl represents a figure with five triangular peripheral extensions from a circular band, and alternating with these are five bundles[15] of feathers of the symbolic form shown in figure *9*. This design is probably a sun emblem, although in figures of the sun tail-feathers in four clusters are more common.

The symbol of the feather shown in figure *9* likewise occurs on the head of a snake and that of a bird which is figured on the inside of a ladle found at Sityatki. It is also represented on the upper surface of several vases in the same relative position to the orifice as those already described and illustrated (figure *3*).

The symbol of a feather with the markings shown in figure *10* is likewise a common one in the decoration of ancient Hopi ceramics. The design here reproduced (figure *10*) is a section of a small, beautiful

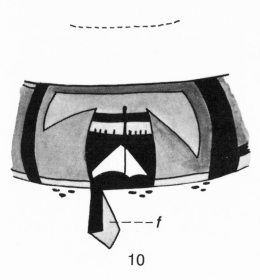

10

vase, with the decoration confined to the equatorial region. From this zone hang symbols of feathers, one of which is plainly indicated. These zones are repeated at intervals around the vase. They may be comparable with the feathers tied about modern ceremonial vessels to which I have elsewhere referred.[16]

I have attempted in the preceding pages to show the symbolic forms assumed by one letter, the feather, in the alphabet of design on ancient Hopi ceramics. These designs, or some simple modifications of them, occur in almost three-fourths of all the decorated ancient vessels of Tusayan. With a little practice the student can readily recognize them, thus rendering comprehensible a most important element in ancient Hopi symbolism. There are two or three other known letters in this alphabet, representing two or three other types which can be identified with the same ease, but limited space prevents a consideration of them in this article.

As would naturally be the case with an element of decoration so constantly duplicated as the feather, there are numerous instances where it has become so changed that while a figure was probably intended for a feather symbol, it is difficult to prove that it was such. These doubtful cases are not, therefore, discussed from the uncertainty which hangs about their identification.

I believe enough has been written above to show that the feather was regarded by ancient Hopi potters as an important decorative motive, and that its symbolism had significant differentiations, so that even different kinds of feathers were indicated by different markings on those symbols.

Considering also how strong a hold the feather has on the modern Hopi mind in ceremonial usages, I am led to the belief that its influence on the ancient mind was of the same general character. Thus we come back to a belief, taught by other reasoning, that ornamentation of ancient pottery was something higher than simple effort to beautify ceramic wares. The ruling motive in decorating these ancient vessels was a religious one, for in their system everything was under the same sway. Esthetic and religious feelings were not differentiated; the one implied the other, and to elaborately decorate a vessel without introducing a religious symbol was to the ancient potter an impossibility. This union is weaker in the mind of the modern Hopi, yet still potent; but as the new conception of beauty has crowded out the religious element, the character of the pottery and its decoration have deteriorated. Many patterns which once had a religious symbolism are mechanically followed, through conservatism, and pottery of fair character is still made, but every Pueblo shows a marked decadence in the potter's art. As time goes by and the Hopi are more modified by their new environment— contact with civilization—the white crockery of the traders will replace the aboriginal wares. This will lead to a still greater degeneracy of native ceramics, and, if they survive at all, it will be more as a commercial product than a medium of religious expression. It can readily be seen that the decorations on pottery made "for the trade" will no longer be a spontaneous expression of aboriginal art, but imitative of types of beauty which please the purchaser. Into that condition much of the pottery made in pueblos along the railroad has already drifted, and Hopi potters are not behind their neighbors in recognizing those decorative designs which please the buyer and those which are most often rejected. Quite in line with what is said above is the feeling which leads some of the best potters of the East Mesa to imitate ancient forms of decorations. These copies are adorned with old patterns because ethnologists ask for ancient ware and purchase vessels with imitations of ancient symbols more eagerly than modern. Trade cannot revive the old religious feeling which expressed itself on ancient Hopi ceramics or resuscitate the defunct intimate union of esthetic and religious inspiration.

Finally, and this is embraced in the primary reason why I am interested in the archeology of the Southwest or any other region, a study of the religious decorative symbols of ancient pottery is an investigation not alone of the peculiarities of one cluster of men and women in ancient Arizona, but of religion in a characteristic environment.[17] A psychologist devises experiments in which he places individual men or animals under conditions to observe how they are thereby affected. Nature has performed a psychological experiment on a grand scale for the ethnologist in the semideserts of Arizona, and has set tribes of men in a special environment for our study. The problem of the ethnologist is to consider the effect on religion as shown in the products or expression of the same. The most important ethnic characteristic of man is his religion. It distinguishes him from other animals and embraces all other mental characteristics, sociology, language, and arts.

Man can transmit his religious feelings to posterity by legends and paleographic records. The former, if not recorded, may suffer changes in transmission, may be colored by successive generations, which have heard them from their elders and passed them along to their children. Paleography does not change. The ancient pictures are the same as when buried in the ancient graves. We may not be able to fully interpret them, but we are sure they have not been materially changed in the years which separate our time from that in which they were drawn. Imperfect as this picture-writing is as a means of transmitting to us the religion of prehistoric Tusayan when compared with written documents, it will in connection with legends yield a rich harvest to the student of the history of the Pueblo beliefs. The investigator who neglects this element in them misses the soul of the study.

VENTILATORS IN CEREMONIAL ROOMS OF PREHISTORIC CLIFF DWELLINGS

J. Walter Fewkes

Fewkes wrote this paper in 1908, and it remains a small gem of limited topic expostulation in Southwestern archaeology. It may be reasonably objected to that we have no evidence that Mesa Verde people *invented* ventilators, but Fewkes in fact does not expand on this statement and so it has no importance to the paper as a whole.

The paper is closely reasoned and shows the willingness to use ethnological analogy that was the hallmark of this period and this group of archaeologists-ethnologists. At the time Fewkes wrote, there was considerable argument as to the real function of these shafts. Fewkes discusses the alternative hypotheses; entryways, chimneyways, and ventilator shafts, and finds the evidence for the latter to be convincing. Since Fewkes's time, experiments in a reconstructed Kiva in Spruce-tree House in Mesa Verde have demonstrated that the ventilator shafts work with striking efficiency and Fewkes's position is virtually universally accepted today.

The object of this article is to show that the inhabitants of the prehistoric cliff dwellings of the Mesa Verde, in Colorado, invented and used ventilators to supply pure air at the floor level in certain of their subterranean rooms.

The special chamber set apart by Pueblo Indians for ceremonial purposes was called by the early Spanish discoverers an *estufa,* or stove, a name no doubt suggested by the great heat of the room when occupied. An estufa is commonly designated by the Hopi Indians a *kiva,*[1] which term is rapidly replacing the older name. It is found that prehistoric ruins as well as modern pueblos have kivas and that specialized rooms of this kind likewise exist in cliff dwellings.

The kiva is the most important and generally the best constructed room in a pueblo, ancient or modern. In certain pueblos of the Southwest the kiva is the oldest room, and, from the very fact that it is devoted to religious practices, it preserves archaic features of construction, being less affected than secular dwellings by sociological changes. It is found in examining kivas of both modern and ancient pueblos that they differ in structure, form, size, and numerous minor peculiarities. It also appears that certain geographical areas have similar kivas and that other forms when found in these areas are intrusive. An examination of architectural variations and their distribution is important as bearing on the special subject of this paper.

Exceptional advantages were presented to the author to study the construction of kivas while in charge of excavation and repair work at "Spruce-tree House," one of the large cliff dwellings of the Mesa Verde National Park.[2] This locality was particularly favorable for this study, as nowhere else in the Southwest are Cliff Dwellers' kivas better preserved or more instructive in their teachings.

The type of kiva at Spruce-tree House is identical with that of other Mesa Verde ruins, and has a wide geographical distribution. It follows the San Juan River and its tributaries as far west as the cliffs of the Cañon de Tseyi, or Chelly, and as far south as the great Chaco ruins in New Mexico. The kivas of the McElmo[3] and lesser cañons of the San Juan are morphologically the same as those of Spruce-tree House. Although aberrant examples of this type can be recognized a considerable distance from the Mesa Verde, the type reached its highest development on this tableland. Certain inhabited pueblos still retain the form of ceremonial rooms found in the Mesa Verde, but circular rooms of this kind do not occur in the western part of the Pueblo area or in the vast region extending from the Hopi villages to the northern boundary of Mexico.

There are two types of pueblo and cliff-house kivas: one circular, the other quadrilateral. The kivas of Spruce-tree House belong to the former group and architecturally are among the highest in development of all these ceremonial rooms. In order to consider intelligently the kiva structure of which this article treats, the author has given below a brief description of the construction of the circular type.

The eight kivas of Spruce-tree House—except possibly [one exception]—are subterranean and constructed on the same general plan. In no instance are they built inside quadrilateral buildings, as is said to be the case with circular kivas elsewhere. The top of the roof is level, and continuous with the floor of the adjacent plaza; the main entrance being through a hatchway, descent into the room was by means of a ladder. Their walls are made of dressed stone, with plastered surfaces of mud and sand of different colors.

We may describe the walls forming the enclosure as double, or as consisting of an outer wall and an inner wall, the latter ending a short distance from the floor. Between the top of the inner and the base of the outer wall there are six recesses separated by the same number of buttresses which project from the outer wall into the kiva, so that the surface of the buttress facing the center of the kiva is flush with that of the inner wall. The horizontal portions of the recesses are banquettes that are generally paved with flat stones but are sometimes smoothly plastered.

The inner wall of each kiva has a rectangular opening, capped on the upper side by one or more flat stones forming part of the banquette. This opening is spacious enough to admit a man's body, the smoothly plastered inner surface showing no signs of smoke or fire. Its cavity narrows, as it recedes from the room, into a passage,[4] which, after extending horizontally a few feet, turns upward, opening externally at the level of the plaza. Here as a rule its walls are now broken, although in some instances evidences still remain that it did not formerly end at the level of the plaza. The vertical shaft probably turned again in a horizontal direction and opened externally through the wall which forms the front of the whole village, enclosing the plaza on the western side. This tunnel, which we may anticipate by calling a ventilator, is the subject of this paper and will be considered more at length later.

In addition to this opening in the side of the room, several kivas have also other lateral passageways situated between their floors and banquettes. These communicate with other rooms situated some distance away, or in some cases open exteriorly in the middle of the adjoining plaza. Through these subterranean tunnels one may with difficulty crawl from an outside room into a kiva, and at least one of these tunnels is furnished with steps to facilitate the passage of one entering the room.[5] While a majority of the kivas are destitute of these tunnels, none lacks the vertical openings called ventilators.

The masonry buttresses separating the recesses and the banquettes above mentioned, are square, or nearly so, in horizontal section, invariably provided with short pointed pegs attached to their tops,[6] upon which the priests formerly hung the ceremonial paraphernalia. As in all sacred rooms, small niches, or cubby-holes, were constructed in the walls at convenient intervals. Meal or paint was formerly kept in these recesses, and in one kiva a small-necked bowl of coarse ware, set into the banquette, evidently served a similar purpose. As a rule, however, no niches of this kind exist in the upper walls or the sides of the buttresses.

The floor of a Spruce-tree House kiva is generally plastered, but in one instance is formed by the smooth surface of rock in place. When [this kiva] was built, the rock surface projected unevenly, and, not being low enough for the kiva floor, was cut down six or eight inches on one side, presenting one of the most remarkable examples of rock cutting en masse the author has seen.

The circular fireplaces, situated a little to one side of the middle of the floor, were found to be packed solid with wood ashes. These fireplaces are merely deep cavities in the floor and apparently are lined with cement, not, as is usually the case, rimmed with slabs of stone set on edge, or with a raised border of adobe.

A flat upright stone, often replaced by a low wall about two feet high, projects from the floor between the fireplace and the kiva wall. This may be designated an "air deflector." The passageway to the ventilator, by which fresh air enters the kiva, is situated back of the deflector, in the lower or inner wall of the kiva.

There is a small circular opening in the floor representing symbolically the entrance to the underworld, called by the Hopi the *sipapû,*[7] between the fireplace and the wall of the kiva directly opposite the deflector. This hole is only a few inches deep, and its sides are lined with the neck of a vase, the body of which is sometimes buried beneath the floor. The *sipapû* is the most revered place in the kiva, and about it are performed some of the most sacred rites.

The most complicated structure in a modern pueblo house is the roof, and the roof of a circular kiva was the most ambitious attempt at building undertaken by the prehistoric inhabitants of cliff dwellings. All eight kivas of Spruce-tree House were roofed in the same way, but none of them had more than a few beams of the original roofing still in position. In clearing out the kivas, however, several well-preserved roof-beams of considerable size were brought to light.

Although Nordenskiöld[8] claims to have seen in the Navaho country a *hogan* with roof constructed in the same way as a Mesa Verde kiva roof, it is believed that he was mistaken. The coverings of these kivas have no likeness in construction to Navaho *hogans* as figured by Mindeleff[9] or as observed by the author. The roof of a cliff-dwelling kiva does not resemble that of any known form of habitation of nonagricultural people, and it was devised to meet architectural conditions foreign to nomadic culture.

The roof rests upon buttresses, which apparently were represented in some ancient kivas by upright logs. These supports, six in number, are placed equidistant[10] around the room. They serve as foundations for eighteen cedar logs which are arranged peripherally and horizontally in threes, each triplet so placed on its supports as to span an interval between adjacent buttresses. Upon these rests another set of eighteen logs, also arranged in threes spanning the sextants including the buttresses. On this second set are numerous other logs. It is to be noticed that, as each row of cedar logs is added crosswise on the row below, the size of the uncovered part of the kiva diminishes and the height of the roof is increased.

Two stout rafters extend diametrically across the kiva, with their ends resting on the outer wall. They are equidistant from and generally parallel with the last set of peripheral logs, or those supported by the buttresses. These large logs serve as the main supports of the roof, especially its middle, where the strain is the greatest. Between them, midway in their length, lies the hatchway[11] through which one enters the kiva. The intervals between these logs and the last layer of crosswise peripheral logs arranged in threes are filled with sticks, the space between the two large beams being occupied by smaller poles resting on split beams. The last-mentioned beams form opposite sides of the kiva hatchway, and support the ladder.

Inserted in the crevices and openings between the logs above mentioned there are small sticks, split logs, and brush, and over the whole is spread a layer of shredded cedar bark. This covering supports a thick deposit of mud filling all spaces above the supports and raising the roof level to that of the top of the outer wall of the kiva.[12] Nothing is visible on the roof of the kiva but a level floor broken by a hatchway in the center of a circle of stones marking the outer wall. This floor is continuous with that of the neighboring plaza when such exists.

The roofs of two of the kivas of Spruce-tree House were restored, following as a model those in the Square-tower House (Peabody House), where there is a considerable section of a kiva roof still fairly well preserved.[13] A kiva with covering constructed in the way described is somewhat more capacious than one with a flat roof resting on parallel rafters, although the height of the walls is the same. The inner surface of the roof is vaulted and its height considerably increased by the manner in which the logs are placed one above the other.

[One] kiva[14] in Spruce-tree House presents the remarkable feature of a partially double-walled chamber, or of a circular room built inside an oval one. A section of the walls of the two is duplicated, the remainder being fused into a single wall. This kiva has an exceptional site, having been originally constructed close to the rear wall of the cave, while others are situated on top of the talus in front of the dwellings. Its floor is at a relatively higher level than the others, and rooms formerly stood in front of its outer walls. It is probable that some time may have elapsed between the period of construction of the two parts of the double wall, and the larger is believed to be the older. The only explanation that has suggested itself to the author to account for the double wall of [this] kiva is the following: It may have been that after the larger kiva was finished and roofed the ventilation was found to be insufficient or such that the smoke and vitiated air were not properly carried off. The smaller kiva was built within the other and nearer the ventilator, to obviate this defect.[15]

The construction of the different parts of the kiva and their significance have been considered by several investigators, among whom may be mentioned Mindeleff and Nordenskiöld, the latter the most prominent student of the Mesa Verde ruins. It should be pointed out that Mindeleff's studies of circular kivas were made in Cañon de Chelly, while those of Nordenskiöld were conducted at the Mesa Verde. It is possible that there is some difference in the construction of ceremonial rooms in these two areas, notwithstanding the kivas in them belong to the same general type.

The plan of the principal kiva in Mummy-cave ruin, in the Cañon de Chelly region, as given by Mindeleff,[16] shows a style of architecture morphologically identical with that of the kivas of Spruce-tree House. A ventilator and a deflector are present, but the fireplace and *sipapû* are absent.[17] These kivas appear to have had only a few buttresses, and not many banquettes and lateral recesses. Their present form would indicate that Cañon de Chelly lies on the outskirts or periphery of that cultural area in which the circular type of kiva reached its maximum development.[18]

Nordenskiöld has given a fairly good general sketch of a typical kiva of the Mesa Verde ruins, from which the following quotation is made:

> Between the fireplace and the outer wall stands a narrow curved wall eight-tenths of a meter high. Between this wall in the same plane as the floor a rectangular opening one meter high and six-tenths of a meter broad has been constructed in the outer wall. This opening forms the mouth of a narrow passage or tunnel of rectangular shape which runs 1.8 meters in a horizontal direction and then goes straight upward on into the open air. The tunnel lies under one of the six niches which is somewhat deeper than the others. The walls are built of carefully hewn blocks of sandstone; the inner surface being perfectly smooth and lined with a thin yellowish plaster. On closer examination of this plaster it is found to consist of several thin layers each of which was black with soot. It is difficult to say for what purpose this tunnel has been constructed and the slab of stone or the wall erected in front of it. As I have mentioned above this arrangement is found in all the estufas.[19]

Each kiva of the cliff dwellings of Cañon de Chelly, according to Mindeleff, was erected inside a rectangular room, and in a "few instances the space between the outer rectangular wall and the inner circular wall was filled solid and perhaps was so constructed, but usually the walls are separated and distinct." Although an outer quadrilateral wall enclosing the circular kiva does not exist in Spruce-tree House, it is not unknown in Mesa Verde ruins. This feature was probably a necessity in Cañon de Chelly, where the rooms were built above ground on account of the exigencies of the rocky site. In no better way could the ancient inhabitants fit buildings of circular form into angular spaces than by enclosing them in quadrilateral rooms.

No structural difference between circular and quadrilateral kivas is more radical than in the mode of building the roofs. According to Mindeleff in the Cañon de Chelly "the roof of the kiva was the roof of the chamber that enclosed it." However this may be in the roofing of the circular kivas referred to, it does not apply to those of Mesa Verde. The author predicts that when the method of roofing circular kivas in Cañon de Chelly is determined by scientific excavation, it will be found to be the same as in the Mesa Verde.[20] According to Nordenskiöld: "The simplest way of roofing an estufa, an example of which was observed in another estufa at Square-tower House (Peabody House), is to lay poles horizontally across the room—poles of sufficient length may easily be procured of piñon or cedar. This form of roof is also the general one in all quadrilateral rooms." The author believes that the roofs of both the Peabody House kivas were constructed in a style not unlike that which has been restored in [one] kiva of Spruce-tree House. In studying roof construction Nordenskiöld overlooked the two main rafters of one kiva of Peabody House, and supposed that the beams spanning the opening of another indicated a difference in the manner of building the roofs. It is believed that there was no radical difference in the construction of these two roofs, but that both were built in the same general way.

Four theories have been presented to account for certain lateral openings, or "chimney-like structures," in the circular kivas: (1) that they are chimneys; (2) that they are passageways or entrances; (3) that they served some ceremonial purpose; (4) that they are ventilators. The theory that they were chimneys seems to have been dismissed by all authors, for they exhibit no sign of smoke. The expression "chimney-like" structure may however persist as a good, although misleading, term by which to designate them. The third theory is too vaguely stated to be discussed.

In considering the second theory, or that these lateral passageways are entrances to the rooms, it must be borne in mind that in some of the kivas of Spruce-tree House, and probably in others of the same culture area, the kivas sometimes have underground lateral openings of two kinds, some of which are entrances. The size and structure of the former, or that by which one enters a kiva from a neighboring room or plaza, and that of the latter—the problematical structures—are quite different, although their openings into the kivas closely resemble each other. When seen from a subterranean chamber they might readily be mistaken one for the other, and without excavation the observer would be at loss to know how to distinguish them. One of these doubtful passageways was described by Professor Holmes[21] many years ago, in a ruin not far from those under discussion. Mindeleff, in considering his description, refers the structure designated as a "covered passageway" to the same category as the "chimney-like" structures of the Cañon de Chelly, but points out that "the tunnel is much larger than usual and the vertical shaft, if there were one, has been so much broken down that it is no longer distinguishable." The tunnel in the ruin described by Holmes might be either an entrance to the kiva or a ventilator, but as no sign of the more constant structure called a ventilator is seen in his ground plan, it is possibly the latter.

The strongest and probably a fatal objection to the second theory of vertical passageways in the Spruce-tree House kivas is that they are too small to allow the passage of even a child, much less an adult. The fourth theory is supported by all the known facts, and the objection to it turns out to be of a most specious nature when analyzed.

Nordenskiöld finds the entrance and chimney hypotheses unsatisfactory. He is not satisfied with the ventilator theory, but does not state his objections. Mindeleff regards all three theories untenable, and thus writes regarding the ventilator: "Ventilators according to this method [the introduction of fresh air on a floor level, striking on a deflector and being thus distributed in the room[22]] is a development in house architecture reached by our own civilization within the last few decades." He adds, however, the following paragraph which shows that he is not wholly opposed to the third theory: "There can be little doubt that the chimney-like structures were not chimneys and no doubt at all that they did provide an efficient means of ventilation no matter what the intention of the builders may have been."

In quadrilateral kivas thus far described, except possibly the kiva of Wukoki, a ruin at Black Falls on the Little Colorado, mentioned by the author,[23] no air flues have yet been found. Modern Hopi kivas, which like those of Spruce-tree House are subterranean, but unlike them in being quadrilateral, have no air vent except the kiva hatchway. As a rule quadrilateral kivas are much larger and their roofs higher than those of circular kivas, so that the ventilation, which is also facilitated by a more capacious hatchway, is not a matter of great concern. The suggestion—it could hardly be regarded as more—that the discovery of the principle of supplying fresh air to a room at the level of the floor was too advanced for a people whose knowledge of architectural principles is said to have been so limited as that of the ancient Cliff Dwellers is contrary to observation, which shows that the Cliff Dwellers had discovered this principle and applied it in their kivas. They were compelled to discover it, for otherwise it would have been impossible for one person, much less for several, to remain in a subterranean chamber so small as these, even with a moderate fire burning. Without adequate ventilation, smoke would have driven them out.

9

ABORIGINAL TURQUOISE MINING IN ARIZONA AND NEW MEXICO

William P. Blake

This very interesting paper published in 1899 points up the importance of the turquoise trade between the Southwest and Mexico proper and the great importance of aboriginal Southwestern turquoise mines, especially the Cerrillos Mines near Santa Fe, New Mexico. It is now generally conceded that Southwestern turquoise was in demand in the great Mesoamerican centers to the south, just as it was of interest to the early Spanish explorers and colonists. Indeed, some Southwestern scholars (including especially Charles DiPeso, J. Charles Kelley, Jonathan Reyman, and Carroll L. Riley among others) now believe that ancient exploitation of Southwestern turquoise deposits by Mesoamerican organized traders (Pochteca), at first in terms of the crude ore and later in the form of craft products (such as mosaics, necklaces, and similar ornaments), may have led to Mesoamerican acculturation of the culturally much less advanced Southwestern aborigines. Considerable support for this thesis has been provided by the discovery that just such a mining exploitation, probably including turquoise in the products mined, existed on a fantastically large scale in western Zacatecas and southern Durango, Mexico, in the period circa A.D. 300–600, near the old town of Chalchihuites, Zacatecas (Weigand, 1968).

Blake's discussion of the meaning of the word *chalchihuites* is now mainly of historical interest. A Nahuatl word, it clearly did denote jade or jadeite in general in Mesoamerica, but just as clearly was used (at least as an alternate form) to mean turquoise in northern Mexico and the Southwest, quite probably in pre-Spanish time and certainly in early Spanish colonial period.

Parenthetically, the early Spaniards in the Cabeza de Vaca and Coronado *entradas* made it clear that they were discussing turquoise in the context of the Southwest by using also the Spanish term *turquesas*. The Cerrillos Mines described by Blake still produce turquoise, but they are no longer worked commercially. However, they were exploited commercially during the Spanish colonial period, the United States territorial epoch, and, in fact, until very recent years.

Recent explorations for turquoise at Turquoise Mountain in Mohave County, Arizona, twenty miles from Kingman, show that mining operations were carried on there during the Stone Age. It is evident that the object of this mining was to secure a supply of *chalchihuitl,* or chalchuite, more generally known as turquoise. The outcropping rocks at this locality are seamed and veined with this gem so highly prized and generally used by the Aztecs and aboriginal tribes of this region and Mexico.

The ancient mining is made evident not alone by the ancient excavations in the form of trenches, cuts, and pits, now filled in with rubbish and overgrown with mezquite trees, but by an abundance of stone implements.

There are benches or terraces cut in the side of the mountain, where, apparently, the ancient miners lived or camped, and probably sorted out the best pieces of chalchuite. In making an excavation upon one of these terraces, a pit or shaft was found by Mr. A. B. Frenzel of New York, who has recently published a notice of the discovery in the columns of the *Engineering and Mining Journal* of New York. " . . . Pictures [in the article] show the mouth of the chief pit, or shaft, and a number of the stone hammers, or mauls, picked up nearby. The shaft was filled up with earth without stones, and apparently with the object of concealing it. It is well cut into the hard rock, and appears to have been made not only by pounding away the rock, but, also, by the use of fire. There is also a cut, some twenty-five feet in length, extending into the side of the hill."

In cleaning out the openings a variety of implements were found, but mostly mauls, or stone hammers, of various sizes, from four or five inches to nine or ten inches in length, and weighing from four pounds to over fifteen pounds each. The great size and weight of some of these implements indicate great strength of the men who used the hammers. In some of them the groove around the boulder (for boulders they probably originally were), made to receive the raw-hide band, or with handle, is about half the distance from end to end, or midway of the stone; but in others, it is cut nearer to one end than to the other, conforming in this respect to the general form of the stone axes of the Salt River Valley.

All the implements bear evidences of hard usage. But few of them are in a perfect state. Great flakes of the stone have been split off the sides, from the points or ends backwards toward the groove, and some are broken across. These implements closely resemble those found in the prehistoric pits and cuts upon the croppings of some of the copper-bearing veins on the borders of Lake Superior.

Another locality of chalchuite in Arizona, which shows aboriginal workings, is in Cochise County, twenty miles east of Tombstone, on the eastern slope of the Dragoon Mountains, in the district known as Turquoise. Here there are large excavations and dumps giving conclusive evidence of extensive working.[1]

Chalchuite was also obtained across the Arizona line in New Mexico, not far from Silver City, in the Burro Mountains; but none of these localities compare, for extent, with the great excavations at Las Cerrillos, not far from Santa Fé, in New Mexico, which appears to have been one of the chief sources of the gem in Aztec times. Its extent and the overgrowth of trees indicate great antiquity.for the chief excavations. There is, however, a tradition that in the year 1680, a large part of the mountain, which had been honeycombed by the long continued excavations of the aboriginal miners, caved in, burying many of the miners and precipitating the uprising of the Indians and the explorations of the Spaniards. Modern explorations of this locality, by shafts and tunnels, have revealed caves, or subterranean chambers, made by the ancients.

In one of these chambers, the modern miners found a stone hammer with its handle attached. The weight of this hammer was thirteen and three-tenths pounds. An account of this, and other results of the modern exploration of the Cerrillos locality, and of turquoise generally, may be found in the admirable book *Gems and Precious Stones of North America,* by George F. Kunz [New York, 1890; 2nd ed., 1892], pages 54–65. The first account of this Cerrillos locality and the identification of *chalchihuitl* of the Aztecs with turquoise was given by me in 1858, after my return from Santa Fé, where I found this gem in use by the Pueblo Indians.[2]

Other localities of chalchuite are found in Mexico and north of Arizona in Nevada. Enough has been cited to show that there were several localities, or sources, whence this stone was procured by ancient mining, and that these localities were far separated upon the great tableland of Anahuac or Ancient Mexico.

It is unnecessary to give all the evidence here of the high esteem in which the turquoise was held by the ancient inhabitants of this region. We know from the narrative of Bernal Diaz and the journals of the Coronado expedition, that it was in general use for personal adornment, and that it was most highly prized, and was an object of trade or commerce between the various tribes. It was also reported as in use at Cibola for the adornment of the portals of chiefs' houses, by inlaying. Thus, the Friar Marcos de Niza, in his reconnaissance in Sonora and northwards in search of the seven large cities of Cibola, was informed that he would there find the chief doorways ornamented with turquoise.

On his way, he met Sonora Indians, returning from the north, who explained that they had been to Cibola to get turquoises and cow (buffalo) skins. Turquoises were suspended in their ears and noses, and they wore belts adorned with turquoises. At one village the chief men were adorned with collars of turquoise, while others were allowed to use them in their ears and noses only. When Casteñada reached Tusayan, the people presented him with some turquoises. Mendoza, in his letter regarding the seven cities, says: "They have turquoises in quantity." Vasquez reported the use of turquoises in worship, as offerings to the gods, and he adds that generally they were poor ones. In Casteñada's narrative mention is made of presents of turquoises to the devil by the inhabitants of Culiacan and, also, that a certain clan of women were decorated with bracelets of fine turquoises.

In the celebrated Coronado expedition northwards from Mexico to Cibola, 1540–1542, the Negro explorer Estévan, who went with the party, gave the good friars great trouble and anxiety by his greed in collecting turquoises and objects of value from the natives. Estévan appears to have been always ready to press on in advance, an explanation of which may probably be found in his desire to get the first pick of the gems. He was loaded with them on his arrival at the outposts of Cibola, where he was killed and his turquoises confiscated.[3]

In their journals, or narratives of exploration, we do not find any reference to the source or locality of the chalchuite. We may assume that such information was carefully withheld. The mines were considered as sacred to the followers of Montezuma, Kunz records,[4] on the authority of Major Hyde, who was exploring the Cerrillos locality in 1880, that the Pueblo Indians from Santo Domingo warned him that the mine was sacred, and that the turquoise (chalchuite) he was taking from it, must not go into the hands of those whose saviour was not Montezuma.

We have abundant evidence of the use of chalchuite for ornaments and decorative works by the ancient race of this great valley—the Salt River Valley of Arizona. Fragments of the gem chalchuite, or portions of the necklaces and pendants in the form of small, oblong, tabular pellets, are found amongst other relics in the earth of the ruins. And other more important objects have been unearthed here and will be briefly noticed.

A few years ago, I was shown a marine shell from the ruins of this valley, which was encrusted with pitch, and a fine mosaic of tesseral of chalchuite. Kunz mentions and gives a figure of a similar object, found about ten miles from Tempe, Arizona. It was enclosed, or wrapped, in asbestos and placed in a decorated Zuñi jar, thus indicating its source and the ancient communication with the Zuñis. This unusual object was in the form of a toad, the sacred emblem of the Zuñi people. The mosaic, composed of chalchuite and garnets, was arranged upon a foundation of shell covered with black pitch. The colored figure given by Kunz[5] is very striking and satisfactory.

Mr. Frank H. Cushing, of the Hemenway Expedition, found in the same region a sculptured object, resembling a prairie dog in form, having eyes of turquoise.

There is in the British Museum, London, a human skull completely overlaid with tesseral of chalchuite. This is believed to be the same specimen formerly in the museum of the late Mr. Henry Christy, a drawing of which was made by Waldeck, and was published by the French Government. A reproduction of this drawing was published by the late E. G. Squier, who also[6] refers to a modern mask similarly encrusted. The eyeballs were made of nodules of iron pyrites, cut hemispherically and highly polished. I am not able to state the locality from which these large objects were obtained, but they were probably from Old Mexico.

The use and high valuation and esteem of chalchuite, or the turquoise, may thus be traced from the country of the Navajos and Zuñis in the northern part of Arizona, southwards into Old Mexico and beyond. The wide geographical distribution of the sources of the gem, and the fact that all the localities found by us have been anciently worked, indicate the universal desire to obtain it. These facts appear to me to be good evidence of the substantial unity of the races which formerly held sway from the Navajo and Zuñi country to the capital of the Montezumas.

The Identification of Chalchihuitl with Turquoise

Before my visit to New Mexico in 1858 and the finding at Santa Fé of green turquoise in use for necklaces by some of the Pueblo Indians, the occurrence of turquoise in America had not been announced or known. Taking pains at that time to learn the name given to this stone by the Indians, I found that it was known to them as *char-chee-wee tee* (spelled phonetically), or as *chal-chi-hui-tee*. On consulting the narrative of Bernal Diaz, I found that certain highly valued green stones corresponding in their external character to the turquoise were called *chalchihuitl* by the ancient Mexicans when visited by Cortes. I could not but recognize in this name the equivalent of that given by the Pueblo Indians of the north to the turquoise of the Cerrillos. But this identification has been questioned by the late E. G. Squier in the memoir already cited. He taking the view that the name *chalchiuitl, chalchihuitl,* or *chalchuite,* was intended to signify *any* green stone of uncommon value, notably jade or emerald. He says, "The word chalchuitl is defined by Molina, in his 'Vocabulario Mexicana' (1571), to signify *esmeralda baja,* or an inferior kind of emerald." The precious emerald, or emerald proper, was called *quetzalitzthi,* from *quetzal,* the name of a bird with brilliant green plumage, and *itzhi,* stone.

There is nothing in Molina's definition militating against the identification of the word *chalchiuitl* with the turquoise of Mexico; more especially with the stones from near the surface, which are generally green. The old writers all discriminate between the chalchuite and the emerald, or *emeraldus.* Neither do I find, in the other citations given by Squier, good reason to question my original identification of *chalchihuitl,* or *chalchuite,* with the green turquoise of New Mexico and other places. Squier applies the name to the series of carved specimens of the hard green stones, known to us as jade or nephrite, which he obtained from ancient ruins on the borders of Chiapas in Central America. Such relics are rare and have not been found north of Mexico. They are sculptured objects and do not conform to the mention of gemlike stones in general use for personal ornament and decoration.

References made in Dana's *Mineralogy*[7] to this subject note the conflict of opinions, as expressed by myself, by Squier and by Professor Raphael Pumpelly. Thus Pumpelly, on his return from his explorations in China,[8] appears to identify the name *chalchihuitl* with the *feitsni,* or jade, of the Chinese, probably because he had seen the jade ornaments in Squier's collection called *chalchihuitl* by Squier; but he refers, also, to the inlaid mask in the collection of the Museum of Practical Geology, London, which is a mosaic of turquoise, and not of jade.

I am still of the opinion, after careful consideration of all the evidence to this date, that my original identification of chalchuite with turquoise was correct. However opinions may differ, the fact remains that the Pueblo Indians of today apply the name to turquoise, and to turquoise only. If a Pueblo Indian of New Mexico or Arizona is asked for chalchuite, he produces green turquoise, and not emerald, jade or jasper, or other green stone.

It will be noted that I have modified the orthography of *chalchihuitl* to *chalchuite,* the latter being shorter and conforming to the usual terminal syllable of names of mineral species. It should, however, be pronounced *chal-chee-we te.*

10

ABORIGINAL TRADE ROUTES FOR SEA SHELLS IN THE SOUTHWEST

Donald D. Brand

At the time Donald D. Brand published this article (1938), the implications of the widespread trade from the Pacific area, the Gulf of California, and the Gulf coast region into the Southwest were not sufficiently understood. In the post–World War II period, however, a variety of workers began to see the implications of the wide-scale trade into the Southwest demonstrated by actual finds of sea shells (and, indeed, many other things not studied by Brand). In the last quarter century, the work of J. Charles Kelley, Edwin Ferdon, Emil W. Haury, Charles C. DiPeso, Albert H. Schroeder, Bertha Dutton, Carroll L. Riley, and a number of others has demonstrated the high level of interchange of ideas and actual objects between the Southwest and its various peripheries. Shell, worked and unworked, came from all the areas mentioned by Brand, while from Mexico came parrots and macaws, rubber balls, copper objects, and a flood of new ideas, religious, ceremonial, political, and social. The Southwest, in turn, exported turquoises, perhaps other semijewel stones and doubtless other things both material and nonmaterial. In a very real sense, therefore, this article by Brand is a landmark paper, only now being fully utilized.

Sea shells, when found in archaeologic ruins and middens of the Southwest, may provide data concerning prehistoric customs, techniques, and trade. This paper attempts to outline the methods and results of a study into prehistoric trade routes in the Southwest, based upon the distribution of marine shells. The study was initiated by examining all possible literature on, and museum collections from, the area (arbitrarily taken as all of Arizona and New Mexico, most of Utah, and portions of adjacent entities) for mentions or exhibits of molluscan shells.[1] The following difficulties were encountered almost immediately:

1. A great many of the reports on excavations failed to mention shells at all, or used such vague terms as *shells, molluscs, clams, snails,*

and the like. At some sites, especially toward the northeastern interior, a lack or paucity of shell material might be expected, but such a condition on middle tributaries of the Colorado River is rather difficult to explain. Probably, in most of such reports, neither the excavators nor the reporters were either interested or versed in malacology, and consequently failed to grasp the importance of preserving and recording all shell material—both worked and unworked. Only in recent years has more than a paragraph or two been devoted to discussing the molluscan finds of an excavation.[2]

2. In the reports that made some pretense to listing the individual species, there was a wide variation in completeness, method, and accuracy of nomenclature. Some monographs gave only common names (such as white olivella, large Pacific clam, conch, whelk, cockle, scallop, and the like) which seldom could be narrowed down to the proper genus and practically never could be identified with a species. Quite often, seemingly, the excavators made their own field and museum identifications. It is possible that this procedure has conditioned the preponderance of *Olivella, Glycymeris, Oliva, Conus, Haliotis, Cardium,* and *Pecten* identifications, since these seven most commonly mentioned genera probably are the seven easiest for the layman to recognize. Even when experts have been called in,[3] there has been much discrepancy in the manner of citation and in the checking of obsolete or less valid synonyms. An example of this is one of the olives, which has been cited as: *Oliva hiatula, Agaronia hiatula* Gmelin, *Agaronia testacea* Lamarck, etc. One should not object, however, to many specific uncertainties in identification since most archaeologic shell material cannot be identified because of being (a) too altered by work (as is true of nearly all disc beads), (b) too fragmentary, or (c) too decayed.

3. Much of the archaeologic Southwest has not been worked, either in time or in space. This is especially true of the so-called Developmental or Pueblo I and II periods (roughly A.D. 600 to 950) of "culture time," and of the Eastern Periphery, Middle Rio Grande, Chihuahua, and Sonora areas. Consequently, any study in distributions must contain lamentable hiatuses.

After determining what genera and species had been found (with subsidiary notes on use and culture period), the next step was to establish the actual, most probable, or possible provenience of each genus and of each species. This was the most difficult portion of the study because of disagreements among conchologic authorities as to terminology, synonyms, and areal distribution.[4]

In general the areal disagreement was along lines unimportant for this study, e.g., whether a species was only in the Gulf of California or extended around to Magdalena Bay, or whether a species was found southward only to San Diego or extended to Cedros Island. In a few cases bad errors may have been introduced, as in Boekelman's identification ([Harold S.] Gladwin, et al., *Excavations at Snaketown* [1937]) of a shell as *Alectrion vibex* Say (of Atlantic origin) when the shell probably was *Nassarius (Alectrion, Nassa) tiarula* Kiener (of Pacific origin). These two species are so similar that it might be said that they differ geographically rather than morphologically. Also, it is possible that *Pecten gibbus* var. *irradians* (identified by Wing for [Paul H.] Nesbitt, *Starkweather Ruin* [1938]), of Atlantic origin, may be one of the Pacific varieties since *Pecten gibbus* is well represented on the Pacific Coast, as in *Pecten gibbus* var. *circularis,* etc. The following list presents alphabetically, within classes, the areas of origin of all identified genera and species known to the writer.

Provenience of Shells

GULF OF CALIFORNIA

Gastropoda:

Acmaea fascicularis Menke

Agaronia testacea Lamarck (*A. hiatula* Gmel., *Oliva hiatula* Gmel., *O. testacea* Lam.)

Anachis (Columbella) coronata Sowerby

Cerithidea albonodosa Carpenter

C. mazatlanica Carpenter

Cerithium stercus-muscarum Valenciennes

Conus fergusoni Sowerby

C. princeps Linn.

C. purpurascens Broderip

C. regularis Sowerby

Galeodea patula Broderip (*Galeodes patulas, Pyrula patula*)

Melongena patula Brod. & Sow. (*Pyrula patula, Galeodea patula*)

Murex (Phyllonotus) radix Gmel. var. *nigritus* Phil.

Nassarius (Alectrion, Nassa) complanatus Powys

N. leucops Pils. & Lowe

N. moestus Hinds (*N. brunneostoma* Stearns)

Nerita bernhardi Recluz

Neretina picta Sowerby

Oliva angulata Lamarck (*O. incrassata* Sol.)

O. verulata-hemphilli Johnson (*O. spicata* Bolt. var. *hemphilli* John.)

Olivella dama Mawe (*O. dama* Gray, *O. dama* Wood)

O. tergina Duclos

O. (Oliva, Lamprodoma) volutella Lamarck

Pyrene (Columbella) major Sowerby

Strombus galeatus Swainson

S. gracilior Sowerby

Turbo (Astraea, Callopoma) fluctuosum Wood

Turritella leucostoma Valenciennes (*T. tigrina* Kien.)

Pelycypoda:

Arca pacifica Sowerby

A. tuberculosa Sowerby

Chama echinata Broderip

Glycymeris (Pectunculus) bicolor Reeve

G. giganteus Reeve

G. maculatus Broderip

Macrocallista (Pitar, Cytherea) squalida Sowerby

Pecten vogdesi Arnold (*P. excavatus* Anton)

P. (Lyropecten) subnodosus Sowerby

Pteria (Avicula) Peruviana Reeve

PACIFIC COAST

Gastropoda:

Cerithidea Californica Haldemann (*C. sacrata* Gould)

Conus Californicus Hinds

Erato vitellina Hinds

Haliotis cracherodii Leach

H. fulgens Philippi

H. rufescens Swainson

Northia (Searlesia) dira Reeve

Olivella (Oliva) biplicata Sowerby

Pelycypoda:

Pecten circularis var. *aequisulcatus* Carpenter

PACIFIC COAST AND GULF OF CALIFORNIA

Gastropoda:

Polinices (Neverita) recluzianus Deshayes

Trivia solandri Gray

Vermetus (Aletes) centiquadrus Valenciennes

V. (Aletes) squamigerus Carpenter

Pelycypoda:

Cardium (Laevicardium) elatum Sowerby

Chama buddiana C. B. Adams

Dosinia ponderosa Gray

Pecten (Aequipecten) gibbus var. *circularis* Sowerby

Spondylus princeps Broderip (*S. limbatus* Sow.)

Tagelus Californianus Conrad

ATLANTIC WATERS

Gastropoda:

Fasciolaria distans Lamarck

Nassarius (Alectrion, Nassa)
   vibex Say

Neritina reclivata Say

Oliva sayana Rav.

Strombus gigas Linn.

S. pugilis Linn.

Pelycypoda:

Cardium robustum Solander

Noetia (Arca) ponderosa Say

Pecten gibbus var. irradians

GENERA POSSIBLE FROM ALL WATERS
(SPECIES NOT DETERMINED)

Cadulus sp.

Cypraea sp.

Tritonalia sp.

Chione sp.

Tivela sp.

Altogether, 132 archaeologic sites were reported to contain from one to 33 species each of marine shells, which provided a total of 41 genera and 66 different identified species. Thirty-eight of these species could have been obtained only from the Gulf of California; another ten species could have been secured from either the Gulf of California or the Pacific Coast of California, or both; and an additional nine species could have come only from approximately the present Southern California Coast. Thus, a total of 57 species were of general Pacific origin, and nine came from Atlantic waters. In this connection it is interesting to note that subtropical and tropical waters, rich in molluscan fauna, contributed all of the identified species. The subtropical Pacific (Southern California—Point Conception to Cedros Island) and Atlantic (Northern Gulf of Mexico) faunal zones contributed nine species each, and the tropical Gulf of California zone (essentially Cedros Island or, better, Magdalena Bay to the Tres Marias Islands) produced at least 38 species. This latter production is not surprising in view of the observation that the richest molluscan collecting grounds on the west coast of North America are around La Paz, whence have been obtained 90 bivalve and 110 univalve species.

It should be observed that the three classes of the phylum Mollusca represented archaeologically in the Southwest are present roughly proportional to the absolute number of species in each class. Class Gastropoda (49,000+ species) is represented by 46 species; Class Pelycypoda (7,000± species) is represented by 20 species; and Class

Scaphopoda (200± species) is represented by one genus, species undetermined. The reason for such a distribution of species by classes does not, however, lie entirely in the relative abundance of species in the various classes. It should be kept in mind that the peoples of the interior Southwest did not obtain the various marine molluscs for food at all (unless it were a small amount of dried shellfish), but rather for ornamentation and ceremonial usage.[5]

Fully ninety percent of the marine shells found in archaeologic sites have been worked in some fashion, which might indicate selection of shell for elaboration rather than as the natural containers of food. Furthermore, an inspection of the shells found in kitchen middens of the San Francisco Bay, Southern California Coast, and Seri Indian areas shows that *Mytilus, Macoma, Ostrea, Cardium, Tapes, Purpura, Cerithidea, Haliotis, Acmaea, Tivela, Solen, Astraea, Pecten,* and *Polinices* along the California Coast were most prized for food; *Pitar, Arca, Tivela, Chama, Paphia, Glycymeris, Dosinia, Macrocallista, Pteria, Mactra, Pecten, Cardium, Murex, Polinices, Mytilus,* and *Turbo* were most utilized along the Sonoran Coast; and, of these 25 genera most commonly used for food by aborigines along the coasts, only *Glycymeris, Haliotis, Cardium,* and *Pecten* (in that order) are at all common in the Southwestern ruins. Specifically, *Glycymeris maculatus, Haliotis cracherodii,* and *Haliotis fulgens* were the only molluscs, much used for food on the coast, whose shells were traded inland in large numbers.

There is no archaeologic or ethnologic evidence for use of marine molluscs for dye, textile, or currency in the Southwest. Although worked and certain unworked shells were (and are) highly prized, all the indications are that the values were primarily aesthetic and ceremonial, and that shells never have functioned as measures or units of value. This Southwestern disregard for shells as currency is in decided contrast with the attitude of the tribes of the Middle Atlantic (peak or wampum of clams), Northwest American (strings of dentalia), and Californian (money of worked abalone, *Olivella,* etc.) coasts.[6]

In the Southwest sea shells were used predominantly for ornament, in the form of beads (mainly *Olivella, Oliva, Conus, Haliotis, Turritella, Cerithidea, Nassarius, Trivia, Vermetus,* and various bivalves which were ground into disc beads and are very difficult to identify), pendants (chiefly of *Haliotis, Glycymeris, Cardium, Pecten,* and *Turritella*), bracelets (principally of *Glycymeris*), rings, placques, etc. Presumably ceremonial in utility were such forms as trumpets (*Strombus, Melongena, Murex*), receptacles for corn pollen, ground turquoise and the like (usually whole *Haliotis*), and eccentric figures and forms carved usually from large heavy walled marine shells. In general marine shells were preferred over land and fresh water shells because the latter were less durable and not so massive, and consequently were not so well suited for carving. Only infrequently were shells used for tools such as needles, awls, and hooks.

In absolute numbers, and by sites at which they have been found, shells of the genera *Olivella* and *Glycymeris* were most important. The approximate order of other common genera is: *Oliva, Conus, Haliotis, Cardium, Pecten, Nassarius, Turritella, Pyrene (Columbella), Cerithidea,* and *Strombus.* In terms of spread in time and area, *Olivella, Glycymeris, Haliotis, Oliva,* and *Conus* have been most important in the Southwest. All five of the above genera have been present in the Southwest since Basketmaker cultural time (possibly since 1500 years ago). It will be noted that *Oliva sayana* is the only species from the above group which is of Atlantic origin, and this species was not found in Basketmaker time. The implication is that all early trade routes in marine shells were from the Pacific and Gulf of California coasts. During the next cultural period, the Developmental Pueblo (Pueblo I and II, more or less A.D. 600 to 950), species of the genera *Cardium, Cerithidea, Strombus,* and *Turritella* were introduced. In succeeding time the number of genera was increased very considerably for the so-called Anasazi or Basketmaker-Pueblo Plateau area, which is the northeastern portion of the Southwest. In the Hohokam-Trincheras area (the southwestern portion of the Southwest) introductions were probably much earlier in the case of every genus originating from western waters.

Worked shell is most commonly found in inhumations and with cremations. Unworked shell, discards, and fragments occur most frequently in refuse. The number of sites with reported marine shell is largest in Arizona and northern Sonora, followed by northern Chihuahua and New Mexico, with western Texas, Utah, Nevada, and Colorado in descending order. This distribution probably represents three factors: 1) distance from the sea, 2) amount of archaeologic work carried out and reported upon, and, 3) nature of barriers to occupation and communication. The sites with the greatest number of reported species and/or genera are, in order, Snaketown and Los Muertos in the Middle Gila drainage, Pecos on the upper Pecos River, Chaco Canyon (five sites within a radius of one mile) on a tributary of the Colorado–San Juan, Tuzigoot (on a tributary of the Gila-Salt), Tusayan (several nearby ruins in Little Colorado drainage), Aztec Ruins (in San Juan drainage), and Cameron Creek Village in Mimbres drainage (see circles on map). It will be noted that all of these sites but two are in Gulf of California–Colorado River drainage. The three sites richest in species are situated near a confluence of Pacific and Gulf of California trade routes (Snaketown and Los Muertos), and at an outpost of Rio Grande Pueblo culture against the High Plains and on Pecos–Rio Grande–Gulf of Mexico drainage (Pecos). Even at the Pecos site, in Atlantic drainage, less than ten percent of the shells were of Atlantic origin.

The accompanying map incorporates the main conclusions as to probable routes of shell movement. With reference to this map the following comments should be made:

1. The absolute and relative amount of shell trade from the Gulf of Mexico to the Southwest was small. Only ruins along the Pecos River, in northern Chihuahua, and in the Mimbres drainage possess any appreciable number of Gulf of Mexico shells. All such areas are east of the Continental Divide. Two sites in Pacific drainage have had one species each reported from the Gulf of Mexico. These are Snaketown (*Nassarius vibex*) and the Starkweather Ruin (*Pecten gibbus* var. *irradians*). Previously there has been pointed out the strong possibility of error in both cases. Although Pacific and Atlantic waters have many genera in common, most malacologists will not allow common possession of any species. It is possible that *Alectrion vibex* and *Pecten gibbus* are exceptions and, therefore, invalid as indicators of provenience.

2. *Haliotis* sp. and possibly *Olivella biplicata* into southwestern Colorado, and *Haliotis* sp. into the Panhandle of Texas, constituted the most north and eastward spread of Pacific Coast shells. Also, other than these two genera, no shells of purely Pacific Coast origin have been reported east of the Rio Grande. Nor have any Pacific Coast shells been reported from Sonora or the Big Bend region of the Rio Grande.

3. No Gulf of California shells were worked along the Pacific Coast of upper California, nor eastward into Nevada. The spread of Gulf of California shells into Utah and Colorado was slight and comprised chiefly *Glycymeris* sp., *Olivella dama,* and *Olivella volutella.*

4. Seemingly there were two main western routes (one from the California Coast, the other from the Sonora Coast) that converged upon the Middle Gila area. The northern route carried mainly *Haliotis* sp. and *Olivella biplicata;* the southern route provided the bulk of the shells found in the Southwest. From the Middle Gila–Lower Salt area routes diverged northward and eastward into the drainage basins of the Little Colorado, San Juan, and the western affluents of the Rio Grande. The natural setting was such as to make the shores between the Colorado and Yaqui deltas the chief gathering grounds, nearby sites (principally in the Altar and Sonora drainages) places of primary elaboration of some of the larger and heavier shells (e.g., *Glycymeris*), and settlements

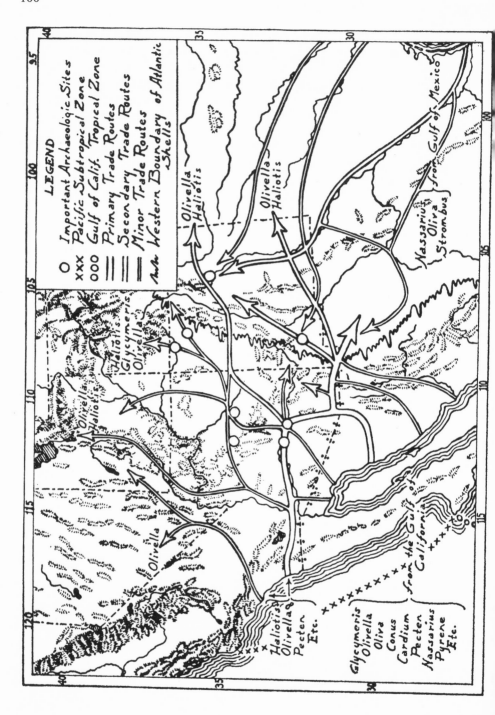

in the Gila Valley (near the crossroads afforded by the Santa Cruz–Salt and Lower and Upper Gila) the final elaborators, arbiters of style in shellwork, and middlemen for both worked and unworked goods going northward and eastward. Subsidiary routes up the Sonora and Yaqui rivers probably delivered the bulk of shells received in the interior drainage basins of northwestern Chihuahua, and continued to join with the Gila routes in feeding the Mimbres and Rio Grande areas. Trade routes up the Brazos, Colorado, and Rio Grande–Pecos brought in the bulk of Gulf of Mexico shells, which were principally *Nassarius vibex, Oliva sayana,* and *Strombus* sp. The vicinities of Pecos Pueblo, Ojinaga, and El Paso were in strong crossroads position, which strength of location was expressed in comparative richness of marine shell material.

5. Future work will undoubtedly add to the species and genera and will fill in details of distribution, but there should be little change in proportion of Atlantic to Pacific shells, major trade routes, or relative importance of the already identified species.

11

PREHISTORIC CULTURES OF THE SAN JUAN DRAINAGE

A. V. Kidder

In 1917, A. V. Kidder published a short account (edited by F. W. Hodge) of the level of knowledge and of the problems that archaeologists of his time faced in their examinations of the San Juan area. Many of the problems posed by Kidder have been answered; for example, it is now accepted that the Basketmakers were the cultural and physical precursors of Puebloan peoples; his "Slab-house" culture is now fitted into the late Basketmaker sequence; and his Kiva culture is now referred to as Anasazi Pueblo. Kidder's speculation as to the affinities of the San Juan Kiva culture with other Puebloan peoples has proven correct. His suggestion that the San Juan may have been a center and original source for what we now call Anasazi is certainly an oversimplification, but his belief that influence from the San Juan reached the Rio Grande Valley is demonstrably true, though the full implications of San Juan–upper Rio Grande relationships in the period A.D. 1200–1300 still have not been worked out.

Most significantly, Kidder's speculations in this paper, taken together, result in the following putative developmental sequence for the Puebloan cultures: (1) Basketmaker culture (later Basketmaker II); (2) Slab-house culture (Basketmaker III); (3) Unit House culture (Pueblo I–II); (4) San Juan Kiva culture (Pueblo III); (5) Rio Grande Kiva culture (Pueblo IV); (6) Historic Pueblos (Pueblo V). Thus, as early as 1917 he had conceptualized essentially the same Basketmaker-Pueblo sequence (the "Pecos Chronology") that was adopted ten years later by Southwestern archaeologists meeting at Pecos, New Mexico, in August 1927. The Pecos Chronology was modified slightly later, actually bringing it more in line with Kidder's thinking in the present paper by combining Pueblo I and II into Developmental Pueblo, but it remains until this day the accepted Anasazi (Basketmaker-Pueblo) cultural sequence. Truly, the reasoning used in this paper, and the research that led to it, represents a monumental accomplishment in view of the permanent impression it left on the thinking of Southwestern archaeologists.

The physiography and climate of the San Juan watershed in Utah, Arizona, New Mexico, and Colorado, are too well known to archeologists from the excellent papers of Dr. Prudden and Professor Cummings to require extended description. Suffice it to say that the region is rough, barren, and essentially arid, a country of deep cañons and high, barren mesas. In spite of these seemingly unfavorable conditions, the thirty thousand square miles drained by the San Juan and its tributaries are almost crowded with the relics of former sedentary inhabitants in the form of the ruins of pueblos, cliff dwellings, watch towers, and shrines. Today, however, all are deserted, nor have we evidence that any of them have been occupied since the discovery of America. These ruins have been studied by many archeologists and described by a few of them, notably by Dr. Prudden, whose writings on San Juan antiquities must always form the basis of any research. No grouping of the extensive data that we have, and no attempt to classify the remains has, however, yet been made. This paper is intended as a beginning in that direction, although it should be understood that in the present state of our knowledge few final conclusions can be reached.

The earliest sedentary or at least agricultural inhabitants of whom we have knowledge were the so-called Basketmakers. Discovered by the Wetherill brothers in the Grand Gulch region of southeastern Utah, the remains were first brought to the notice of archeologists through papers by Mr. Pepper, describing collections made by the Wetherills and other professional diggers, and quoting statements made by them.

According to these accounts the Basketmakers occupied round subterranean rooms dug in the compact earth floors of the large caves that they always seemed to inhabit. They built cists, both plain and stone-lined—primarily for storage, secondarily for burial. The crania found in the graves were all undeformed and the bodies were always accompanied with baskets. Baskets indeed were evidently one of the chief products of the people, for they occurred in the caves in large numbers and of most excellent workmanship. Pottery vessels, on the other hand, were scarce and crude, and usually bore on their bottoms the imprint of the baskets in which they had been formed. Also characteristic of the culture was the use of the atlatl, or throwing-stick, and the weaving of peculiar square-toed sandals. It was definitely stated by the Wetherills that these remains were often found underneath typical stone cliff dwellings. The range of the culture was given as Grand Gulch, the adjoining cañons, and possibly the Cañon de Chelly.

Recent field work by the Peabody Museum in Marsh Pass and Monument Valley, on the south side of the San Juan, has served to confirm all these statements, to extend the range of the Basketmakers to that district, and to add some details to the summary given above, such as the identification of the Basketmaker pipe, a squat, conical affair; the determination of the twined-woven, banded sack as a characteristic Basketmaker product; and the recognition as typical of certain painted pictographs of square-shouldered human figures. No trace of loom weaving could be discovered.

Apparently coming between the Basketmakers and the later Cliff Dwellers were people who left behind them traces of what we may tentatively call the Slab-house culture. At present it is known definitely from only one small area in northeastern Arizona, the Monument Valley country. The site that gives us our evidence for stating that the group is older than the cliff dwellings was found in a cave in Hagoé Cañon, a tributary of Gypsum wash. Here beneath a well-defined stratum of typical Cliff Dweller remains were found the ruins of a series of round and oval semisubterranean rooms the lower sides of which were made of flat slabs set edgewise in adobe, and whose upper parts were built of large chunks or "turtlebacks" of adobe patted on wet and added above each other as the walls grew. Most of the rooms were small, but in the center of the cave was a single larger chamber, round, entirely subterranean, and formerly provided with a low, tipi-like roof. The rubbish in these lower strata contained a larger number of bone and chipped stone implements than is commonly found in like deposits in the later cliff dwellings. The most striking difference, however, was in the pottery. Instead of the red-and-yellow and finely made black-and-white of the Kayenta types which occurred in the upper layers of the cave, the rubbish in and about the lower slab-rooms contained only a coarsely finished black-and-white ware, very neatly decorated with symbols quite distinct from those of the upper stratum and a dark ware of particular interest in that it seems to show, in the few heavy coils that encircle the necks of all the pieces, the first stages of the beautiful corrugated technique that later became so marked a feature of San Juan pottery. Of perishable objects, such as sandals, basketry, and cloth, unfortunately nothing was preserved, nor were any burials found. An open-air site with numbers of slab-houses of the same rounded form and with pottery of the same types was found some twelve miles to the east in the "Great Comb."

The known range of the Slab-house culture is very small, but there is reason to suspect that it will eventually prove to be much greater. Pottery very similar in appearance was found in the rubbish below a large cliff-house in the lower Chinlee; Professor Cummings describes ruins in Sagi-ot-sosi that seem to be typically Slab-house,[1] and in the same publication he refers to turtleback adobe walls as far north as Moab, Utah.[2]

The third and latest culture is that of the cliff-houses and pueblos. This I call for convenience the Kiva culture, because with few exceptions[3] all the principal ruins of the San Juan contain highly specialized ceremonial rooms called kivas. While these rooms have local variations, too numerous to mention in this paper, all of them are round and subterranean, although the exigencies of the site may sometimes have warped the shape or forced the room, so to speak, partly out of the ground; all have a firepit near the middle of the floor; a masonry, slab, or wattle-work screen in front of it, and a small horizontal passage entering at the floor level and connecting with the outside by a vertical shaft. For purposes of classification and for clearness I venture to propose that no structure among the San Juan ruins be called a kiva, unless it conforms to these general specifications.

As was said above, all or nearly all the ruins of stone community houses, be they cliff dwellings or surface pueblos, contain kivas, and it is safe, I think, to group them together on this basis. Common ownership of so peculiar and highly specialized a feature as the kiva must imply some degree of relationship.

The general culture of the cliff dwellings and pueblos is well known from the writings of Nordenskiöld, Fewkes, and Cummings. Pottery making was an important industry, the leading wares being the black-and-white and the corrugated. Corn, beans, and squashes were grown, and the turkey was domesticated; fine cotton cloth was woven, as well as excellent rush matting. While the manufacture of coiled basketry was practiced, it was not carried on to any such extent as it was in the Basketmaker culture, nor were baskets commonly used as mortuary offerings. Much more research must be done before we can finally classify the ruins, but at present it is possible to recognize certain definite subdivisions of the culture, each characterized by peculiarities of pottery, architecture, and kiva construction. These are: Chaco Cañon, Mesa Verde, Montezuma Creek, Chinlee, and Kayenta. Further study will undoubtedly lead to the recognition of others. The subgroups are named from the localities where they seem to have reached their highest developments, but each of them is found over a considerable area and several of them invade each other's territory. The description of the subcultures and the consideration of their interrelation cannot be undertaken in this paper, in which the Kiva culture is treated as a unit.

To sum up: We find that the Basketmaker is the earliest known culture of sedentary corn-growing type. In the matter of housebuilding, pottery making, and loom weaving, the people were very little advanced;

in the arts of basketry, bag weaving, and sandal making, on the other hand, their products were abundant and of the very finest quality. Stone masonry, pottery making, and the loom being typically Southwestern developments, we are led to suspect that the Basketmaker culture was an intrusive one that had brought with it its peculiar textile arts and was in process of acquiring, either by natural development or possibly from contact with already established cultures, a knowledge of stone masonry and pottery. This is, of course, theoretical, but at least it sets before us definite problems and indicates lines of research necessary for their solution. First, we must have more data, both on the culture itself and on its range. Second, when the culture is well enough known for analysis of its component parts—the weaves of its basketry, sandals, and bags; the technique of its wood, stone, and clay working,—we must prosecute a thorough search, both in the Southwest and in all directions beyond its limits, to ascertain the relationship of the cultural traits that our intensive study has established. Third, the same analytical and comparative methods must be applied in somatological research. Most important results may be expected from this branch of our investigation, as material is abundant, and the deformation and nondeformation of the head (apparently an invariable difference between the later people and the Basketmakers) provides a very useful starting point.

No less important than questions of origin and contemporary relationship are those of later development. Was the Basketmaker ancestral to the later cultures, or did it die out; was it pushed aside or was it assimilated? Here again analytical methods must be followed—pottery technique, basket-weaves, sandal types, implements, weapons, and ornaments, all should be compared with those from the slab-houses and cliff dwellings.

In the consideration of our next culture, that of the Slab-houses, we are confronted by a serious lack of data. We have no conclusive evidence that the slab-houses should be placed between the Basketmakers' remains and those of the Cliff Dwellers. The pottery of the Slab-house culture, however, is so much like that of the Kiva culture that a fairly close relationship seems certain, and as we know that both Basketmaker and Slab-house are earlier than Kiva, it is probable that the Slab-house should occupy the middle position. The Slab-house is, as we have just said, undoubtedly related to the Kiva culture and probably lies between it and the Basketmaker; but whether or not it is truly transitional remains to be determined. I am inclined to think that it is. The semisubterranean rooms show in their attempts at masonry construction an apparent development from the merely excavated rooms and slab cists of the Basketmakers to the stone dwellings of the Kiva culture. Lack of data handicaps us in any attempt to determine whether or not the round underground room uncovered in Hagoé Cañon should be regarded as a forerunner of a true kiva.

Slab-house pottery is particularly interesting. If the black wares with their few heavy coils at the neck show the beginning of the corrugated style, it means that smooth pottery had been long in use and had even developed a complex painted symbolism before corrugated wares were even attempted. This would rather effectually disprove Cushing's theory of the origin of Southwestern pottery in the conscious imitation in clay of coiled basketry. Another interesting feature, but one which requires further study, is the resemblance between Slab-house black-and-white ware and certain styles found in the Chaco Cañon subgroup of the Kiva culture.

Textiles and other perishable objects we have unfortunately not yet found, but their recovery is merely a matter of further exploration. One hint we do get: Professor Cummings describes a ruin in Sagi-ot-sosi, Arizona, in which a late building was found above the ruins of rooms made of upright slabs and otherwise corresponding closely to the Slab-house remains in Hagoé Cañon. Among the objects found in these rooms were woven headbands and cord sandals with peculiar scooped-out toes. If these relics be accepted as belonging to the Slab-house culture, and the only reason for thinking that they do not lies in the coarseness of the pottery as described by Professor Cummings, the scoop-toed sandals, intermediate in shape between the square-toed Basketmaker type and the pointed-toe Kiva-culture type, at once become objects of much morphological significance.

Of the Kiva culture, the last and most important of our San Juan groups, we know really extremely little. We are aware that the region is full of ruins of stone community dwellings, ranging in size from tiny three- or four-room affairs to such enormous and splendidly built structures as Pueblo Bonito and Hungo Pavie. We have also a good idea of the material culture of certain of the more striking groups, such as Chaco Cañon, Mesa Verde, Kayenta, and Chinlee; but as to the interrelation of these groups—whether, for example, they were all inhabited at one time or whether a single body of people, drifting slowly across the country, built, inhabited, and deserted them one after another—we are entirely ignorant.

It would be futile to attempt, in the present state of our knowledge, to theorize on these matters, but it may not be amiss in closing to point out a few striking features that have not hitherto been emphasized and to indicate a line of research that may perhaps lead to more definite information.

First. The San Juan Kiva culture is in its broader aspects, such as sedentary community life, agriculture, and general pottery type, allied to all the other Puebloan cultures. It is, nevertheless, a true culture and not merely a convenient geographical unit, for the reason that it is distinguishable, especially in its more highly specialized phases, by traits peculiar to itself, such as its pottery, many forms of which are unmistakable, and particularly by its high development of the round subterranean kiva. Deeper analysis of the culture will undoubtedly reveal still others.

Second. The San Juan Kiva culture seems to be, so to speak, the headquarters for or the breeder of those elements which serve to divide all Southwestern cultures into two large divisions. One of these is the northern and eastern, comprising the San Juan, all of puebloan Utah, the Rio Grande, the Upper Gila and Salt, and parts of the Little Colorado. The other is the southern and western, embracing the lower Gila, southern Arizona and New Mexico, and the Casas Grandes country in Chihuahua. The northern and eastern division is marked by the arrangement of small rectangular cells into generally terraced buildings, by the use of circular ceremonial structures, and by a great development of black-and-white wares and corrugated cooking pottery. The southern and western, on the other hand, tends to produce more loosely knit structures of large rooms and compounds, rectangular ceremonial apartments, and, in pottery, colored wares and uncorrugated cooking vessels. Closer study and more data will go to show, I think, that while these contrasted traits mingle in such zones of contact as the middle Gila, the Mimbres, and the Little Colorado, they become purer as they recede toward their points of origin. That point, for the northern and eastern division, will, I believe, be found in the San Juan basin.

Third of these general observations is: that while the culture died out in the San Juan itself, it survived elsewhere, and in its greatest purity in the upper Rio Grande. This is to be seen, for one example, in the so-called "biscuit ware," the most typical of the later Rio Grande ceramics, which, in my estimation, is the direct descendant of some San Juan class, most probably the Mesa Verde. The survival is also to be seen in the Rio Grande kivas, which are round, subterranean, and provided with the ventilating shaft; furthermore, the round kiva, subterranean as at Taos, above ground as at Nambé, Santo Domingo, and other villages, survives only in those of the modern Pueblos of the eastern or Rio Grande group.

The foregoing observations are hesitatingly put forward because they are founded on such incomplete evidence. They show, however, the need for gathering further data, and particularly for careful analytical and classificatory research. If the San Juan country was indeed a breeder and disseminator of cultural traits, it is of the first importance that *its* culture be thoroughly understood. That can be accomplished only by working back to its very earliest phases. What these may have been was shown in our very brief review of the Basketmaker and Slab-house cultures; some later stages, however, must have intervened between the crude attempts of the Slab-houses and such architectural triumphs as Cliff Palace and Pueblo Bonito. They are presumably to be found in the small "unit type" ruins so well described by Dr. Prudden. As, however, it is easier and safer to work backward than forward, it would be best, I think, to study carefully and to classify thoroughly the large and important ruins that may reasonably be assumed to mark the later stages of the culture. When we have them well in mind and really know their architecture, kivas, textiles, and pottery, we can then follow the culture back through smaller and less highly developed groups to the generalized type which, theoretically at least, must have been the ancestor of them all.

12

AN ANALYSIS OF SOUTHWESTERN SOCIETY

William Duncan Strong

Strong's magnificent survey and synthesis of the social organization and some related ceremonial practices throughout much of the Greater Southwest must be viewed in terms of the historical development of anthropological research in the area. During the period of circa 1880–1905, classic ethnographic studies such as those of Cushing, Fewkes, Dorsey, Bandelier, Stevenson, Hodge, Mindeleff, Voth, Matthews, and Russell had concentrated primarily on the Pueblo, secondarily on the Navajo and the Pima. From about 1915 to 1927, and continuing thereafter, a new wave of studies of the various pueblos by Parsons and others, and of various California tribes and Shoshonean groups by Kroeber, Gifford, Lowie, Benedict, and others, had been made. In the interim, archaeological research beginning in the 1880s had reached a climax in 1924 with the publication of Kidder's remarkable synthesis of Southwestern archaeology, *An Introduction to the Study of Southwestern Archaeology.*

Strong took all of this new and old ethnographic data and considered it with relation to the new conceptualization of Southwestern archaeology. It appears that he immediately recognized that between southern California and the Puebloan Southwest there were certain shared basic principles of social and ceremonial organization that carried an unmistakable implication of former close cultural relation, putatively interrupted later in terms of geographic distribution by incursions of Yuman-speaking peoples and Shoshoneans from the Great Basin. Strong interpreted these early widespread fundamental cultural practices—essentially, the group house, priest, fetish complex and associated ritual (largely concerned with rain-bringing and fertility)—to an ancient wave of diffusion into the Southwest, probably from Mexico, that affected all these groups at a time when they had a continuous geographic distribution.

His chart 2 entitled "Theoretical Reconstruction of Southwestern Society," is actually a reconstruction of Southwestern cultural history that not only was congruent with archaeological interpretations then current but one which also tended to interpret them in terms of the development of social and ceremonial factors.

Strong's paper, published in January 1927,[1] probably influenced the thinking of the archaeologists who developed the Pecos Chronology in August of the same year. Certainly it led directly and immediately to the writing of Kroeber's significant paper, "Native Cultures of the Southwest," in 1928, as Kroeber himself attests. Today, as a wave of new knowledge of the culture history of northwestern Mesoamerica and the Greater Southwest has brought us to the threshold of a better understanding of Mesoamerican-southwestern relations, it is both exciting and gratifying to see how close Strong came to postulating many events just as we now visualize them. It is remarkable how valuable his synthesis of the data of his time still is today in clarifying the culture history of both areas. Strong's paper clearly is a classic contribution to southwestern studies.

As new material on the native peoples of the southwestern portion of the United States has been added to our knowledge of aboriginal culture, an historic relationship between the Pueblo area and southern California has become more and more evident. With only the outlines available twenty-odd years ago, the relationship seemed decidedly tenuous and based solely on details of material culture.[2] Later, with the addition of new facts, it became clear that certain of the Pueblo mythologies shared their fundamental motifs with the Luiseño and other South Californian groups;[3] while in the possession of clans and moieties there appeared in their societies at least superficial resemblances.[4] Further work in the southern California field carried on by the author during the winter of 1924 and 1925 brought to light still other features of social organization which seemed to further the probability of such a connection.

In the light of this new viewpoint, it appears worthwhile to make a more extensive comparison of the society of all southwestern peoples in regard to whom we have available data than has heretofore been attempted. For this purpose the term *southwestern* is extended beyond its customary ethnologic connotation, and made geographically inclusive of the entire southwestern United States.

It is hoped that an approach from the western periphery of the Pueblo area may to some extent shed light on the complexities of social organization there presented. The complex ritualism and society of the Pueblos themselves, with the added difficulty of obtaining information in regard to those in the Rio Grande region, forms a problem for the specialist in this area. It would seem, however, to be a problem that might well be supplemented by a consideration of those areas which apparently came under the influence of the early Pueblo or a related culture, and which may in certain respects retain the elements from which the more elaborate societies arose. It is with this hope that the present comparative study has been made.

In the present paper the social factors to be considered are limited to those of group organization and do not include ceremonial features save where the latter are intimately connected with the units of society and must be considered in relation to them. A few words in regard to the present use of some of the terms for social groupings may be in order. In all cases an attempt has been made to cling to the most generally accepted meanings for the terms employed, but the variety of social groupings in the area and their shifting nature seem inevitably to make necessary some degree of redefinition.

The *lineage*[5] is a unilateral kinship group, all members being united through descent from a common ancestor: where descent is patrilineal, the lineage includes a male, his offspring, and their descendants through males. In other words, the lineage, in contrast to our bilateral family, is equivalent to Rivers'[6] *joint family* and Goldenweiser's[7] *matrilineal family* or *patrilineal family*. A clan may include more than one lineage but is a similar unilateral group, which may be composed of assumed as well as real kinsfolk. As used herein the term *clan* is synonymous with *sib* and has no implication of matrilineal reckoning of descent. The sense of kinship in both lineage and clan tends to prescribe exogamy, but this often applied criterion is not used in the present paper; the characteristic features of the groups coming under these classifications are discussed as they are encountered.

A *phratry* is a major group including a number of clans, or comparable social units which preserve a sense of distinctness. Whether this major group has come about by the linking of the subdivisions, or by some other process, is not implied by the term *phratry*. Whenever these major groups are only two in number each is called a *moiety;* however, a moiety may represent an undivided half of the political unit, the emphasis being on the occurrence of a dual organization of society. Tribal organization, as here used, in part complies with the definition given by Rivers:[8] "A tribe is a social group of a simple kind, the members of which speak a common dialect, have a single government, and act together for common purposes such as warfare." Strangely enough, the Miwok lineage[9] for example, conforms to this definition of a tribe in as much as it is a localized, politically independent, and dialectic unit. Thus the possession of group consciousness over and above that based on real or assumed relationship must be added as a criterion to distinguish these large warlike tribes from such small autonomous units. These features, with certain others to be discussed later, constitute a

majority of those factors of social organization which are most fundamental in the area under consideration, and we will discuss them from
the standpoint of their distribution, qualifying the broad definitions
listed above by the particular features of the phenomena described.

For the use of as yet unpublished material bearing on this problem
the author is greatly indebted to the following persons: to Dr. Robert
H. Lowie for the use of his notes on the social organization of the Hopi,
gathered under the auspices of the American Museum of Natural History in 1915 and 1916; to Dr. Leslie Spier for the use of his paper
on the Havasupai, shortly to be published in the *Anthropological Papers*
of the latter institution; to Dr. Gladys Reichard for material on Navajo
society, and to Miss Ann Gayton for information on the Yokuts. Statements in regard to southern California peoples for which no references
are given are taken from a paper now in preparation by the present
author, on "Aboriginal Society in Southern California," to be published
in the University of California series.

Distribution of Social Elements

POLITICAL ORGANIZATION

The coastal peoples of California appear to have had nothing resembling
the tribe as it has just been defined. The Yokuts are reported by
Powers[10] as a group of warlike tribes, but a condition of localized bands
occupying rather large areas quite peacefully, seems to be revealed by
more recent investigation.[11] The Chumash and Gabrielino people apparently acted as village units on their brief war excursions, and the
rest of the neighboring California Shoshonean groups were similarly
united in either villages or localized clans. The Plateau Shoshoneans,
such as the Chemehuevi, appear to have been organized in more or
less isolated bands, as were their linguistic kinsfolk of the Great Basin.[12]
The degree to which the dialectic groups were united in former times
is not very clear.

With the Yuman people of the Colorado River we first encounter
large, united and warlike tribes, including the Mohave, Yuma, Cocopa,
and other, now extinct, peoples.[13] These groups, ranging from 500 to
5000 souls, formed quite coherent units in their war expeditions, which
utterly distinguishes them from their loosely organized and peaceful
Shoshonean neighbors to the west. The Yuman Diegueño, however, resembled their Cahuilla and Luiseño neighbors in their aboriginal condition of local groups or autonomous lineages.[14] Apparently the Walapai
and Yavapai resembled the Havasupai in possessing somewhat the same
tribal organization as their downriver Yuman neighbors, but were too

few in numbers to carry on such extensive campaigns. According to data secured by Spier, the Havasupai have six chiefs today, one of whom occupies a superior status, with, however, only limited powers. Formerly in war any chief might assume directive capacity. No data on the otherwise similar Walapai and Yavapai being at hand, we must assume much the same condition of a rather vague unified or tribal sense for them.

The Uto-Aztekan Pima were, at least in historic times, confederated in one tribe, each village having a chief, and all village chiefs electing a head chief.[15] According to Russell the tribe acted as a unit against the Apache, but accounts of campaigns[16] seem to indicate individual village or war party movements rather than tribal mass action. In Southern California it can be clearly demonstrated that the Desert Cahuilla clans, formerly independent, were nominally united under one clan chief through Mexican influence. In the light of the revocation of the Pima head chiefs' commission in 1864, by the United States Bureau of Indian Affairs,[17] it seems possible that this condition among the Pima was brought about in the same manner through Caucasian influence. However this may be, there is no doubt that the Pima were a strongly organized people as their successful competition with the warlike Apache and Colorado River tribes indicates. It is probable that the Papago organization was very similar to that of the Pima.

The Athapascan Apache and Navajo appear to have been in historic times distributed in more or less localized bands over a large area.[18] The Jicarilla Apache have at present two chiefs, elected from each of the two bands.[19] A similar condition prevails among the Navajo, according to Goddard,[20] although the Franciscan Fathers state that in early days the tribe was represented by twelve chiefs, who assembled in council.[21] This latter appears rather mythical, especially in its legendary formalization, and it would appear more probable that a condition of independent bands occasionally uniting, then as now, characterized the Navajo. The Pueblo-dwelling peoples, as far back as data are obtainable, appear to have been organized in town units, under a priestly hierarchy.[22] As a rule the individual Pueblos seem, save for temporary alliances, to have been largely independent. Passing beyond the area under consideration, to the north and east, the typical nomadic tribes of the plains are encountered, such as the Kiowa, Comanche, Cheyenne, and Arapaho, all of which were quite strongly united and warlike groups.[23]

PHRATRY AND MOIETY

The northernmost California people possessing the moiety organization are the Miwok. These divisions were called respectively "land" and "water," and were strictly exogamous in theory and probably in practice until modern Caucasian influences broke down the rules. The northern Miwok seem to have been peripheral to this system compared to the southerly groups.[24] All nature in theory was divided between the two, and as a result among other natural phenomena, we find all birds and animals thus divided. The division of these was arbitrary, many land animals belonging to the water moiety, and vice versa. All individual names applied indirectly to objects classified in the moiety and as such were vaguely totemic. Reciprocal functions between the moieties occurred in the funeral, mourning ceremony, girls' puberty ceremony, and the *ahana* dance. In the ceremonies the southern Sierra Miwok indicated moiety by means of painting the face, the land moiety being indicated by stripes, the water moiety by spots.[25] The southwestern neighbors of the Miwok, the Yokuts, possessed the same moiety organization in the majority of their bands on which we have data. Among certain of the southern Sierra groups it does not appear so far as is now known. In regard to the majority of the northern hill and central valley Yokuts the main characteristics of the Miwok moiety appear: reciprocity, animal association with the moiety, moiety paints, and among the Tachi Yokuts a dual or moiety chieftainship is indicated. The Yokut names appear to be meaningless but a totem or "pet" animal is inherited from the father instead. The moieties are called "upstream" and "downstream," are exogamous and acquired in the paternal line.[26]

The eastern Shoshonean neighbors of the Yokuts, the Western Mono, possess a moiety organization while the Eastern Mono do not.[27] The moiety of the Western Mono is patrilineal, but not exogamous, and each moiety is subdivided into two non-exogamous phratries. Associated with the moieties, and necessarily with the phratries, are certain birds and animals which are passed from father to son as "pets" or totems. As only the North Fork division of the Western Mono have been reported on, this condition of subdivided non-exogamous moieties among the Mono is not clear and must await further investigation. The North Fork Mono, like the Tachi Yokuts, are reported to have a dual or moiety chieftainship; and reciprocity in funeral and mourning ceremonies occurs between the phratries rather than the moieties.[28]

The coastal peoples of southern California in this regard, as in most other matters of detailed ethnology, present almost an unknown quantity to the problem. Through early Caucasian and Mission influences the coastal peoples such as the Chumash, probably the most highly developed groups of the region, have vanished; leaving behind almost no knowledge of their society, save for tantalizingly suggestive and equally fragmentary comments from their white contemporaries.[29] I am told by Mr. E. W. Gifford that Mr. J. P. Harrington stated a moiety organization occurred among the Chumash. Mr. Harrington has done ethnologic work with some of the very few survivors of these people, but further efforts to gain more information from him have been unavailing. The Salinans to the north of the Chumash were divided into moieties characterized by a bear and deer totem.[30] Brief as these statements are, they form important links in tracing out the spread of the moiety idea.

For the Gabrielino and their neighbors, the Juaneño and San Fernandeño, we have no direct evidence, although I have been told by neighboring Serrano and Cahuilla that the former of the three had a "wildcat" and "coyote" division.[31] Such evidence is, however, next to worthless. Among the Luiseño the moiety is practically nonexistent, but there was at Saboba among a prevailing Luiseño population a division into a wildcat and coyote moiety.[32] This occurrence was verified by Luiseño at Rincon who agreed that such a condition existed at Saboba but not among themselves. No definite traces of a dual organization could be discovered among any other Luiseño, but a myth of definite Luiseño provenience, recorded by Du Bois, tells of a contest between the "uplanders of the east" and the "westerners of the coast,"[33] which brings in a division of the animals among the contestants, some belonging to one and some to the other division. This tale would appear to be either a borrowing, or a reflection of a former division among the Luiseño. It is worth noting that the Luiseño word *paha'*, used by the Cahuilla also, means "red racer" (*Coluber flagellum*). The *paha'* is the ceremonial assistant and is painted vertically, half red and half black, on the theory that the male snake is red and the female black.[34]

The Serrano, Cahuilla (all three divisions), and the Cupeño were all divided into moieties, called respectively "wildcat" and "coyote." Among the Serrano, definite reciprocity occurred in regard to funerals and mourning ceremonies. There are traces of reciprocity to be found among the Pass and Mountain Cahuilla south of the Serrano, and it occurred quite definitely among the Cupeño. The Desert Cahuilla had no rules of moiety reciprocity whatsoever, although the custom of calling in another clan with whom the clan giving the ceremony was much intermarried brought about natural rather than enforced reciprocity through exogamy. Among the Serrano, Cupeño, Pass and Mountain Cahuilla, reciprocity was limited to ceremonies connected with death, mourning, or puberty rites. The Desert Cahuilla distinguished a girl of the "wildcat" moiety at the adolescence ceremony by the use of spotted paint. The Cupeño distinguished girls at such ceremonies by spotted cheek designs for the wildcat moiety and striped designs for the coyote moiety. The Luiseño had both types of face painting but they were used in separate ceremonies. For the other groups no moiety paints were remembered. The Desert Cahuilla in theory and practice observed strict moiety exogamy. The two other Cahuilla groups observed it as a rule, but actual cases show considerable laxity in observance, especially among the Cahuilla of the San Gorgonio Pass. The Serrano and Cupeño both had definite rules of moiety exogamy, but especially in regard to marriages outside their dialectic group, they were quite lax.

None of the Plateau or Kern River Shoshoneans, with the exception of the Western Mono, seem to have possessed any sort of a moiety division. This includes the Chemehuevi, Kawaiisu, Tübatulabal, probably the Koso, and the Eastern Mono.[35] This condition also prevails for the Shoshoneans of the Great Basin so far as they are known.[36] The Yuman Diegueño, Mohave, Yuma, Cocopa, and Havasupai likewise show no traces of a moiety division.

East of the Colorado River the moiety first appears among the Pima and Papago. That a moiety division of patrilineal descent occurred seems clear, but the alignment of clans in moieties given by the various authorities is decidedly variable. These discrepancies are shown by the following lists. The clan names on which all authorities agree are taken from Russell; for the Pima the data are as follows:

MOIETY ALIGNMENT

Clan Names	Russell[37]	Curtis[38]
Ã'kol	Vulture or Red People (Ants)	?
A'pap	Vulture or Red People (Ants)	Coyote
A pukĭ	Vulture or Red People (Ants)	Coyote
Ma'am	Coyote or White People (Ants)	Buzzard
Va'af	Coyote or White People (Ants)	Buzzard

For the Papago we have the following list:

MOIETY ALIGNMENT

Clan Names	Russell[39]	Curtis[40]	Dolores[41]	Lumholtz[42]
Ã'kol	Vulture or Red Ants	?	Buzzard	White Ants
A'pap	Vulture or Red Ants	Coyote	Coyote	White Ants
A pukĭ	Vulture or Red Ants	Coyote	?	White Ants
Ma'am	Coyote or White Ants	Buzzard	Red	Red Ants
Va'af	Coyote or White Ants	Buzzard	White	Red Ants

The lack of agreement is only too obvious and shows the need of further investigation in regard to the real situation in Pima and Papago society before exact comparisons can be made. Goddard has given a list of these clans and their moiety alignment,[43] but appears to have followed Russell.

There is no rule of moiety exogamy at present, nor according to all information does there appear to have been such a rule within historic times.[44] Members of salt-gathering expeditions "formerly painted their faces the color of the division to which they belonged." Likewise all animals having red about them belonged to the red people.[45] This is true of the Papago, and probably of the Pima.[46] Among the Papago the "white" people are most numerous, the "red" people being in a minority. According to their myths the "red" people once owned the country but they were conquered and nearly exterminated by the "white" people.[47] It is apparent that the exact nature of the moiety, its characteristic paints, and actual application to society may only be determined by further study.

No exogamous moiety division occurs among the Navajo or Apache so far as present data are concerned. The Jicarilla Apache have a moiety division for pleasurable rivalry in certain games, but no mention of exogamy is made.[48] None of the Eastern Apache as far as known have clans or other divisions regulating marriage. The Western Apache, however, have exogamous clans which are for the most part grouped in unnamed but exogamous phratries.[49] The clans are matrilineal in descent,[50] as are the phratries.

The Navajo have exogamous matrilineal clans, which are similarly grouped in unnamed exogamous phratries.[51] According to Reichard these clan groups are quite evenly divided over the Navajo country, while the clans themselves are definitely localized.[52] This agrees with the interpretation of Mathews[53] and Stephen.[54] "Clan groups," as Reichard calls these larger exogamous unions of clans, seems a more exact definition than phratries, considering that they are unnamed. So far as the literature is concerned, these larger groups do not seem to have been associated with animals, nor did they have distinctive paints. The same may be said for the Apache.

In myth and ceremony there are traces of a moiety division among the Hopi[55] and the Zuñi,[56] but in neither case is there at present any idea of descent or alignment of clans according to moiety. Save for the mythical division of the Dogwood Clan into Raven and Macaw sub-clans, Stevenson makes no mention of any moiety idea in her account of Zuñi.[57] Cushing describes a moiety division of the whole Zuñi people into a Macaw, south or summer people, and a Raven, north or winter people, in the creation myth recorded by him.[58] Kroeber[59] obtained no evidence for any actual moiety at Zuñi and favors Stevenson's mythical account as more accurate than that of Cushing.

Stevenson notes that each of the fourteen A'shiwanni priests has two pots of paint, one of black earth, and one of red earth, which are supposed to have come from the undermost world. Prayer sticks offered for cold rain and snow were colored with the black paint, and those for summer rain with the red paint.[60] Parsons believes that at Zuñi the winter ceremonies of the curing societies and the summer ceremonies of the rain priests, the seasonal distinction between two sets of sacred clowns, the winter cacique (rain priest of the north) and summer cacique (speaker to the sun), as well as the double grouping of the six kivas in regard to war cult and *santu* ceremonials, are all reflections of the moiety idea, which is more definitely expressed among the Rio Grande Pueblos.[61] All recent authorities seem to agree that moiety exogamy is definitely lacking among all of the Pueblos.

A system of linked clans, or unnamed phratries, occurs among the Hopi, at Zuñi, and to a lesser extent among all the western Pueblos. According to Fewkes, the Hopi have seven such phratries,[62] but he gives a list of fourteen according to clan traditions.[63] Curtis lists twelve groups of linked clans among the Hopi.[64] Kroeber has demonstrated that this linkage appears much the same for all the Pueblos, and notes that in each clan there is a tendency toward polarity, repeated whenever that clan occurs.[65] Parsons does not find this polarity among Laguna clans, and appears to doubt the application of Kroeber's pattern to the eastern Pueblos.[66] Such linked clans do not seem to limit marriage choice among the members.

The Western Keresan Pueblos have a moiety classification that enters considerably into their ceremonial life. At Laguna, during the war and *santu* dances, certain of the clans are assigned to buildings on one side of the plaza, the remainder to the other side. They form the West group and the East group. One division of the *k'atsina* dancers is assigned to the cloud spirits of the North, identified with winter, another is assigned to the cloud spirits of the South, associated with summer.[67] A man may dance in both of these groups if his father's clan is in the opposite group from that of his mother; a fact that emphasizes the non-exogamous nature of the ceremonial grouping. There is no clear association of kiva with moiety, but the two buildings from which the groups come strongly suggest the eastern Pueblo pattern of double kivas.[68]

The Eastern Keresan Pueblos have the double kiva system for the two moieties. The latter are called Turquoise and Squash and are associated with the ideas of summer and winter. At Jemez the same pattern prevails.[69] Stevenson in her account of Sia makes no mention of the moiety, but notes the small importance attached to clan affiliations there, as compared to Zuñi.[70] An analysis of Starr's census of Cochiti[71] leads Kroeber to the conclusion that moieties or phratries made no difference in actual marriages between clans.[72] Among the Eastern Keresan, the moiety is inherited in the male line, the woman often joining the kiva of her husband.[73]

Among the Tewa, especially at Santa Clara and San Ildefonso, there is a strong tendency for the moieties to be endogamous.[74] The moieties are named for summer and winter.[75] At San Juan the moiety is the outstanding social group, taking the place held by the clan in the social consciousness of the Zuñi and Hopi.[76] Among the eastern Tewa, and at Taos, there is a double town chieftaincy, one chief having control in summer, the other in winter.[77] Among the southern Tigua, at Isleta, the two moieties are called "black eyes" and "red eyes," ceremonial clowns of the first being painted black, of the second red and white, thus giving the moiety names.[78] At present there are no clans at Taos,[79] the patrilineal moiety apparently having taken over all ceremonial functions. It has been stated that the general Pueblo classification of clans with moiety gives the winter people the Day, Bear, Lizard, and Eagle clans, while the Geese, Corn, Chaparral Cock, and Parrot clans are usually summer people. With the former is associated the Flint society, with the latter the Fire society.[80] In the present state of knowledge I presume this classification to be more a suggestion than an established fact. In regard to the more esoteric features of the moiety among the Rio Grande pueblos there seems to be little on record.

While this briefly sums up the available information on the moiety in the area under consideration, it is well to note that a moiety classification varying in degree of importance, exists among neighboring Plain's tribes such as the Kiowa[81] and Pawnee,[82] and farther still to the north and east among the Omaha, Ponca, Osage, Kansas, Ouapaw, Oto, Iowa, Missouri, and Winnebago.[83]

LINEAGE AND CLAN

Beside the moiety organization previously described, the Miwok of central California were organized in small male lineages which were autonomous landowning units. The lineage territories were held by the group in common and the patriarchal chieftainship descended normally from father to eldest son. As the lineage was composed of closely related kinsfolk it was absolutely exogamous, men of the lineage bringing their wives to their own hamlet, daughters of the lineage going to the hamlet of their husbands. The lineage name was always a place name, and though in the valleys Caucasian influences tended to amalgamate the lineages into villages, the old lineage place names are still remembered, while the groups remaining in the mountains have clung to their own territories until recent times.[84] The North Fork Mono, south of the Miwok, were also organized into male lineages in addition to the phratry and moiety grouping already discussed. What the exact relationship between these three social groupings was, may only be determined by adequate genealogical data.[85]

The central Yokuts, especially those of the foothills, seem to have been grouped in villages having two or three chiefs of equal power. Within these villages were paternal families, with meaningless personal names inherited in the male line. Each one of these families had an animal which was called its *posha,*[86] apparently akin to the "pet" animals of the Mono phratries previously described. Save in rare cases where the family of a chief sometimes kept an eagle, prairie falcon, or bear cub as its *posha,* these animals were not actually kept by the families. They did not, however, kill or eat their *posha.* While actual blood families were exogamous as far as kin could be traced, the possession of the same *posha* by two distinct families did not bar marriage between them. The central Yokuts had no family ownership of land as far as known, and even the village groups had no clearly defined boundaries. The various southern villages seemed on the whole to have maintained friendly relations and more or less commonly used territories. North of Tulare Lake there seems to have been a stronger feeling of village boundaries, and against trespass by outsiders.[87] Further work in this area, as among the Mono, should, when such intervening groups as still exist are known, give a more coherent and detailed picture of society in the great southern valley of California.

No details of social organization among the Salinan peoples are extant save for the bare mention of the moiety.[88] Portola's estimate of the Chumash, Esselen, and Costanoan villages between the sites of San Luis Obispo and Monterey in 1769, gives an average of over 100 people in each of the 10 towns seen.[89] As for the Chumash, nothing is on record of their social organization other than lists of the coast and island villages visited by Cabrillo and later Spanish explorers.[90] For the Gabrielino, Juaneño, and San Fernandeño, we have the interesting but not detailed accounts of Boscana and Hugo Reid. The former, speaking of the Juaneño and probably Gabrielino, mentions individual villages and rancherias, each with its chief, and in which most of the people were related.[91] Speaking of the Indians of Los Angeles County, Reid states that there were approximately 40 villages in aboriginal times, and states that there were from 500 to 1000 huts in each village.[92] This probably applies to the Juaneño, San Fernandeño, and Gabrielino. The details of village government given by him seem identical with those given by Boscana, and I am inclined to believe that these large villages he speaks of are the result of native exaggeration. He carefully notes that at the time he writes no such conditions exist and that only a few survivors remain. Other evidences to be discussed later seem to indicate a similar if not identical condition existing among the aforementioned groups and the Luiseño, save that the village groupings of the coastal peoples were in all probability larger.

To what degree the Luiseño in pre-Mission times were grouped in villages is not clear. A village at San Luis Rey in post-Mission times, composed of twenty families or clans under one hereditary chief, has been recorded,[93] and a somewhat similar case at Saboba as well.[94] I am inclined to believe that this condition was largely due to modern influences for the following reasons. In the eastern and mountainous parts of the Luiseño territory, notably at La Jolla, the Luiseño were grouped, even in post-Mission times, in small family units or male lineages each owning a certain territory. I have preferred calling these *clans,* however, because the central feature of their organization was a patriarchal chief or priest, distinguished by living in the ceremonial house and having in his possession a sacred bundle of reed matting called *ma'swut,* containing ceremonial paraphernalia and objects sacred to the clan. Thus in addition to kinship such a group was further united by the important clan ceremonial bundle concept. In such a clan group a woman always retained her own lineage or clan name but was ceremonially affiliated with the activities of her husband's clan.

In the mountains there appears to have been a tendency for these individual groups to exist as autonomous units for a considerable time after the decay of the Missions. Genealogies indicate that about every three generations the lineage tended to divide, a branch moving away to a new territory and acquiring a new name, usually a nickname applicable to some important individual or individuals in the group. A new ceremonial house was built, a new bundle acquired, and the new group became an autonomous unit, although the feeling of relationship and consequent avoidance of marriage with the parent group persisted. Thus the groups were always quite small, save in the more habitable valley areas where larger clans composed of many collateral branches of the original lineage probably existed. After the Mission period a new influence came in, likewise based on the ceremonial bundle, in the formation of "parties."[95] Small clans decimated in numbers, lacking efficient ceremonial leaders or paraphernalia, tended to merge with more active clans possessing powerful *ma'swut,* into "parties." These were mainly ceremonial groups, composed of once individual clans, under one chief or *not,* but they are not exogamous as were the clans.[96] The parties would appear as the logical outcome of the powerful ceremonial leaders or chiefs possessing *ma'swut,* drawing into their organizations the fragmentary clans released from the Missions. At the present time these parties are very loose affairs and merely serve to maintain the fragments of Luiseño ceremonialism that still persist. I am inclined to believe that the parties as such, are entirely post-Mission affairs. Previous to the Mission period, however, the localized autonomous clan group, named as a rule for natural objects or verbal derivatives of natural objects, and composed of one or more lineages, appears to have been the basis of Luiseño society.

The same state of affairs existed among the Cupeño who were, at least in Mission and post-Mission times, grouped around the Warner's Hot Springs. Five of the Cupeño clans were each composed of one lineage while the sixth clan included three separate lineages. Each lineage, however, had individual food-gathering territories in the mountains back of the springs. The independent clans each had a chief, a ceremonial house, and a *ma'swut* bundle. The Serrano clans were very similar, but the equally important clan fetish concept was rather complicated due to more complete moiety reciprocity in ceremonies.

The Mountain and Pass divisions of the Cahuilla were in aboriginal times apparently grouped into localized and independent clans, each owning various food-gathering areas, and each possessing a clan head or priest, a *ma'swut* bundle, and a clan ceremonial house. Genealogies indicate that these clans usually consisted of one male lineage, but as this lineage included collateral male lines for four or five generations the groups were fairly large, consisting usually of fifty or more persons. The kinship system of the Cahuilla indicates that they reckoned lineal descent back five generations from the speaker,[97] the term for great-great-grandfather, *nañaa,* being translated "from the beginning." Thus collateral branches four or five generations removed tended to form new clans, which naturally belonged to the moiety of the parent stock, but in the course of time lost the sense of actual kinship. The historic Luiseño clans, as has been stated, seem only to have included collateral branches for three generations back, and as a result the groups were smaller. This bears out Gifford's surmise that the Luiseño may have represented a more finely spun fabric of clan organization than did the Cahuilla.[98] Even in aboriginal times it is extremely probable that certain of the more favorably located Cahuilla clans, for example, that at Palm Springs, may have been composed, as they seem to be at present, of several lineages. Where this occurs it does not seem in any way to invalidate the rule of clan exogamy. The Cahuilla clans seem to have place names in the majority of cases, but natural objects or their derivatives, as among the Luiseño, appear in many of their names.

The same condition of independent clans held for the Desert Cahuilla, whose clans were likewise united by the same kinship and ceremonial bonds. Scarcity of water on the desert, however, seems to have brought several clans together, forming villages at the available wells and water holes. Up to the present the Desert Cahuilla have clung to their independent clan organization for ceremonial purposes, although modern reservation and farming conditions have caused new land-holding arrangements. The Mountain Cahuilla and certain of the Pass Cahuilla clans, brought much earlier under Caucasian influence,[99] in many cases formed parties similar to those among the Luiseño. The decimated or ceremonially disorganized clans tending to affiliate themselves with ceremonially intact and active clans. The basis of Luiseño, Cahuilla, Cupeño, and Serrano social organization, however, seems to be the localized male lineage, augmented by the power of the clan priest, clan ceremonial bundle, and clan ceremonial house, a complex which will be discussed hereafter.

The units of Tübatulabal, Kawaiisu, and Panamint social organization are not known in detail, but would appear to resemble the Chemehuevi and other Plateau Shoshoneans in a more or less loose grouping into bands. Whether the lineage is at the basis of their organization is not known, but no clans have been reported for them. Their northeasterly neighbors of the Basin, the Paviotso, Ute, Moapa, and Shivwits Paiute had neither clans nor lineages, the bilateral family forming the only unit within the band.[100] It is probable that the more southwesterly members of this Basin group have much the same organization, but the extent to which western influences have affected them may only be known when more is on record concerning them.

Spier has shown the unilateral family to be the outstanding unit of Yuman Diegueño social organization;[101] thus they resemble their Luiseño and Cupeño neighbors in possessing male lineages.[102] They seem also to have had in part the group ceremonial priest, bundle, and house complex common to the latter.[103] The Yuman peoples of the Colorado River have a quite different clan organization, and while it has been suggested that the male lineage may be the basis of their present system,[104] there seems hardly enough evidence at hand to make this more than guesswork. The Mohave, Yuman, Cocopa and probably others of the downriver Yuman tribes share a system of patrilineal exogamous nameless clans of totemic reference.[105] All the women born in a clan bear an identical name, although they may also have other nicknames. This clan name has totemic import and indirectly alludes to some natural object, such as sun, moon, wind, beaver, quail, etc. Apparently these derivative clan names are archaic stems, disguised allusions, or equivalents of the objects connoted. Totemic taboos are slight, although the Cocopa do not kill their totems.[106] The clans do not enter into religious activities as far as known, and the entire system apparently rests lightly on the cults or actual organization of society. The clan members are scattered over the tribal territory, and while little groups of kinsmen, and therefore of clansmen, live at favorable sites during shifting periods,[107] the clans as a whole do not appear to be localized. While the house is ritually significant among the Yuma and Mohave in myth and song, it is not employed to any extent in actual ceremonies.[108] There is no trace of priest or sacred bundle.[109]

If we may judge from the Havasupai, on whom we have information,[110] the upriver Yuman tribes, such as the Yavapai and Walapai, have no clan or gentile organization of any sort. The two latter tribes, however, being nearer the Mohave, may reflect their social institutions more than do the Havasupai. The basis of the Havasupai life is the bilateral family; there is no indication of any other than blood family kinship. Groups of relatives associated through patrilocal residence are merged into camps within the village, but within these the married couple and their progeny are the unit. Land and chieftainship are inherited in the male line. There is no trace of a ceremonial group-house,[111] group-priest, or sacred-bundle concept.

The Pima and Papago east of the Colorado River have somewhat the same clan organization as the Mohave. These clans, which have been previously listed, are five in number. The names of the clans have in the main lost their meanings but they appear to have been totemic.[112] These names descend in the patrilineal line and apply to the father.[113] There is no clan exogamy, nor any evidences of clan organization.[114] According to Lumholtz, wives joined the clan of their husband.[115] To call these clans rather than phratries is purely arbitrary and largely due to the fact that the smaller units which may make up these clans are not known at present, whereas in the case of the North Fork Mono it has been demonstrated that the phratries are made up of male lineages. Among the Papago the villages were exogamous, although all clan groups might occur in each village.[116] There is, moreover, a sacred ceremonial lodge, priest, and sacred bundle in each village,[117] as nearly as can be ascertained from the description given by Lumholtz. In the face of this it is hard to escape the belief that we have here a lineage or localized clan organization, as well as a loose intervillage phratral system.

Material on the social organization of the Athapascan peoples of the Southwest is not overly clear or abundant, but enough is extant to show the general nature of their clans. According to Goddard[118] the Eastern Apache, as far as known, have no clans, while the Western Apache are organized in about thirty or more. These latter are exogamous and to a certain extent control the social duties of their members. Clan names are usually place names, and among the White Mountain Apache the clans do appear to be somewhat localized.[119] The clans are matrilineal, and in the majority of cases localization exists more in theory than actually. Certain of the political bands are likewise associated in the Apache mind with certain clans. In about fourteen cases the clan names of the Apache coincide with those of the Navajo,[120] although the same territories do not seem to be implied in the name. Only one clan, named for the dragonfly, has any animalistic connotation, although a few seem slightly totemic. As has already been stated, they are more or less grouped in exogamous unnamed phratries.[121]

The clans of the Navajo are very much the same as those of the Western Apache, and are about 40 or 50 in number, being exogamous and matrilineal in descent.[122] Matrilocal residence is the rule. Mathews and Stephen both state that localization is one of the striking characters of the Navajo clan.[123] Reichard[124] agrees as to localization and states that place names are usual; only a few clans have names such as "sun" or "turkey," which may be Pueblo in origin. The Navajo do not believe in a common clan ancestress, but in a common local group as the basis of each clan. As among the Western Apache the clans are grouped, the groups being quite evenly distributed over the Navajo country.[125] It is interesting to note that in their mythology each clan had a "pet" animal that accompanied it on its journeys.[126] Among the Navajo there is no clan priest, no sacred bundle, or permanent ceremonial house.[127] The same apparently applies to the Apache.

The exact nature of the Pueblo clan is a somewhat disputed matter but certain general characteristics stand out. The clans are exogamous, usually matrilineal in descent and totemic as to name. The same clan names occur in many of the pueblos, and while all clans are not represented in each, where clans of the same name occur in different pueblos the members are usually considered as ceremonially related. The main ceremonies of the Pueblos are carried on by groups (fraternities) of priests, not directly by the clans. Among the Hopi these ceremonies are said to be motivated mainly by a desire to bring rain, at Zuñi for both rain-making and curing, and among the eastern Pueblos mainly for curing.[128] Native theory, expressed in the clan migration legends, deals with each clan as a once-independent unit, and this viewpoint was largely taken over by early investigators in the area.[129] At present the clans appear at integral parts of the entire Pueblo social structure, rather than independent autonomous units loosely fused by town or communal dwelling. This viewpoint was to a large extent brought out by Kroeber's analysis of modern conditions in Zuñi.[130] Similar methods employed by Parsons, Lowie, and others seem to shift the emphasis from the clan as a whole to the individual matrilineal families as the ceremonial units of Pueblo society.[131] The problem is extremely complex, but a brief survey of clan status in the various Pueblo groups may be of value.

It was at one time believed that the Hopi clans at Oraibi were definitely localized in the town,[132] but later analysis of the data leads to a negative rather than a positive conclusion.[133] A similar analysis of the data presented by Fewkes[134] on association between clans and fraternities of the same name leads Kroeber to the belief that the membership in the fraternities is not made up of representatives of clans of the same name, any more than those of other clans.[135] Lowie, on the basis of censuses obtained on the First and Second Mesas, agrees with Kroeber's general conclusions but points out the important fact that the preferential (similarly named) clan supplied the head priest, and that in certain cases all such clansmen are conceived as at least potential participants in the ceremonies of such a fraternity. He is strongly impressed with the connection between fraternity officers and membership in certain clans. The fact that entrance into the Snake fraternity, for example, may be effected by anyone desiring to be cured of snakebite, clearly indicates why all clans may be represented in any one of the curing fraternities. Offices, both ceremonial and political, are associated with the clans through the principle of matrilineal descent;[136] that is, an office descends from brother to brother or maternal uncle to sister's son within what Goldenweiser calls a maternal family[137] and I have called here a female lineage.[138] In the absence of matrilineal kin the privilege devolves on an unrelated clansman, and if none such exists, on some member of a linked clan. In regard to relation of lineage and family, Lowie found that of the thirteen Mishongnovi clans, there were six which coincided with single lineages, and of the remainder, the majority were composed of only two lineages.[139]

Parsons, on the basis of independent research, coincides with this new interpretation and adds the following details.

> Each one of the maternal families has a name, a maternal or stock house where fetishes, masks, etc., are kept, and a male head or chief together with a female head, "our oldest mother," as a Hopi will refer to her, the senior or representative woman of the stock house. The male head is also closely associated with this house. He is also the chief of any ceremony which is "handed" as the Hopi say, by the clan. In other words, a ceremony is primarily in charge of a maternal family or family connection, rather than of the clan as a whole.[140]

It is further pointed out that these female lineages (maternal families) are stable organizations, while the clan of which they are part is socially unstable and subject to different combinations in different towns, and even at different periods in the same town.[141] As a result, clan composition, and therefore clan linkage, appears to be a varying phenomenon and not uniform for all pueblos as Kroeber believed.[142] The entire question of clan linkage is, however, too complicated for analysis at the present time. It may be noted that among the Hopi the feeling of the equivalence among the linked clans is very strong and appears to be largely due to a desire to share in certain clan ritualistic privileges.[143]

All Hopi proper names have some reference to the clan totem of the person giving the name, not its possessor. This reference to the totem is often indirect. Such clan names apply not only to people but to kivas, pipes, etc.[144] Curtis agrees that all Hopi names are clan owned and are the property of the name-giver's clan, the majority being given by the clan of the father.[145] The totemism of the Hopi clans is not very clear as to degree or nature. Lowie notes that the Butterfly clan had a winged fetish of cottonwood bark; the Horn clan, horned masks; the Snake clan, a bow with a snakeskin tied to it; the Bear clan, a small stone bear effigy; and the Kachina clan, masks and fetishes resembling little children. The Rabbit clan was supposed to own all deer and rabbits; but aside from such distinctions little regard seems to be paid to the totems of the various clans.[146] It has been noted that certain clans had special territories for hunting eagles.[147]

Of the fifteen clans at Zuñi in 1916, the largest contained 400 people, the smallest 3 or 4. Marriage into the mother's clan was forbidden and into the father's clan disapproved. Such groupings of clans (phratries) as occurred had no social significance. The clans were not localized save in a fragmentary way due to household growth. There were no clan totems or taboos noted, and each clan appeared an equivalent unit, distinct from all others. Kroeber also notes that certain houses were distinguished as clan name "having," and these often contained the clan fetish.[148] Parsons stresses this point of the clan house, and shows that while women are usually the keepers of the fetishes, men rather than women are supposed to know the songs and prayers associated with the fetish. There is a great reluctance to remove the fetish from a house as long as any women keepers are alive, but as men marry out of the house and households may become extinct, in some cases fetishes are kept by people "out of" the clan house. The tendency to leave the fetish in the clan house, however, seems to account for the cases of Rain priests and clan fetishes in different houses at Zuñi. The Rain priests at Zuñi are the outcome of the house fetish complex of the clan and the weather control and curing functions of the society or fraternity. Assistants to ceremonial offices are chosen from the incumbent's household, which leads to family or household association with the societies.[149]

Both Kroeber and Parsons emphasize the social importance of the family, as we know it, among the Zuñi, but the latter brings out the importance of the household (or female lineage) as an important unit within the exogamous clan of several lineages. The ceremonial importance of the clan is brought out by the fact that in Cushing's time the ruling priesthood was elected from the Parrot clan,[150] which also owns the ceremonially important salt lake.[151] The exact degree to which ceremonial offices are inherited through clan, lineage, or blood family relationship at Zuñi is not entirely clear, although it is quite probable that inheritance of the different positions may be along different lines.[152] The fact that the whole ceremonial life of the Pueblos is pervaded by kinship conceptions is best shown by the rite of exchanging terms of relationship, noted among the Hopi,[153] at Zuñi,[154] and probably applicable to some of the eastern Pueblos as well. As among the Hopi, totemism at Zuñi is very obscure. It may be noted, however, that Parsons[155] objects to Kroeber's statement[156] that there is no spiritual connection between the clan and the object or animal from which it derives its name. It is pointed out for example, that the Bear clan at Zuñi is associated with the war gods, who in turn are associated with the bear.[157] Also according to Cushing, there is a connection between the Eagle and Coyote clans and the same pair of prey gods.[158]

The Western Keresan Pueblos (Acoma and Laguna) have maternal clans. At Laguna the clans are divided into the moieties,[159] but at Acoma this division is obscure.[160] While in theory the clans are exogamous, marriages into both father and mother's clan do occur. Residence is matrilocal in theory, but in reality quite frequently patrilocal.[161] For ceremonial purposes, changes of clan take place,[162] a thing not known for the western Pueblos. At Laguna the clans formerly had senior members, usually men but sometimes women. These clan elders each kept in a basket completely kernelled ears of corn, fetish animals, and terraced medicine bowls. They directed the communal work of the clan and possessed knowledge of the ritual that was the basis of their leadership. In cases of dispute in the clan it was carried to the oldest clan member, not necessarily the clan head, for settlement.[163] In the *k'atsina* cult certain masked impersonators belong to certain clans; leadership in the cult was vested in the Badger clan.[164] Names were usually clan owned and given by the father's clan.[165] The latter applies to Laguna; at Acoma the child may be named by a medicine man or any relative.[166] Laguna, being made up to a great extent of alien Pueblo clans, shows in its records the interesting fact that at no time did any one of the clans migrate en masse to the site, but tended to come by families.[167]

The Eastern Keresan Pueblos, as has been noted,[168] seem to have attached little importance to the clan as a social group. In 1889 there were only six active clans at Sia, only two of which had more than one or two members, while a list of fifteen extinct clans was obtained. It was regarded as wrong to marry into the clan of either the father or the mother.[169] At Santa Ana the Dove, Mouse, Coyote, Lizard, and Bear clans belong to one moiety; the Turkey, White Shell, Eagle, Corn, Water Turquoise, Parrot, and Fire clans to the other. The Ant clan is regarded as belonging to either moiety.[170] The northeastern Keresan Pueblos are said to be patrilineal in descent,[171] and at Cochiti residence is commonly patrilocal.[172]

The clans of the eastern Tewa seem likewise to have largely lost such importance as they may once have possessed. According to Parsons there are three or four clans in each town, but these are mere names, without even the function of regulating marriages.[173] According to Harrington[174] and Freire-Marreco,[175] clans among the Tewa are patrilineal in descent. The latter states that the bilateral family has become the primary unit in society, and the kinship system is used inconsistently, descriptive compound terms being introduced to remedy the confusion. The Tewa do not use kinship terms as clan terms because they do not regard people bearing the same clan name as necessarily related.[176] While there is considerable restriction of marriage, it is not to avoid matings of clan mates, but to prevent those between either matrilineal or patrilineal kin.[177] The moieties, it should be noted, are likewise patrilineal.[178] How far this patrilineal, almost clanless, condition is due to alien influence, and how much to native pattern, remains to be determined.

Among the Tigua there seem to be marked differences, for in the southwestern group at Isleta there are eight clans which do not seem to be aligned in the moiety classification.[179] There are clan heads and clan fetishes employed in the ceremonies,[180] but the nature of postmarital residence, exogamy, and descent does not seem very clear. At Taos, the most northeasterly of all the pueblos, on the other hand, there are no clans at present,[181] although several Taos clans were formerly recorded by Bandelier.[182] A comparison of early and late clan lists from the Rio Grande pueblos shows a constantly decreasing number of clan names, but here again the question whether this is due to aboriginal conditions or to long-continued Caucasian interference remains to be answered.

THE GROUP-HOUSE, GROUP-FETISH AND GROUP-PRIEST COMPLEX

The great importance of the house, fetish, and priest in Pueblo society has been emphasized by many workers in the field, but the first clear statement of the combination of house and fetish as a definite complex seems to have been made by Parsons.[183] The new data on social organization in southern California, in connection with a survey of the literature on the remainder of the southwestern area, shows that the group-house, group-fetish, and group-priest are so often associated that they also form an actual complex, rather than a mere accidental association of three different traits. A survey of the area in question shows this complex to have been present in the social systems of many of the groups.

Whether the Chumash of the southern California coast or the Salinans, their northern neighbors, had this complex in their social organization is not positively known. The Chumash had a large ceremonial chamber, apparently dirt-roofed, with steps leading up to the top, and entrance from the roof which was effected by means of a ladder. The town chief evidently enjoyed unusual influence and honor, and if we may judge by the southern neighbors of the Chumash, played more the part of a priest than of an actual ruler or leader. He summoned neighboring groups to ceremonies and received food and shell money from the people.[184] While such fragmentary evidences are interesting, they would alone have small bearing on the present problem were it not for the definite occurrence of the complex among all the peoples bordering them on the southeast, peoples, moreover, who seem to have been influenced to a considerable extent by the Chumash.

To the northeast of the Chumash the complete complex does not seem to have penetrated, at least so far as the existing data are concerned. More intensive work, however, may show that the Yokuts and Miwok had traces of the triple institution.

The Juaneño, San Fernandeño, and Gabrielino quite evidently possessed this complex, for while the early literature in regard to them is fragmentary, it brings out the following points: Boscana states that all the esoteric knowledge of these groups was "confined to the chiefs of their tribes, and the old men who officiate as priests," and adds that all ceremonies were conducted in an esoteric language "distinct from that in common use."[185] According to the same authority, the first commandment of Chinigchinich, the god who brought the individual people power to bring rain, dews, acorns, etc., was to build a temple to worship him and to offer sacrifices. This was called *Vanquech* (similar to the Luiseño *wamkish*), and no others than the chief and the *puplem* (shamans) were allowed to enter its sanctuary.[186] "These temples erected by the command of the god Chinigchinich . . . were invariably erected in the centre of their towns, and contiguous to the dwelling-place of the captain, or chief."[187] They consisted of an oval enclosure made of stakes, inside of which were two other enclosures made of mats and brush. In the inner one was "a kind of hurdle" on which was placed a figure of the god, Chinigchinich, which consisted of the skin of a coyote or *gato montes* (wildcat) with head and feet attached. Inside of this were placed feathers of particular bird species, talons, mountain lion's claws, deer horns, and projecting from the mouth, a few arrows. Next to the figure was placed a bow and more arrows. When all the people had been called together, the shamans drew "a very ridiculous figure" on the ground before Chinigchinich, which all the people worshipped, and to which they presented offerings or *bateas* (special instruments). This inner enclosure could only be entered by the "Chief, Puplem and elders," on feast days. A profound silence was maintained, and sometimes the chief or one of the shamans danced before the altar. The ceremony closed by all present partaking of food from the same vessel.[188] While the chiefs had much ceremonial importance, were distinguished by black paint, a hair-cord wrapped around the head, a decorated bull-roarer, turtle-shell rattle, and feather skirt, they had little actual power. Food was given to the chief to store for all the people, but if he squandered it he might be deposed, a new chief in the paternal

line being appointed.[189] Nearly all the people in the village were related.[190] It is interesting to note that the priests who danced before the
altar were painted red and black, as were the sons of chiefs when they
were initiated into the ceremonial rites.[191] A similar picture, but with
less detail, is presented by Hugo Reid.[192]

From new material, obtained by the present author in the winter
of 1924–25, it appears that the Luiseño, Cupeño, Cahuilla (three divisions), and Serrano all possessed this complex in its full form. The importance of the ceremonial leader (*not*), the fetish bundle (*ma'swut*),
and ceremonial house (*wamkish*) among the Luiseño has already been
discussed.[193] Among all these groups the fetish bundle, or wrapping
called *ma'swut,* is the most important part of the fetish concept. According to theory, these matting bundles came from the western coast, where
according to the Cahuilla creation story they were brought out of the
ocean by Coyote. Actually the Cupeño and Cahuilla seem to have used
moutain reeds for their *ma'swut* bundles. The Serrano used either reeds
or cactus fibre[194] for their fetish wrappings. The mats were from four
to six feet in length, and about three feet wide.

Among all the groups, ceremonial objects were wrapped up in this
mat which was cared for by the chief. The Cupeño wrapped up crystal-
bearing wands, turtle-shell rattles, eagle feathers and eagle-feather
skirts, eagle-down headdresses, feather wands, and shell money in their
bundles. Those were always hung up in a dark corner of the ceremonial
leader's house, which was likewise the dance-house. The matting was
used to make images of the dead, for burning at the mourning ceremony. Small portions of *ma'swut* were given to other ceremonial leaders
in time of mourning or great stress. When the latter occurred, it was
necessary for women in the leader's household to accompany the
ma'swut and feed it acorn meal and other food. It was considered to be
alive, and baskets and other presents were made to it. The chief or priest
obtained his power from this *ma'swut,* and he talked to it in the
ma'swut language. The bundle and the house in which it was kept were
very sacred.

The same concept held for the Cahuilla groups; *ma'swut* was
known as "the heart of the house," and was passed on from one clan
leader to his successor in the paternal line. It was said to be very powerful, and by talking to the *ma'swut* in its own esoteric language, the
clan leader could bring misfortune to members of the clan who failed
to obey his judgments. The different clans had different objects wrapped
up in the bundle; on the desert one clan had a sacred stone pipe, another
at Palm Springs had a whistle made of the pelvis of a California grizzly

bear, certain of the Mountain Cahuilla clans had stone concretions, eagle-bone whistles, and strangely shaped sticks. Always the ceremonial belongings of the group, barring purely personal or shamanistic paraphernalia, were included in the bundle. The nature of this material varied with the rites performed by the clans, the distribution of which cannot be considered here. The main fetish of the Serrano was the long string of sacred feathers.[195] A similar string was possessed by the southern Mountain Cahuilla.

At the week-long Mourning Ceremony of the Palm Springs Cahuilla, observed by the author in 1925, the importance of the *ma'swut* concept was well brought out, as was the importance of the priest and the ceremonial house. Three days prior to the ceremony the "net" (clan priest) "retreats" within the *kishamnawut* ("big house," e.g., dance-house) and spends a considerable part of this time conferring with the *ma'swut* in the inner room. When the ceremony begins the clan shamans seek advice from the "little witch doctors" of the four directions, who through the *ma'swut* tell the priest if the time is favorable. In the middle of the week, after dark, the priest and his assistant extinguish all lights in the dance-house and the priest brings the *ma'swut* bundle into the center of the house. All present are very silent, for in the old days, it is said, the *ma'swut* killed any one who made a noise. Unfolding the fetish bundle in the dark, the priest prays over it in the "*ma'swut* language," asking it to bless the house; then all the men kneeling blow cigarette smoke over the bundle, and it is put away in the inner room until the next ceremony. Formerly the priest's assistant, called the *paha'*, blew on the bear-bone whistle at this time, a sound that would kill any noisy or irreverent person. Now, however, they say this whistle has disappeared. The *ma'swut* is "the heart of the big house," which gives the clan priest his power and sanctifies the ceremonial house.

Even today, sadly broken down as the old ceremonials of the southern Californians are, it was impossible for me to examine the *ma'swut*, and only a few of the old men would talk about it. When the last active clan of the Mountain Cahuilla gave up their ceremonial activities, the clan priest buried his *ma'swut* in a distant cave and sent his ceremonial shell money to the active clan at Palm Springs. It can safely be said that the clan-priest, "big house" and *ma'swut* complex is the most important factor in the aboriginal society of southern California today, as it undoubtedly was in pre-Mission times.

The complex seems to have been lacking among the Yuman Diegueño, and as far as known among the Chemehuevi and other Plateau

Shoshoneans. None of the Colorado River Yuman peoples[196] had it in its full form, for while in myth and ritual the house seems to have been ceremonially important among the Yuma and Mohave,[197] there were no priests or fetish bundles, and in actual ceremonies the house was little used. Somewhat the same state of affairs occurred among the Apache and the Navajo. The former have personal fetishes, especially the shamans, and use a symbolic four-pole lodge in the girls' puberty ceremony in which a priest is hired.[198] There seem to be no references to group-priests, group-houses, or group-fetishes, and on the whole such resemblances to the complex as do occur seem to be rather pale imitations of Pueblo ceremonies, instead of fundamental concepts of Apache society. The Navajo also seem to reflect the Pueblo, especially the Hopi ceremonials, in their house dedications,[199] hunting and flock fetishes,[200] sun symbol in basket at the Night Chant,[201] ceremonial tobacco smoking,[202] and carved images which are talked to in a foreign language, presumably Hopi.[202] I would hesitate to ascribe all these features to comparatively late borrowing were it not for the statement made by Reichard that, with one exception which is not clear as yet, there is no relation between any priest, fetish, or ceremonial house and the Navajo clan organization.[204] The view that these Pueblo-like features possessed by the Navajo represent comparatively late borrowings has been previously stated by James Stevenson[205] and the Franciscan Fathers.[206]

The previous discussion of the moiety and clan organization of the Pima and Papago has shown how obscure and contradictory are many of the data concerning their society. In spite of this confusion, enough material is extant to indicate quite strongly that the Pima and Papago possessed the group-house, fetish, and priest complex in its full form. In the description given by Lumholtz,[207] striking analogies to both Californian and Pueblo rituals appear. During the Papago Sahuaro feast, strings of eagle feathers were stretched across the dance-house from east to west, while "rock crystals and queer objects" were used to procure rain.[208] The group-fetish is described as a

> long basket of enormous proportions placed between east and west on the ground at the foot of the western pole, near the doctors. It was of the same oblong shape as the ordinary medicine basket of so many tribes, and serves as a receptacle for the sacred paraphernalia of the lodge. Here the string of eagle feathers hanging near by is kept during the year. It is provided with a cover of the same material, considered by the Indians as its blanket, which when the basket is in use, is placed on the ground for it to "sit on."[209]

During the ceremony the medicine man blew and breathed over the sacred stone (taken from the basket) "making peculiar noises." These actions were for the purpose of bringing rain.[210] Lumholtz was refused permission to examine the contents of the basket, for the priest said it was very dangerous and might harm the beholder.[211] After the great annual harvest feast in August the sacred paraphernalia are put away in some distant cave.[212]

The lodge is a circular dome-shaped grass hut, the ancient form of Papago habitation, and is larger than the dwelling house. It is called *kúki*, "big house."[213] When a dispute arose between Lumholtz and one of the local Papago, the latter stated that "He was going to bring the matter before the Big House, . . . " and when he had done so, the priest reprimanded Lumholtz for proceeding without the permission of the "big house," saying, "In this house I tell people what to do, and this is the place where any undertaking should begin."[214] This ceremonial leader or priest who is in charge of the lodge and its sacred objects is elected for life. "He lives near by and is called Keeper of the Smoke, which means tobacco smoke."[215] When this information is considered in connection with the fact of village exogamy among the Papago,[216] the village unit, ceremonially held together by the group-house, fetish, and priest complex, appears more fundamental than the loose non-exogamous clan or phratry system.

Russell mentions the council house of the Pima, which, like the other Pima houses, was built by the men.[217] He likewise mentions that families kept owl feathers in a long rectangular box or basket of maguey leaf,[218] and that cottonbound medicine sticks were used by the shamans in connection with other paraphernalia.[219] He gives little data on ceremonial organization, but it seems highly probable considering their community in moiety and clan organization, as well as material culture, that the Pima and the Papago both had the group-house, fetish, and priest complex. The uniformity of the two systems has also been assumed by Goddard.[220]

Among the Pueblo peoples the complex under discussion enters so fully into their involved ceremonial life and appears to be of such antiquity that only a résumé of its most salient characteristics may be given here.[221] The kiva itself is found in association with practically all Pueblo ruins in the Southwest[222] and is also associated with ruins of the pre-Pueblo culture.[223] The fetishes, usually stone concretions, express their antiquity in their appearance and in their associations.[224] The antiquity of the priest concept is harder to trace but may be assumed from ethnological evidence. While the association of these three concepts as a complex seems to have been more or less assumed by writers on the Southwest, it has, so far as I know, never been treated as such, and as a result references to it are decidedly scattered.

Among the Hopi, clans are not necessarily associated with individual kivas, but one clan is usually considered as the builder and nominal owner of the kiva.[225] Clan names are moreover often applied to the different kivas.[226] Later work confirms this view of clan association with individual kivas and adds the fact that, should a clan grow too large, additional kivas may be built.[227] The four lines drawn on the wall of the Hopi dwelling during natal ceremonies, symbolizing the "house," with similar symbolic "house" rites performed in nearly all secret ceremonies, shows how deeply the concept of the ceremonial house enters into the consciousness of the people. The "house of the clouds" figures in certain ceremonial songs.[228]

Fetishes, and with them fetish bundles, are associated with every house,[229] clan,[230] and fraternity[231] of the Hopi. The household fetish is a stone animal and is the property of the woman, who feeds it daily. It is the guardian of her house.[232] The sacred paraphernalia of the secret fraternities are supposed to have their peculiar charm or influence, especially the altar paraphernalia, which cannot be touched or even seen without danger.[233] The nature of the clan fetishes has been previously indicated. It appears that the clan fetish is in the hands of one lineage in the clan, and that this is the clan unit in so-called "clan" migrations.

> The custodian of a clan fetish believes that were he to migrate all his clans-people would have to follow him, and no doubt those who attached importance to the fetish would indeed follow him. Now the members of the custodian's maternal family are those who most value the fetish and who would stay by it. So that when a Hopi refers to migration of clan he is really referring to a migration by a fetish-holding maternal family, to him the heart of the clan.

The Hopi individual does not readily discuss this fetish concept, first because it is so clear to him, and second because he does not care to discuss or even refer to the fetishes. "And yet in native philosophy it is the clan fetish or the clan mask (*wöye*)—every clan has a *wöye* . . . —which holds the group together."[234] Lowie states that during the flute ceremony at Walpi, feather offerings are laid out on a Havasupai basket, which is carried to a dark section of the ceremonial chamber and placed in front of the altar.[235] Goddard mentions very antique-appearing images of the twin war gods, and stone mountain-lion fetishes, which are placed by the symbolically colored (directional) sand painting during initiation rites.[236] The use of the quartz-crystal sun symbol in the center of the sand painting called the "house of the sun" likewise brings out the importance of both house and fetish concepts. The fetishes are consecrated by breathing and blowing clouds of smoke over them from the cone-shaped pipe called "cloud producer."[237] The whole idea of ceremonial smoking on entering the kiva, to consecrate paraphernalia and to bring rain clouds, is fundamental in Hopi ritual, and without this no ceremony would be considered efficacious.[238] Corn meal is sprinkled over the altar, fetishes, and in the flute ceremony over the ceremonial basket containing offerings.[239] The blowing of eagle-bone whistles into the medicine bowl[240] during all extended Hopi ceremonials is important.[241] Prayers are offered by the priest before the altar and fetishes.[242] The intimate relationship of the priest to the fetish and to the kiva is well known in a general way, but the exact relationship is decidedly involved. Such facts as are clear have been brought out previously in the discussion of Pueblo clans.

According to Cushing the Zuñi fetishes are designated as "What they live by," and are relics of the gods given directly to mankind.[243] The myths relating to these fetishes which are usually natural concretions are full of archaic and esoteric terms. The images themselves are regarded as possessing the actual breath and life of the Prey God animals they represent. Thus, they are mediators between the priests who hold them "in captivity" and the gods. On the day of the "Council of the Fetishes" the priests pray over the fetishes and the other members respond.[244] Each rain priest possesses one of these most sacred fetishes, which according to legend were "brought into the world wrapped in a mat of straw in a crude basket."[245] When the mythical Zuñi ancestors were divided into clans each became associated with such a fetish, which though at present used by successive rain priests, must remain in the possession of the women of the clan, passing from mother to daughter or sister to sister.[246] These fetishes are often simple reeds or bundles of reeds. From the fetish the priest, after a short prayer and meal sprinkling, draws "the sacred breath."[247] The ceremonial importance of tobacco smoke as the offering that brings rain clouds appears as great among the Zuñi[248] as among the Hopi. Corn-meal sprinklings, plume offerings, and other rites are performed for the altars and fetishes, as among the Hopi. A new expansion of the clan may lead to the manufacture of a new fetish, and in case of a threatened extinction of the clan the keepers of the fetish may bury or definitely dispose of it.[249] The room into which the priests retreat prior to ceremonies is usually directly above the chamber of the fetish, and meal is sprinkled through an opening onto the fetish. At other times this opening is sealed up.[250] This period of retirement prior to a ceremony is characteristic of the priesthood in all the pueblos. The guardianship of the fetish is a strictly clan affair, the house where it is kept determining its clan proprietorship.[251] It is worth noting that the fetish of the Shu'maakwe fraternity at Zuñi, "is distinctly different from the others." The songs connected with this fetish are in the Pima language.[252] All students of Zuñi bring out the importance of the fetish concept in definitely shaping the social organization. In this regard, Kroeber says in part:

> I believe that the truest understanding of Zuñi life other than its purely practical manifestations, can be had by setting the ettowe [fetishes] as a center. Around these priesthoods, fraternities, clan organization, as well as most esoteric thinking and sacred tradition group themselves, while in turn kivas, dances, and acts of public worship can be construed as but the outward means of expression of the inner activities that radiate around the nucleus of the physical fetishes and the ideas attached to them. In other words he who knows all that is knowable concerning the ettowe, must necessarily understand substantially the whole of Zuñi society.[253]

The central and eastern Pueblos conform in all essentials to the complex concept just outlined; a few details, however, may be recorded. The most sacred fetish of the Western Keresans is a corn ear; it is encircled with abalone shell and olivella beads, and wrapped in unspun cotton. Fetish stones are used on the altars and are wrapped in corn meal and corn husks at other times.[254] Corn meal offered the fetishes is first breathed upon.[255] Certain masks are associated with certain clans, and when no one is qualified to inherit such a mask, it is buried in the river.[256] The clan heads go into retreat for four days and make images of the sun. Each has a basket with arrow points attached, which contains fully kernelled ears of corn of which fetishes are made. They likewise keep stone fetish animals and terraced medicine bowls. Knowledge of the rituals is the basis of leadership, and this also applies to the rain priests at Zuñi.[257]

Among the Eastern Keresans at Cochiti and Sia, details of organization are obscure, but it seems clear that ceremonial priests, fetishes, and kivas are of paramount importance. At Cochiti, the Cacique is called the father and mother of his people; he prays for the whole world and is a man of peace. His office is characterized by the possession of a small black staff with eagle feathers attached and a small jar of unknown content. He gives advice and counsels harmony; and at certain periods communal hunts are organized by the war captain to secure food for him.[258] The relation of the Cacique to the clans or clan leaders is not known. At Sia there is one chief rain priest appointed for life from one of the three clans; he also is supposed to be absorbed with religion and is never supposed to leave the village.[259] There is a stone in the village laid by the priest, emblematic of the heart of the village ("for a heart must be, before a thing can exist").[260] Stone animal fetishes are employed, a line of meal laid before them, allowing the spirits of the animals they represent to enter during the ceremonies. The priest doctors of the warrior society possess slat altars, and those who practice through the power of the prey animals have sand paintings as well. The fetishes are carefully stored in different houses between the ceremonies. During the ceremonies the priests blow smoke from ceremonial cigarettes over the altar and fetishes and draw the "sacred breath" from the latter. When water is poured into the sacred "cloud bowl," whistles are blown. Offerings are made to the fetishes.[261]

Among the eastern Tewa the clans appear to be functionless, the priesthood, kivas, and I presume certain fetishes, being associated with the moieties. The southern Tigua are likewise dominated by the double-kiva, moiety idea. There are clans, however, and clan heads who go into retreat before ceremonies, while fetishes are also employed.[262] At Taos, in the north, the moiety is dominant, with two kivas and priests, but the details of organization are unknown.

This complex appears among a number of the Plains tribes[263] and well to the northeast, the Winnebago being an excellent example of the frequent combination of moiety, clan, and fetish complex.[264] A study of these organizations would be highly significant in regard to the history of the complex, but is beyond the scope of the present paper.

Interpretation of Distribution

So far we have merely mapped out the distribution of social groupings in the area under consideration (see Chart I), and it now remains to compare these and draw whatever conclusions seem permissible from the data at hand.

A true tribal sense seems to characterize, and in certain respects set aside, the Yuman tribes of the lower Colorado River. Similarly the Pima and Papago, their neighbors and intermittent enemies, seem to have acted together when the need arose. The Navajo, in theory or legend, had twelve chiefs that met in council, but in actuality they seem to have acted in independent bands, as did the Apache. The people

CHART I DISTRIBUTION OF SOCIAL FACTORS

Tribes W. to E.

Social Factors	Salinan	Miwok	Yokuts	Chumash	Gabrielino	Luiseño	Diegueño	Cupeño	Cahuilla	Serrano	Chemehuevi	Basin Shosh.	Mohave	Yuma	Havasupai	Pima	Papago	W. Apache	Navajo	Hopi	Zuñi	W. Keresan	E. Keresan	Tewa	Isleta	Taos	E. Apache	Kiowa Apache	Pawnee
Warlike Tribe	x	x	x	?									x	x		x	x											x	x
Moiety	?	x	x	?	?	x	x	x	x	x						x	x			?	?	x	x	x	x	x	?	x	x
Group-fetish	?		?	?	x	x	?	x	x	x					x	x	x			x	x	x	x	x	x	x	x	x	x
Group-priest	?	?	?	?	x	x	?	x	x	x				?	x	x	x			x	x	x	x	x	x	x	x	x	x
Group-house	x	x	x	?	x	x	x	x	x	x			?	?	x	x	x			x	x	x	x	x	x	x	?	?	
Nonlocalized clan	?				?								x	x		x	x			?	x	x	x	x	?				
Localized clan	?	x	x	?	?	x		x	x	x					?	?	?	x	x	?									
Localized lineage	?	x	x	?	?	?	?	?	?	?	?	?	?	?	?	?	?	?	?	?							?	?	?
Moiety descent	?	P	P	?	?	P	P	P	P	P			P	P	P	P	P	M	M	M	?	PM	P	P	P	P		M	M
Clan descent	?	P	P	?	?	P	P	P	P	P			P	P	?	P	P	M	M	M	M	M	P	P	P	P		?	?
Lineage descent	?	P	P	?	?	P	P	P	P	P			?	?	?	?	?	M	?	M	M	M	MP	P	?	?	?	?	?
Moiety exogamy	?	x	x	?	?	x	P	x	x	x			?	?	?	?	?												
Clan exogamy	?	x	x	?	?	x	x	x	x	x			x	x		x	x	x	x	x	x	x	x	x	?	?			

Explanation: x = present; blank = absent; ? = data not clear or lacking.

of the Plains were organized in strong warlike tribes, but in the present survey we have not considered them in more than a general way. For the rest of the area, localized clans or lineages and bands appear to have been the political units.

The distribution of the moiety over the Southwest presents an intricate problem.[265] In the light of new information it seems practically certain that in southern and south central California the various moiety groupings arose from one source. The names given the divisions differ in various parts of the area, but the ideas of exogamy, reciprocity, paternal descent, divisions of natural phenomena (especially animals), and distinguishing moiety paints are nearly always present wherever the moiety occurs. Thus we have the bear and deer divisions of the Salinans, the land and water divisions of the Miwok (also associated strongly with bear and deer in moiety names),[266] upstream and downstream of the Yokuts and Mono, and the coyote and wildcat of the Cupeño, Cahuilla, and Serrano. The latter names for the two divisions probably arose among the Cupeño by the association of Shoshonean and Yuman people at Warner's Hot Springs, the clans of the former being called coyote, and the latter wildcat. The former animal is important in Shoshonean, and the latter in Yuman mythology;[267] and it seems probable that the animal name most commonly associated with each group was given to the moiety grouping common to southern California.

Among the Miwok, spotted face design indicated the water moiety, stripes the land moiety; while among the Cupeño, spotted face designs indicated the wildcat, stripes the coyote moiety. Whenever moiety paints were remembered they fit this pattern. In addition to the Saboba dual division and the moiety myth of the Luiseño, I am inclined to believe that the body paint of the ceremonial assistant or *paha'*, half red and half black, supposedly symbolizing the male and female red racer (*Coluber flagellum*), was due to early moiety influence. This name was employed by Luiseño and Cahuilla. According to Boscana, Gabrielino priests were also painted red and black.[268]

The apparent breaks in the distribution of the moiety in southern California are more impressive on the map than actually significant. The central groups without any moiety organization are the Kawaiisu and Tübatulabal.[269] The latter are of the Kern River Shoshonean branch, and while their residence in the area may have been as long as that of the Southern California Shoshonean branch, they are a small isolated group, probably more in touch with the Plateau culture than that to the west. The Kawaiisu are Plateau Shoshoneans and appear to be comparatively latecomers to the area.[270] The Plateau Shoshoneans such as the Chemehuevi and the Yuman tribes of the Colorado River are without the institution and form a barrier between the moiety-organized peoples of the west and east. Thus it seems clear that the two main factors in obscuring the moiety relationship in southern California appear to be intrusions from the north and east of non-dichotomous groups and a fading of the institution in areas where it was longest in vogue. Added to this we have practically no data in regard to the moiety for the Chumash, Gabrielino, or Juaneño, who may well have been at the center of its western dispersal. The fact that the moiety idea had practically disappeared among the Luiseño may indicate that the same condition occurred among their western neighbors.

The nearest people to the east having a moiety division are the Pima and Papago of the allied Uto-Aztekan linguistic stock. It appears there as an outworn custom having no function in their present-day society. However, the appearance of characteristic face paints for each moiety, as well as a division of all animals between them, is similar to the moiety in California. The two colors symbolizing the moieties are red and white. Descent of the moiety is patrilineal, but there is at present no moiety exogamy.

The Apache and Navajo have no traces of any dual division, but the western Pueblos have traces in both myth and ceremony. At Zuñi, red and black paints are associated with prayer sticks for summer rains and winter rains, respectively. There are other ceremonial manifestations of the moiety among both the Hopi and Zuñi. Among the eastern Pueblos the ceremonial importance of patrilineal, non-exogamous moiety is clear. The association of red and black paints with the two moieties at Isleta has also been noted. Whether the rather obscure custom of assigning animal-named clans to different moieties among the eastern Pueblos can be compared to the California custom of dividing the various animals between the moieties is uncertain but appears quite possible.

For the area under consideration it would seem that the patrilineal moiety is most strongly represented on the periphery, while in the central area characterized by the Pima, Papago, and western Pueblos, it has faded to little more than a myth. Among the Athapascan, Yuman, and Basin Shoshonean peoples, who appear as somewhat late invaders in the area, the moiety is not found at all.

That the Pueblo dichotomous organization is related to that of such Plains tribes as the Pawnee seems probable when we also take into account the bundle-fetish and priest complex of the latter people.[271] But the nature of this relationship, as well as that of the other dichotomous Plains and eastern tribes,[272] is beyond the scope of the present paper.

To presume an earlier connection between all these southwestern groups possessing a moiety organization would be extremely rash were it not for strong corroborating evidence. All the Southern California Shoshoneans and all the Pueblo peoples having a dichotomous organization of varying degree of importance also possess exogamous clans characterized by the clan-house, priest, and fetish complex. Probably this holds for the Uto-Aztekan Pima and Papago as well, but the clans on record for the latter seem to be loose non-exogamous reflections of the Mohave type and really appear more like phratries than clans. They are not localized and are not centered around any clan house, priest, or fetish, whereas the villages of the Pima and Papago are exogamous, and possess the complete house, priest, and fetish complex. This village unit therefore appears quite similar to the south California localized clan, characterized by the fetish complex, also common to the Pueblo clan.

The localized exogamous matrilineal clans and phratries (or clan groups) of the Apache and Navajo seem to be reflections of the strong matrilineal clans of the western Pueblos, but they lack entirely the clan-house, priest, and fetish complex that is so vital to the latter. Similarly the Yuman peoples of the lower Colorado River in their exogamous non-localized patrilineal clans, whose names are borne by the women, may represent the influence of the developed matrilineal clan of the western Pueblos on a patrilineal group. However this unique system arose, I believe that it has spread in a somewhat variant form back to the Pima and Papago, in part covering over their older and more Pueblo-like organization. This may only be proved or disproved by more data from the people in question. In the same way I am inclined to account for the otherwise anomalous phratries of the Western Mono, although this is more hypothetical. The occurrence of the Pima and Papago clans, whose vaguely totemic names apply to the father, to the east of the Yuma and Mohave; and of the Mono, whose phratries are named after the totem animal of the father, to the west of the same people, can best be explained through the diffusion of this indirect clan-naming system from the Colorado River center. The *posha* of the Yokuts appears as the most westerly occurrence of this indirectly totemic clan. It is in accord with observed facts on southern California that while the Yuma and Mohave have influenced their western neighbors in a considerable degree, these influences are underlaid by more widespread and basic concepts found among the Pueblo peoples. The natural inference to be drawn from such a situation is that the Pueblo-like influences (or similarities) are the older, and in the regions nearest the Colorado River have been overlaid by Yuman concepts. Thus, the Western Mono, with their lineages, phratries, and non-exogamous moiety organization, represent a combination of the two sets of cultural influences. When more is known of both Mono divisions and of their neighbors, the situation should clarify itself.

The upriver Yuman tribes, represented in this survey by the Havasupai, like the Basin Shoshoneans have the bilateral family as the unit within the tribe. Thus, they have neither lineages nor clans, as have the Diegueño and lower-river Yumans, respectively.

To sum up the situation, it may be said that the Pueblos, the Southern California Shoshoneans, and probably the Uto-Aztekan Pima and Papago have, in addition to the moiety, male or female lineages fused into paternal or maternal clans, characterized in either case by the complete clan-house, priest, and fetish complex. The Athapascan Navajo and Apache had maternal clans, probably composed of fused lineages, but without the aforementioned complex. The downriver Yumans had paternal clans or phratries, without the complex; and the upriver Yumans, as well as the Basin Shoshoneans, had neither clans nor lineages, having the natural or bilateral family as the unit of society.

Gifford has shown that for most of California the lineage is the aboriginal political unit,[273] and I am inclined to believe this applies to the Pueblo area and to the Pima and Papago. Certainly the data secured by Lowie and Parsons in regard to the Hopi point in that direction.[274] The latter has also shown that the patrilineal moiety of the eastern Pueblos is correlated with male house-owning, while the strong matrilineal clans of the western Pueblos are correlated with female house-owning.[275] The heart of the clan organization being the fetish, and the lineage which possesses it,[276] it would seem that in these two fundamental concepts, house-owning and fetish custodianship, we may have the cause for male or female lineage differentiation. If the woman owns the house and is custodian of the fetish, as occurs among the Hopi and at Zuñi, it seems logical that maternal reckoning of descent might follow. Matrilineal residence would strengthen this tendency, whereas male custodianship of the fetish with patrilocal residence might lead to a paternal clan system as in southern California. Spier has shown that with the bilateral family of the Havasupai, any factor which tended to accentuate either male or female lineage might bring about a unilateral system of descent and a sib organization.[277] The fetish concept, with its correlates, would surely seem to be such a factor.

When the importance of the fetish complex is fully realized and the lineage basis of the clan borne in mind, it becomes clear why the transmission of such an important factor as the fetish complex might lead to either paternal or maternal reckoning of descent in accord with the existing pattern of the receptors. Thus it is possible to regard the predominantly maternal clan system of the western Pueblos as more or less identical with the paternal clan system of southern California, for in their fundamental fetish concept they agree even in minutiae. It is likewise significant that the moiety, wherever found in the entire area, is paternal in descent; for as this institution is more widespread than any single type of clan organization, it may indicate a former condition of paternal reckoning of descent, which owing to special conditions was superseded in the western Pueblos by maternal reckoning. Whether the absence of maternal clans in the eastern Pueblos is significant in this regard depends on how far their present condition is the result of Caucasian influence or due to native pattern.

Probably the Navajo and Western Apache owe their maternal clans to the influence of the fully developed maternal clan among the Hopi and at Zuñi. How far the lineage enters into their clan organization is not clear, but the very important clan fetish complex seems to be entirely absent.

A multiple origin for the clan seems certain from a consideration of southwestern social groupings, and if the foregoing conclusions are accepted, the importance of the fetish complex in clan formation is demonstrated. That it is only one factor is amply illustrated by those groups which do not possess the complex, and yet have clans. The relative antiquity of clan and moiety is not clear, even though the wider spread of the latter appears certain. That the correlation of a dichotomous organization with clans possessing the fetish complex is significant seems indubitable, but in south central California dichotomy seems to have spread beyond the range of the fetish complex. It may be that a moiety idea is more volatile and easily fitted into a culture pattern than the fetish complex, but this again must wait further comparisons in areas where the moiety and the fetish complex both occur. A survey of southwestern social groupings certainly suggests such a correlation.

Conclusions

The Pueblo-like features in the aboriginal society of southern California are found in greatest numbers among the coastal peoples. Such traits as the group-house, priest, and fetish complex, the ceremonial ground-painting, asperging of water brought from a particular spring,[278] placing of plume offerings in certain shrines,[279] ceremonial smoking of tobacco, offering prayers for rain, initiation of boys, ceremonial pole climbing, eagle and whirling dances, clan ownership of eagles and personification of the gods[280] are found in their most complete form among the Gabrielino, Juaneño, San Fernandeño, and Luiseño, and in lesser degree among the Cupeño, Serrano, Mountain and Pass Cahuilla, while among the Desert Cahuilla, well to the east, only a minimal number of such practices occur. From this distribution it seems probable that the connection between the Southwest proper and southern California was severed before the Plateau and more easterly Southern California Shoshoneans occupied their present habitat. Since the Yuman peoples of the Colorado River show comparatively few similarities to the Pueblos, it seems probable that their incursion into their present range, as well as the southwestward movement of the Shoshoneans, presumably from the Great Basin,[281] severed whatever connections formerly existed between the southern coast of California and the early Pueblo culture.[282] Quite probably the Chumash, as well as the earliest Southern California Shoshoneans to reach the Pacific, shared this common heritage of Pueblo-like traits, and from them they were diffused to the east, throughout central and even into northern California west of the Sierras.

Since no absolute records are extant to show that the Shoshoneans, Yumans, and Athapascans caused these breaks by pressing into the intervening areas, it might well be argued that no such migration had occurred and that the traits in question were diffused through the medium of the above peoples. Opposed to this is the fact that the moiety, group-house, priest, and fetish complex, as well as rain-producing ceremonies are fundamental in Pueblo, Pima, Papago, and the coastal cultures of southern California, and tend to condition all other social activities, while in the three intervening linguistic groups they are almost entirely lacking. That once possessing these Pueblo-like traits, the Athapascans, Yumans, and easterly Shoshoneans might have lost them is equally improbable, for there are only superficial traces of such traits among any of them, and their group organization is markedly different. The hypothesis that they were merely passive agents in the transmission of such an elaborate complex and were unaffected by it themselves is untenable when the many superficial features of Pueblo ceremonials now used by Navajo and Apache are considered. In the final analysis it would seem that there had been an intrusion of these peoples at a time when the Pueblo, probably the Uto-Aztekan, and the California coastal peoples had already developed their fundamental social structures under very similar influences.

CHART II

THEORETICAL RECONSTRUCTION OF SOUTHWESTERN SOCIETY

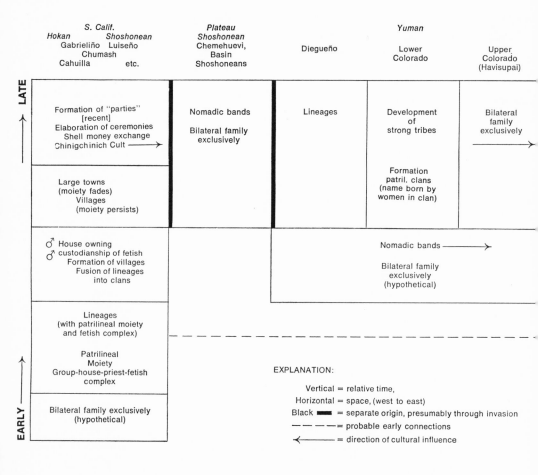

WEST

	S. Calif. Hokan Shoshonean Gabrieliño Luiseño Chumash Cahuilla etc.	Plateau Shoshonean Chemehuevi, Basin Shoshoneans	Diegueño	Yuman Lower Colorado	Upper Colorado (Havisupai)
LATE ↑	Formation of "parties" [recent] Elaboration of ceremonies Shell money exchange Chinigchinich Cult →	Nomadic bands Bilateral family exclusively	Lineages	Development of strong tribes	Bilateral family exclusively →
	Large towns (moiety fades) Villages (moiety persists)			Formation patril. clans (name born by women in clan)	
	♂ House owning ♂ custodianship of fetish Formation of villages Fusion of lineages into clans		Nomadic bands → Bilateral family exclusively (hypothetical)		
	Lineages (with patrilineal moiety and fetish complex)				
↑	Patrilineal Moiety Group-house-priest-fetish complex				
EARLY ↑	Bilateral family exclusively (hypothetical)				

EXPLANATION:

Vertical = relative time,
Horizontal = space, (west to east)
Black ■■■ = separate origin, presumably through invasion
— — — — = probable early connections
◄———— = direction of cultural influence

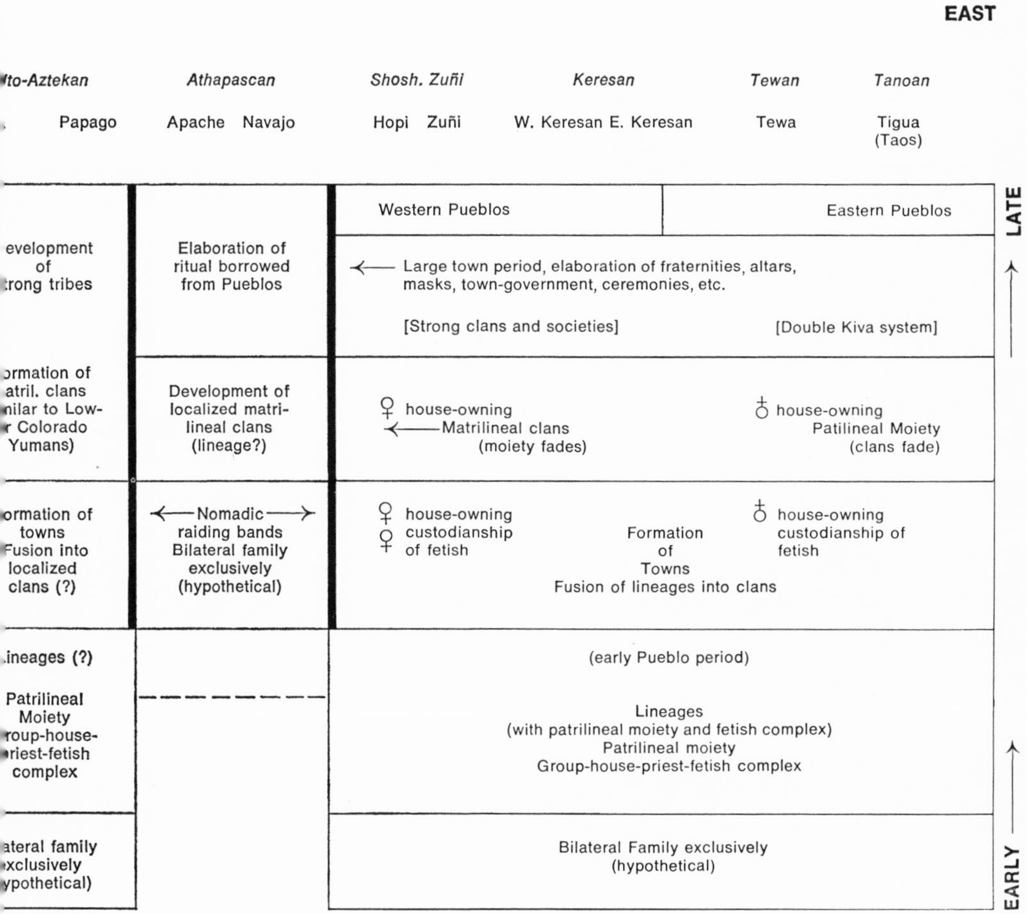
EAST
[U]to-Aztekan
Athapascan
Shosh. Zuñi
Keresan
Tewan
Tanoan
Papago
Apache Navajo
Hopi Zuñi
W. Keresan E. Keresan
Tewa
Tigua (Taos)
Western Pueblos
Eastern Pueblos
LATE
[D]evelopment of [s]trong tribes
Elaboration of ritual borrowed from Pueblos
Large town period, elaboration of fraternities, altars, masks, town-government, ceremonies, etc.
[Strong clans and societies]
[Double Kiva system]
[F]ormation of [m]atril. clans [si]milar to Low[e]r Colorado Yumans)
Development of localized matrilineal clans (lineage?)
♀ house-owning
Matrilineal clans
(moiety fades)
♂ house-owning
Patilineal Moiety
(clans fade)
[F]ormation of towns [F]usion into localized clans (?)
Nomadic raiding bands
Bilateral family exclusively (hypothetical)
♀ house-owning
♀ custodianship of fetish
Formation of Towns
Fusion of lineages into clans
♂ house-owning custodianship of fetish
[L]ineages (?)
Patrilineal Moiety
[G]roup-house-[p]riest-fetish complex
(early Pueblo period)
Lineages
(with patrilineal moiety and fetish complex)
Patrilineal moiety
Group-house-priest-fetish complex
[Bil]ateral family [e]xclusively [h]ypothetical)
Bilateral Family exclusively
(hypothetical)
EARLY

Not only ethnology but archaeology also indicates a very wide range for the early Pueblo culture, which was gradually cut down by the incursion of nomadic peoples.[283] This early Pueblo culture is characterized in its archaeological remains by small ruins associated with the round kiva, and marked by black-on-white pottery.[284] The later ruins increase in size as the range of the culture decreases, presumably due to concentration against invaders.[285] Thus, in the modern Pueblo towns, we seem to have concentrated a culture that at an earlier time extended from Great Salt Lake in the north to southwestern Nevada in the west.[286]

In these small house and kiva ruins it is tempting to see the stage of localized lineages in Pueblo development, similar to those localized lineages in southern California, and perhaps the towns of the Pima and Papago. If the clans of the modern Pueblo towns are made up of separate lineages, as seems probable in the light of recent ethnologic investigation, it appears possible that the clans grew from the lineages due to concentration in larger towns. Such concentration would presumably lead to the present ceremonial elaboration, as well as advance of material culture noted in the Pueblos of historic times. Barring differences in materials of construction, there is a marked analogy between these small ruins of the early Pueblo period and the localized clans of southern California, as well as with the village unit of the Pima and Papago, especially when one considers the fundamental importance of the ceremonial house in each case and the present-day similarities in moiety, group-priest, and fetish complex. Just as the Pueblo towns were formed later, probably after the Athapascan, Yuman, and Shoshonean peoples had severed the wider connections to the west; so in California among the Chumash and Gabrielino larger towns arose, evidently based on a fusion of independent lineages, and unique developments arose in each area. (See chart II.)

Unfortunately such a simple view of direct transmission of basic social organization from east to west cannot be taken on the basis of archaeological evidence, for the black-on-white pottery of the early Pueblo ruins is not characteristic of ruins in Pima territory[287] and is utterly unknown for any period in California. What seems more probable is that prior to the main incursion of nomadic peoples, perhaps at the time of the widest early Pueblo expansion, there was a spread of basic ideas, presumably from the south,[288] which alike influenced the development of the peoples of the south California coast, the Lower Gila, and the early Pueblos to the north. This state of affairs I have attempted to bring out diagrammatically in chart 2 indicating the early relationships between these groups and the later breaks in continuity due to the pushing in of later peoples with subsequent shifts of cultural influence.

The data on the peoples of northern Mexico are sadly inadequate, but it is clear that among the Tarahumare,[289] Cora,[290] Tepehuane, Huichol, and Aztec,[291] the group-house, priest, and fetish complex is well developed. Sprinkling of water, meal, and the ceremonial smoking of tobacco likewise are ceremonially important, and there is every indication that with more knowledge of their organization the relationship between the Pueblo-like cultures of the southwestern United States and adjacent areas, would become more significant.

In regard to the relationship between California and the Southwest, future archaeology in the Salt, Lower Gila, and Colorado River regions may well yield significant facts. The pottery of southern California closely resembles certain plain red types from the Lower Gila,[292] and stratigraphic work there and in southern California may indicate the connection. The fact that the findings of archaeology and ethnology are definitely converging in the solution of problems of American prehistory gives great promise for the future.

Summary

From the new data it appears, that the group-house, priest, and fetish complex in the aboriginal society of southern California occurs among the San Fernandeño, Gabrielino, Juaneño, Luiseño, Cupeño, Cahuilla, and Serrano peoples, and is the most important single factor in shaping their social organization.

This complex is likewise fundamental, and equally important, among the Pima, Papago, and Pueblo peoples, and the complex with its associated ceremonial features is so similar even to minute detail for all these groups, that an historical relationship is thereby implied.

In the area under consideration, wherever the above complex occurs, there is also present a moiety division or ceremonial traces thereof.

Whenever this dichotomy appears, its associated factors are very similar, and a common origin is therefore implied for the Californian, Pima and Papago, and the Pueblo moiety.

The intervening Plateau Shoshonean, Yuman, and Athapascan peoples lack the complete fetish complex and the moiety, and as they form a barrier at present between those areas possessing the two concepts, they would seem to be intruders in their present habitat who had interrupted a once continuous distribution.

Finally, the dichotomous grouping is more widely spread than any single type of clan, and in the area under consideration would appear older than any form of clan save the unilateral family or lineage.

NOTES
BIBLIOGRAPHY
INDEX

NOTES

2 SPECULATIONS ON NEW WORLD PREHISTORY

1. I disagree with Spinden's belief that American cultures rest on a worldwide polished stone "peneplane."

2. It seems to me certain that the Folsom culture, in the western plains at least, must have lasted relatively unchanged for a very long time. Only by such a supposition, or on the much less probable theory of a dense population, can we account for the great numbers of Folsom points which have come to light since 1927. These now number many hundreds, and if it be taken into account that they have been found by a few individuals collecting more or less casually and intermittently, and if it be remembered that they have come from the relatively few places where wind or water have chanced to lay bare the artifact-bearing strata, it can be realized how many scores of thousands of them must still remain undiscovered.

3. The reports of Strong, Roberts, and Haury, to quote only from the literature with which I am most familiar, are models of accuracy and completeness.

4. I follow the terminology recently suggested by F. H. H. Roberts, Jr.

5. I here rather hesitatingly launch a trial balloon. It is now evident, because of the segregation of the Hohokam, that the term *Pueblo* can no longer properly be applied to all the sedentary, agricultural, pottery-making peoples of southwestern United States and northern Mexico. We must speak of Hohokam and Basketmaker-Pueblo. But the latter is an unwieldy designation which also causes confusion when we wish to refer to either of these two sequent elements separately. Might we therefore not use the word *Anasazi*, which has the same meaning ("old people") in Navaho that Hohokam bears in Pima? It would apply to the Northern or San Juan Basketmaker and Developmental Basketmaker; and to those Pueblo groups which

155

can be shown to have derived the basic framework of their culture from the Basketmaker.

3   THE DEVIL'S GROTTO

1.   Rodriguez passed through what is now Presidio in the summer of 1581; Espejo arrived there on December 9, 1582. See [Herbert E.] Bolton, *Spanish Exploration in the Southwest* [N.Y., 1908], pp. 137 ff. and 163 ff.

2.   Ernest Gruening, "The Mexican Renaissance," *The Century Magazine* 107, [1924], 522–23.

4   THE PENITENT BROTHERS

1.   The order was unquestionably of Franciscan origin. In Spanish letters patent of as late date as 1793 we find it referred to as *La Cofradia del tercer orden de Franciscanos*—the Brotherhood of the Third Order of Franciscans.

2.   It is interesting to note that a tribal penance, vicariously done, has been a custom among the Pueblo Indians from time immemorial and is still observed. Twice every year, in each of the nineteen now inhabited pueblos, a penitential fast of four days is kept by allotted parties. In Isleta six men and six women are selected to expiate thus the sins of the whole pueblo; and in some pueblos the whole adult population fasts. Where a small number bear the sins of all, they are shut up in the *estufa* (sacred council chamber), with a *tinaja* of water before each, but they must not drink. Every morning a delegation comes to wash their feet. This fast continues four days. It is the only form of penance known to exist among them now, aside from what is imposed by the Church.

When the Spanish *conquistadores* first entered New Mexico they found traces of a similar custom of then great antiquity. All the tribes had their tribal professional penitents. The word *cacique,* so widely misused, means nothing else. The Tanos Indians, whose pueblos then occupied the country about Galisteo—Santa Fé's present site being also included in their territory—were called by a name based on the method of their penance. This name in the Queres tongue was *Poo-ya-tye,* from *poo-ya,* a thorn. They were the tribe whose *caciques* did penance by pricking themselves with thorns of the *palmilla,* the *maguey,* or cactus. Just how this pricking was done is not known. Whether it was by lying on beds of thorns and lashing prickly burdens to the body, as the Mexican *Penitentes* now do, or whether merely by jabbing the individual thorn through the cuticle, is still a mystery. Prof. Ad. F. Bandelier—now historian of the Hemenway Southwest Expedition and the only real savant in the Southwest except Mr. Frank Cushing—has thus far discovered nothing that will throw more explicit light on this subject. As a tribe the Tanos are now extinct, save at the Tegua pueblo of Moqui.

In old Mexico there is really nothing to be compared to the *Penitentes*. The reign of the *Phariseos* and the Holy Week representation of the Crucifixion and the Resurrection by lifelike automatons belong in a widely different category.

3. A political meeting was held in the *morada* at San Mateo, October 17, 1888, at the call of a very prominent young man of San Mateo, whose education in Washington cost his father thirty-six thousand dollars. The county campaign was very close, and finding that he was losing ground, the young man called upon the *Penitentes* to assist him. He was at that meeting initiated into the Order, and received its seal—six gashes with the flint knife over each kidney. In a speech there he referred to *ese Americano malvado* who had taken the photographs of the Good Friday services. The wife of this young politician, by the way, is a daughter of a prominent Washington official, recently deceased.

ALVAR NUÑEZ CABEZA DE VACA

1. The date of A.D. 1565, results from his dedication of comentarios to Don Carlos of Spain, in which Alvar Nuñez says: "Thirty-seven years have elapsed since that long and perilous expedition to Florida." Reckoning from the year when that expedition was destroyed (1528), this would bring his death to after 1565, and if we depart from 1536, date of his arrival in Sinaloa, it would even carry it beyond 1573.

2. For these and all other biographical details concerning Cabeza de Vaca, I refer in order to cut short an otherwise long biographical list, to the following works. *Voyages, Relations et Mémoires originaux pour servir á l'histoire de la déconverte de l'Amérique,* by H. Ternaux Compans (Paris, 1837). "Commentaires d'Alvar Nuñez de Vaca" (Preface pp. 1–4), in Enrique de Vedia, *Historiadores primitivos de Indias,* vol. I (1852), Preliminares pp. 18, 21.

3. This date is so frequently mentioned that it needs no special references.

4. The term of five years is established by Cabeza de Vaca "Naufragios," Chap. xvi (in Vedia, I, p. 529). "Fueron casi seis anos el tiempo gueyo estuve en esta tierra solo entre ellos y desnudo." Oviedo *Historia*

general *y* natural *de Indias* (edition of 1853, vol. III, lib. xxxv, chap. iv. p. 601). "Vino Cabesa de Vaca a se juntar con essotros, que avia cinco años que lo avian dexado atrás."

5. "Naufragios" (Vedia I, p. 529).
6. Oviedo, *Historia General, etc.* (III, p. 604). "è hicolo Dios tan bien, que lo que no pensaban andar aunque las vida les turara ocho años, la andovieron en diez meses."
7. This date is well settled—Cabeza de Vaca "Naufragios" (Vedia, I, chap. xxxiii, p. 546). "Y pasados quince dias que allí habiamos llegado" (p. 547). "En la villa de Sant Miguel estuvimos hast 15 dias del mes de Mayo." Antonio de Herrera, *Historia general de los Hechos de los castellanos en las Islas y la Tierra firme del mar Ociano* (edition of 1726, dec. VI, lib. I, chap. vii, p. 11 of vol. II), speaks of a certificate issued on the fifteenth of May (old style) and adds: "i haviendo estado alli quince dias."
8. Compare "Naufragios" (chap. xxi, xxii, etc.), Oviedo *Historia general, etc.* (III, p. 603 etc.).
9. In quoting the "Naufragios" I use the copy of it contained in vol. I of Vedia's *Historiadores primitivos de Indias.* I have collated it with the original and found it very reliable. The full title I omit as unnecessary.
10. Edition of 1852 (vol. III, lib. xxxv), or the entire thirty-fifth book (sixteenth of the second part) is devoted to Cabeza de Vaca, his friends, and their adventures.
11. Oviedo *Historia general* (III, p. 592, p. 600) not "Naufragios" mentions the river of "Espiritu Santo" at the latter's mouth. Under that name the Mississippi was known.
12. Oviedo *Historia general* (III, p. 603).
13. It is superfluous to quote here. The allusions are too numerous.
14. *Ut supra.*
15. Oviedo *Historia general* (p. 604) "Naufragios" (chap. xxvii, p. 539).
16. *Historia general* (p. 605). "Naufragios" (chap. xxviii, p. 539).
17. "Naufragios" (chap. xxviii, p. 539). Oviedo (p. 605). "E luego aquella noche enviaron á llamar gente abaxo hácia el mar, y el dia siguiente viniéron muchos hombus é mugeres à ver estos chripstianos è sus miraglos, è à traerlos cosas que les diceon, è aquestos trabaxocon mucho por los llevar hacia la mar."
18. "Naufragios" (chap. xxviii to xxx). Oviedo (pp. 605, 608).
19. "Naufragios" (p. 542). The name is properly given, not to the river, but to the Indians who lived on its shores, but he adds: "y porque aquel río arriba mas de cincuenta leguas, van matan o muchas de ellas."
20. *Ut supra.*
21. Oviedo (p. 609). "Naufragios" (chap. xxxi, p. 544).
22. Ibid.

23. Oviedo (p. 610). "Naufragios" (chap. xxxii).
24. Pedro de Castañeda de Nagera. *Relation du voyage de Cibola* (French translation by Ternaux Compans [Paris, 1838]) says that the "Valle de los Corazones" was below that of the Sonora river (p. 157). He also states that: "Quand l'on fut arrive à Batuco, des Indiens alliès de la vallèe des Coracones vinrent au devant de l'armèe pour voir le gènèral." Consequently it was near Batuco and south of it. Batuco itself belongs to the "Eudeves," a Pima dialect, but the Pimas proper reach as far south as Comuripa. Manuel Orozco y Berra, *Geografía de las lenguas y carta etnogràfica de Mèxico* [Mexico, 1864] (pp. 344 and 351). Compare also: P. Andres Perez de Ribas, *Historia de los Triumphos de nuestra Santa Fe entre Gentes las mas barbaras y fieras del nueuo Orbe; conseguidos por los soldados de la milicia de la compania de Jesus, etc.* (Madrid 1645. lib. vi, cap. 1. page 358). Comoripa, Tecoripa, Suaqui are ascribed to the "Nebomes bajos." "Nebome" is synonymous with Pima, therefore to the lower Pimas. Finally: Juan Jaramillo "Relation du voyage fait à la nouvelle terre sous les ordres da gènèral Francisco Vasquez Coronado etc." (in *Relation du voyage de Cibola,* appendix p. 366) describes the valley of Hearts, and indicates that it lay at least two days march of the Yaqui and north of it. Antonio de Mendoza ("Lettre à l'empereur Charles V," *Cibola,* appendix p. 289) says the "Corazones" are one hundred and twenty leagues (three hundred and twenty-five miles) north of Culiacan in Sonora. That distance would place it in the vicinity of Batuco with Indians from the Corazones. Cabeza de Vaca, "Naufragios" (pp. 546, 547) founded a colony in Sinaloa. Ribas *Hist. de los Triumphos de nuestra Santa Fee etc.* (lib. I, cap. vii, p. 25). The settlement was called Bamoa, on the Rio del Fuerte, "y es de lengua y nacion poblada mas de cien leguas mas la tierra adentro." Orozco y Berra *Geografia de las Lenguas* (p. 333). "La Concepcion Bamoa fuè fundada con los indios pimas, que vinieron acompanando en su peregrinacion à Cabeza de Vaca y à sus companeros."
25. Oviedo (p. 611).
26. "Naufragios" (chap. xxxiv, p. 545). Herrera *Historia general etc.* (dec. vi, lib. i, c. vii, p. 10). F. Antonio Tello, "Historia de la Nueva Galicia" (vol. II, *Documentos para la Historia de Mexico,* 1866, chap. xii, p. 358). Matias de la Mota Padilla, *Historia de la Nueva Galicia* (chap. xv, pp. 80–81).
27. Compare "Naufragios," (chap. xii to chap. xx); also Oviedo (lib. xxxv, chap. iii to v).
28. The description agrees with a small Piñon tree. Oviedo (chap. v, pp. 606 and 607). The tree was found in the Sierras. See also "Naufragios" (chap. xxix, p. 540), "hay por aquella tierra pinos chicos, y las pinas de ellas son como huevos pequenos."
29. Oviedo chap. vi, p. 609).

30. "Naufragios" (chap. xviii, p. 532). Oviedo (Interview de., p. 617).
31. Oviedo (chap. vi, pp. 608 and 609). "Naufragios" (chap. xxx and xxxi).
32. "Vacas Corcobadas"—Thus they are called by Francisco Lopez de Gomara. "Historia General de las Indias" (in Vedia, *Historiadores primitivos, etc.,* vol. I, p. 288).—The reports of Cabeza de Vaca were the earliest notices received in Europe of the buffalo, which were of a positive and well-defined nature.
33. Compare "Naufragios" (chap. xxvi).
34. "Naufragios," (chap. xxx, xxxi).
35. *Idem* (chap. xxx). The Indians knew maize, but they had not planted any for several years, owing to drouth. So they brought what they needed from the west. "Tambien nosotros quesimos saber de donde habien traido aquel maiz, y ellos nos dijeron que de donde el sol se ponia."
36. References to these facts are numerous in Cabeza de Vaca as well as in the joint report, so that quotations are superfluous.
37. See "Naufragios" (chap. xxx).
38. *Idem* (chap. xxix); Oviedo (p. 606). The rattle probably came from the northeast.
39. This is abundantly proven. I refer to the following papers contained in the *Coleccion de Documentos inéditos relativos al descubrimiento conquista y organizacion de las antiguas posesiones espanolas en América y Oceanía, sacados de los archivos del Reino, y musy especialmente del de Indias* [42 vols, Madrid, 1864–84].
    1. Pedro de Bustamante and Hernan Gallegos, "Testimonio" sixteenth of May, 1582 (vol. XV, pp. 83–89).
    2. "Relacion breve y verdadera del descubrimiento del nuevo Mexico," sixth of October, 1583 (vol. XV, pp. 146–47).
    3. Antonio de Espejo "Relacion del Viaje" (p. 109). "Expediente y Relacion, etc." (p. 172).
    4. Juan de Oñate, "Discurso de las Jornadas que hizo el campo de su magestad desde la nueva Espana á la Provincia de la nuevo México" (vol. XVI, p. 250)—and others.
40. "Naufragios" (chap. XXXI). Oviedo (pp. 609 and 610).
41. Orozco y Berra, *Geografia de Lenguas* (p. 345).
42. Compare Ribas, *Historia de los Triumphos etc.* (lib. VI, chap. vii, p. 369–72; chap. xviii, p. 391; chap. ii, p. 360; part II, lib. VIII, chap. ii, p. 471.) P. Francisco Xavier Alegre, *Historia de la Compania de Jesus en Nueva España* (edited by Bustamante in 1841, vol. I, lib. III, pp. 231–35).
43. Oviedo (p. 609).
44. "Naufragios," (chap. xxxi, p. 543).
45. Compare my report in the "Fifth Annual Report of the Archaeological Institute of America," pp. 80–81.

6   FRAY JUAN DE PADILLA, THE FIRST CATHOLIC MISSIONARY AND MARTYR IN EASTERN KANSAS. 1542.

1. Fray Gerónimo Mendieta, *Historia Ecclesiástica Indiana*, p. 742, says there were five "Los Religiosos eran cinco." This is true, but only four reached New Mexico. The fifth, Fray Antonio Victoria, broke his thigh at three days' march from Culiacán, which he had left with Coronado. See Pedro de Castañeda, *Relation du Voyage de Cibola*, p. 39.

2. Compare our "The Discovery of New Mexico, by Fray Marcos, of Nizza," in the *Magazine of Western History*. Also, "La dé Couverte du Nouveau Méxique par le Frére Marcos de Nice," in the *Revue d'Ethnographie*. For the death of Father Marcos, etc., the sources of information are numerous. Mendieta, who knew him personally, says of him, *Historia Ecclesiástica,* p. 541, "y de los grandes fríos que pasó, lo hallé yo cuando vine de España, morador en Jalapa, gafo ó tollido de pies y manos."

3. It is again Mendieta who conveys this information. *Historia*, p. 378, "Otro Francés hubo de Aquitania, llamado Fr. Juan de la Cruz, gran siervo de Dios y buen obrero de su viña"; p. 745, "Era religioso muy observante y de aprobada vido, y por ello muy respetado de todos; tanto que el capitán Francisco Vázquez Coronado tenía mendado á sus soldados se destocasen cuando oyesen el nombre de Fr. Juan de la Cruz." Torquemada, *Monarchia Indiana*, edition of 1723, copies Mendieta.

4. He is not mentioned by Castañeda, neither by Jaramillo, but Mendieta is very positive, p. 745: "Del siervo de Dios no se supo otra cosa mas de que quedó solo en aquel Pueblo de Tiguex (como queda dicho) para enseñar á los indios las cosas de nuestra fé y vida cristiana, de que ellos holgaron mucho, y en señal de regocijo lo tomaron en brazos y hicieron otras demostraciones de contento. Entiéndese moriría martir." Matías de la Mota-Padilla, *Historia de la Nueva Galicia,* 1742, p. 112, mentions him. On page 167 he says: "Dejando, como prelado, lleno de bendiciones, á Fr. Juan de la Cruz"; p. 168: "Del padre Fr. Juan de la Cruz la noticia que se tiene es: Que después de haber trabajado en la instrucción de los indios en Tigues y en Coquite murió flechado de indios, por que no todos abrasaron su doctrina y conbejos, con los que trataba detestasen sus bárbaras costumbres, aunque por lo general era muy estimado de los caciques y demás naturales. Que habían visto la veneración con qué el general, Capitanes y soldados le trataban." See also Vetancurt, *Menología Franciscano*.

5. Fray Luis is called Descalona by Castañeda, *Cibola,* and also by Jaramillo, "Relation." Mota-Padilla calls him Fray Luis de Ubeda.

As there is a place called Ubeda in Spain, we infer that, as was frequently the case, the name of his place of origin was substituted. Of his disappearance at Pecos, all sources at our command treat.

6. This was plainly shown by the action of the Pueblos after they had driven out the Spaniards from New Mexico in 1680. Three years later there was hardly a cow left, in the territory.—"Declaración de un Indio Pecuri Que Dijo Llamarse Juan." MSS., 1683.

7. It is positive among the Zuñi, less so at Pecos, Jemez and Isleta.

8. Mendieta, *Historia Ecclesiástica,* p. 742; Torquemada, *Monarchia,* vol. iii, p. 606 to 611; Vetancurt, *Menología,* edition of 1871, p. 386.

9. Mendieta, p. 742.

10. *Tusayan* is a corruption of *Usaya,* a name given formerly by the Zuñis to some of the principal Moqui Pueblos. *Usayan* is the possessive. Refrain from quoting on the deeds of Coronado, they being too well known.

11. Castañeda, *Cibola,* p. 60.

12. In the third volume of the *Documentos de Indias,* there is a report remitted jointly by Alvarado and Fray Padilla on the expedition to Pecos. It is incorrectly indexed. "Relación del Viaje que Hernando de Soto y Fray Juan de Padilla Hicieron en Demanda de la mar del sur." It should be Alvarado. The document is very important, although Muñoz states he placed no faith in it. Muñoz had not been in New Mexico himself.

13. Castañeda, *Cibola,* p. 72.

14. Coronado. *Lettre A. L'Empereur Charles V.,* Tiguex, October 20–30 of 1541, p. 361.

15. Idem, p. 355.

16. It is superfluous to quote, since the events are too well known.

17. We hold that the crossing was effected south (or east) of the junction of the Canadian with the Rio de Mora. The Pecos river flows at a distance of three miles from the old Pueblo, and they had to cross it at all events.

18. For the facts we refer in general to the numerous original sources. That the Querechos were the Apaches of the plains or Vaqueros, who afterwards became known under the different names of Carlanes, Natajees, Lipanes, Cuartelejos, etc., is established by Espejo, "Relacion Del Viaje." See our *Report on Studies Among the Indians of the Southwest,* 1890.

19. The change in direction of the route is mentioned by various writers. Going first northeast from the Canadian below its junction with the Mora, carried the Spaniards into Colfax County, New Mexico, thence east with inclination to the southeast, to the north fork of the Canadian. Crossing it, they naturally travelled to the banks of the main river near the central portion of the Indian Territory.

20. The Teyas were found too far to the east to be the Jumanos. Still

there is a possibility at the present day that the Jumanos (reduced to a mere fraction) live in northeastern Texas and the Indian Territory. They are mostly confounded with the Comanches. That the Jumanos lived on the eastern plains is abundantly proven.

21. For the short marches we refer to Jaramillo, "Relation." That the Arkansas must have been the stream in question is manifest. There is no great river between the Canadian and the Arkansas. The latter makes a sharp turn to the northeast east of Fort George at Great Bend, and continues to flow in that direction for quite a distance.

22. Coronado, *Lettre à l'Empereur,* p. 353.

23. Idem, p. 360.

24. "Relation," p. 378.

25. *Cibola,* p. 194.

26. Ibid.

27. *Lettre,* p. 354, *et seq.*

28. "Relation," p. 379. He also says, p. 376, that the village of Quivira was built by the side of small but pretty brooks, all of which flowed into the great river Arkansas. "Il y avait, autant que je me le Rappelle, six ou sept villages séparés les uns des autres; nous times route pendant, quatre ou cinq jours sans les quitter, l'intervalle compris entre l'un et l'autre ruisseau n'est pas habite." The last one of these villages was called Quivira.

29. *Lettre,* p. 360.

30. *Journal Historique de l'Etablissment des Francais à la Louisiane,* p. 200, 212.

31. This we infer from the statements of Juan de Oñate about his expedition to Quivira in 1599; from Geronimo de Zarate Salmeron: "Relacioner of 1626," MSS.; from Fray Alonzo de Posadas, "Informe al Rey Sobre las Tierras de Nuevo México, Quivira y Teguayo," MSS., and Torquemada, *Monarchia Indiana,* vol. I., p. 673, *et seq.*

32. Posadas, "Informe"; Francisco Gomez, "Carta al Virrey," 1638, MSS.; Juan Domingo de Mendoza, "Diario de la Formada a Los Jumanos," 1684, MSS.

33. Zarate Salmeron, "Relaciones de Todas las Cosas."

34. Hennepin, *Description of Louisiana;* published by Mr. Shea. On the map there is in latitude 50 north, Thinthonha ou gens des Praires. Compare also p. 200.

35. "Informe al Rey."

36. "Relación Postrera de Sivola y de Quatrocientas Leguas Adelante," MSS., contained in the Libro de Oro y Thesoro Indico. A still unpublished manuscript of Motolinia, in possession of Don Joaquin Garcia y Cazbalceta at Mexico.

37. It appears that Andres Docampo alone went on horseback. The others, including the father, were on foot. These details are given by Jaramillo, Castañeda, Mota Padilla, and later authors also.

38. Coronado, *Lettre.*
39. Idem. He says that he brought Indians from Quivira with him. It is therefore likely that they returned with the friar and the Portuguese.
40. Coronado, idem.
41. All the main sources seem to agree on that point.
42. *Cibola,* p. 194.
43. "Relation," p. 381.
44. *Historia de la Nueva Galicia,* p. 167.
45. *Menologia,* p. 386. Artur von Muenster, in his *Auctarium Marty-rologii Franciscani,* 1650, p. 637, gives no year. He calls the Indians at whose hands the monk perished, "Herzinalen:" "est er endlich von et lichen wilden Leuthen (welche man Herzinalen nennet) mit Pfeilen dur chochossen worden." [Direct quote as in original.]
46. Both of these "Donados" were from Mechuacan. The name of Andrés, the soldier, is mostly written Del Campo, but since he was a Portuguese, it must have been Do Campo. That they returned previous to 1552 is proven by the fact that Gómara mentions it in his *Crónica,* which was completed in that year.
47. Neither Jaramillo nor Castañeda mention the dog. Compare Gómara, *Crónica,* and Herrera, *Historia General.* The latter is usually very reliable, as far as careful compilation goes.
48. Mendieta, *Historia Ecclesiastica;* Vetancurt, *Menologid,* and others.
49. "Histoire de la Colonisation et des Missions du Sonora, Nouveau Mexique, Chihuahua et Arizona, Jusquà l'an 1700" (MSS. at the Vatican). We refer here particularly to the expedition of Pedro de Villazur to the banks of the Platte River, where nearly the whole of the Spaniards perished, at the hands of the Pawnees and French, on the 17th of August, 1720. A monograph on that expedition will shortly appear in the papers of the Archaeological Institute of America. The notorious Jean L'Archévèque, the betrayer of Lasalle, perished in that massacre.

7   THE FEATHER SYMBOL IN ANCIENT HOPI DESIGN

1. For a discussion of the antiquity of Sikyatki, see "Prehistoric Culture of Tusayan," *American Anthropologist,* 1896, and *Report of the Secretary of the Smithsonian Institution,* 1895.
2. J. Walter Fewkes, "A preliminary account of an expedition to the Cliff villages of the Red Rock Country," 1895 *Annual Report of the Board of Regents of the Smithsonian Institution* (1896), pp. 577–88.
3. The reason for this relatively large number of avian over other zoomorphic deities in the Hopi system is not apparent.

4. Compare the combination of *three* feathers in Aztec and Maya symbolism.

5. This figure shows the head below, with the eye well drawn. The continuation to the left is the neck, that to the right a beginning of an elaborate snout [*sic*].

6. A number of these gourds are figured in my accounts of Tusayan ceremony. A vase with attached feathers, called *patne,* is represented on page 43, ["Snake Ceremonies at Walpi,"] *Journ. Amer. Eth. and Arch.* 4 [1894].

7. [J. Walter Fewkes, "A Few Summer Ceremonials at the Tusayan Pueblos,"] *Journ. Amer. Eth. and Arch.,* 2 [1892]: 86, 107; *American Anthropologist* [o.s. 10] (1897): 133, 134.

8. It will be seen on consultation of my article on "Dolls of the Tusayan Indians" that there are several in which the crests of feathers on the heads are represented by sticks with symbolic markings. In some instances we have real feathers instead of symbols. An example of this kind is figured on page 136, ["Morphology of Tusayan Altars,"] *American Anthropologist* [o.s. 10] (1897).

9. [J. Walter Fewkes, "Tusayan Snake Ceremonies," *Sixteenth Annual Report of the Bureau of American Ethnology,* 1897, plate 72.]

10. *Journ. Amer. Eth. and Arch.* 2 [1892]: 120.

11. See male and female lightning snakes on Walpi Antelope altar.

12. The three arrowpoints, figure 4, represent the flint arrowpoints which the mythic bird is reputed to have worn in its feathers.

13. [J. Walter Fewkes, "Tusayan Katcinas,"] *Fifteenth Annual Report of the Bureau of American Ethnology,* 1897, pp. 251–313.

14. "Tusayan Katcinas," *Fifteenth Annual Report of the Bureau of American Ethnology.* A figure of the symbolic sun disk from which the feathers have been removed is given on plate 104 of that memoir.

15. The bundle here figured represents eight feathers.

16. The symbol of the feather was painted on the vase in ancient times, whereas in modern vessels stringed feathers are tied in the same positions. Probably the latter custom was also common in ancient times.

17. It is believed that the religious sentiment permeated and dominated all ancient Hopi art as well as sociology, and that a study of the symbolism of the decorations on ancient pottery is practically a study of religion.

8 VENTILATORS IN CEREMONIAL ROOMS OF PREHISTORIC CLIFF DWELLINGS

1. It is instructive to note that the Hopi word *kiva* has the same elements in composition as *va^aki,* the Pima designation of a ceremonial building

like Casa Grande. In both, ki means "house"; the significance of *va* is not apparent.

2. The excavation and repair work at Spruce-tree House was done under direction of the Secretary of the Interior.

3. Mr. S. G. Morley writes me that he has found similar kivas in the Cannonball ruin on the McElmo, not far from Holly's ranch. The recurrence of kivas of the same kind in rimrock ruins and cliff houses shows a homogeneity in the culture of the inhabitants.

4. Strangely enough, in each of three of the Spruce-tree House kivas a human skull and some other bones were found in the passage.

5. These passages were probably used by the chief priest, and not by others who entered the kiva. The regular entrance was through the roof.

6. Ceremonial offerings, if any, are found on the top of these buttresses at the end of these pegs.

7. This is the first recognition in print of a *sipapû* in a circular kiva.

8. [G. E. A. Nordenskiöld], *Cliff Dwellers of the Mesa Verde,* [Stockholm], 1893.

9. [Cosmos Mindeleff, "Navaho Houses,"] *Seventeenth Annual Report of the Bureau of American Ethnology,* pt. 2 [1898], pp. 469–517.

10. The recess under which the ventilator passes is generally deeper and broader than the other.

11. No Mesa Verde kiva has yet been found with hatchway or ladder in place, but there is every probability that the entrance was in the roof. It is, however, extraordinary that no signs of the stumps of ladders or holes for the same were found in any of the eight kivas of Spruce-tree House.

12. Nordenskiöld's schematic drawing of the roof of a kiva in Square-tower House does not tally with the author's observations. The roof logs in reality are arranged in threes, and not one above another as Nordenskiöld represents.

13. In the restoration of the roof of one of the Spruce-tree House kivas the author was aided by Mr. A. V. Kidder, who has given much attention to the structure of cliff dwellings and whose great help made this work possible.

14. For convenience in reference the rooms of Spruce-tree House are numbered and the kivas lettered, the figures and letters being painted in black on the walls themselves.

15. The shaft partially excavated several years ago by Mr. W. K. Moorehead at Aztec, New Mexico, may later be found to be the ventilator of some adjacent room. See *American Anthropologist,* n.s. 10 (April–June 1908).

16. [Mindeleff], p. 186, fig. 82.

17. These will probably be found through excavation by experienced archeologists in this interesting locality.

18. Kiva B of Spruce-tree House is the closest approximation of all to the Cañon de Chelly kivas.
19. Although, as Mindeleff points out, an inspection of Nordenskiöld's ground plan shows more kivas without this feature than with it, the statement in the text of the above quotation is correct, the ground plans being faulty in this particular.
20. As is known to students of the Mesa Verde ruins, there are several circular rooms that are not kivas.
21. *Tenth Ann. Rep. U.S. Geol. and Geog. Survey* (Washington, 1878), p. 395.
22. The Tobin system introduces fresh air above the level of entrance.
23. [J. Walter Fewkes, "Two Summer's Work in Pueblo Ruins,"] *Twenty-Second Annual Report of the Bureau of American Ethnology,* pt. 1 [1904], p. 49.

9 ABORIGINAL TURQUOISE MINING IN ARIZONA AND NEW MEXICO

1. William P. Blake, "New Locality of the Green Turquoise, Known as Chalchihuite," *American Journal of Science,* II.
2. "The Chalchihuitl of the Ancient Mexicans; Its Locality and Association, and Its Association and Its Identity with Turquoise," *American Journal of Science* 25, (March 1858) p. 227.
3. For the full account of this expedition, and others, reference may be made to the translation of Casteñada's narrative, *Report of the Bûreau of Ethnology* 14 (1896), pt. I, p. 474.
4. [George F. Kunz,] *Precious Stones of North America,* [New York, 1890; 2nd ed., 1892], p. 61.
5. Ibid., 61. This treatise may be consulted for further details and many valuable references to the literature of turquoise, and of the various inlaid, or encrusted, masks in foreign museums.
6. E. G. Squier, "Observations on a Collection of Chalchihuitls from Mexico and Central America," in *Annals of the Lyceum of Natural History of New York* (New York, 1869), p. 22.
7. [James Dwight Dana, "The system of mineralogy of James Dwight Dana, 1837–1868," *Descriptive Mineralogy,* 6th ed., by Edward Salisbury Dana (New York, 1892), p. 371.]
8. Raphael Pumpelly, "Geological Researches in China, Mongolia and Japan." *Smithsonian Contribution* (1866), p. 118.

10 ABORIGINAL TRADE ROUTES FOR SEA SHELLS IN THE SOUTHWEST

1. This portion of the study was carried on through library work, correspondence, and travel—by the writer sporadically from 1930 to the

present and by one of his graduate students, Mr. John M. Goggin, who rendered invaluable aid during 1937 and 1938.

2.   Some of the better reports, in chronological order, are: J. Walter Fewkes, "Pacific Coast Shells from Prehistoric Tusayan Pueblos," *American Anthropologist* o.s. 9 (1896). E. H. Morris, "The Aztec Ruin," American Museum of Natural History *Anthropological Papers* 26 (1919): 1. W. Bradfield, *Cameron Creek Village* (Santa Fe, 1931). A. V. Kidder, "The Artifacts of Pecos," *Papers of the Phillips Academy Southwestern Expedition,* no. 6 (1932). L. R. Caywood and E. H. Spicer, *Tuzigoot* (Berkeley, 1935). Brand, Hawley, Hibben, et al., "Tseh So, A Small House Ruin, Chaco Canyon, New Mexico," *University of New Mexico Bulletin* no. 308, Anthropological Series 2, no. 2 (1937). Gladwin, Haury, Sayles, Gladwin, "Excavations at Snaketown: Material Culture," *Medallion Papers* no. 25 (1937).

3.   Dr. Stillman S. Berry, U.S. Bur. of Fisheries, Redlands, California; Dr. H. J. Boekelman, Curator of Ethnoconchology, Louisiana State Museum, New Orleans; Mr. William J. Clench, Harvard Museum of Comparative Zoology, Cambridge, Mass.; Dr. Howard Hill, Los Angeles Museum, California; Dr. Roy W. Miner, Curator of Living Invertebrates, American Museum of Natural History, New York; Mrs. Kate Stevens, former Curator of Molluscs, San Diego Museum of Natural History, California, have made most of the published identifications during the past twenty years.

4.   The author here desires to acknowledge his great obligation to Dr. Paul Bartsch (United States National Museum), Dr. Leo G. Hertlein (California Academy of Sciences), Miss Viola Bristol (Museum of Natural History, San Diego), Dr. Willard Van Name (American Museum of Natural History), Dr. Bruce Clark (University of California), Dr. Howard Hill (Los Angeles Museum), and Mrs. Kate Stevens (San Diego, California), all of whom aided in unraveling the tangled skein of synonymy. For lack of space no discussion is here given concerning various changes made in the genus and species names of some shells identified in archaeologic literature. Useful manuals were: William H. Dall, "Summary of the Marine Shellbearing Mollusks of the Northwest Coast of America, from San Diego, California, to the Polar Sea," *U.S. Nat. Mus. Bulletin* 112 (1921). U.S. Grant IV and H. R. Gale, "Catalogue of the Marine Pliocene and Pleistocene Mollusca of California and Adjacent Regions," *San Diego Society of Natural History Memoirs* 1 (1931). Josiah Keep, *West Coast Shells,* rev. by J. L. Baily, Jr. (Stanford University, 1935). Mrs. Ida S. Oldroyd, "The Marine Shells of the West Coast of North America," *Stanford Univ. Pub., Univ. Series, Geol. Sciences* 1, no. 1; 2, pts. 1, 2, 3 (1924–27). Mrs. Julia E. Rogers, *The Shell Book,*

rev. ed. (New York, 1931). Walter F. Webb, *Handbook for Shell Collectors* (Rochester, N.Y.: 1936).

5. Sea shells have been used by various peoples for such purposes as food (cockle, scallop, oyster, mussel, clam, whelk, conch, etc.), dye (*Purpura, Murex, Fasciolaria*), pearly ornament (*Meleagrina, Turbo,* etc.), textile (*Pinna*), currency-ornament, (cowry, spiny oyster, *Venus, Mytilus, Dentalium, Haliotis, Buccinum, Pyrula, Olivella,* etc.), trumpets (*Strombus, Melongena, Murex,* etc.), dishes (*Haliotis, Tivela,* etc.), tools (pieces of shell worked into needles, awls, etc.).

6. See R. E. C. Stearns, "Ethno-Conchology: A Study of Primitive Money," *U.S. Nat. Mus. Annual Report,* 1887, pp. 297–334; and other articles by Stearns in *The American Naturalist* for 1869 and 1877, and *Proceedings of the California Academy of Sciences* 5 (1873).

11 PREHISTORIC CULTURES OF THE SAN JUAN DRAINAGE

1. [Byron Cummings,] *Ancient Inhabitants of San Juan Valley* [Salt Lake City, 1910], p. 10.
2. Ibid, p. 18.
3. Betatakin, Bat-woman House. [Byron] Cummings in *American Anthropologist,* n.s. 17 (1915): 277.

12 AN ANALYSIS OF SOUTHWESTERN SOCIETY

1. Strong's paper was originally a dissertation offered in partial fulfillment for the degree of Doctor of Philosophy, University of California, May 1926.
2. A. L. Kroeber, "Types of Indian Culture in California," *Univ. Cal. Publs. Amer. Archaeol. and Ethnol.* 2 (1904): 81–103.
3. H. K. Haeberlin, "The Idea of Fertilization in the Culture of the Pueblo Indians," *Mems. Amer. Anthrop. Assoc.* 3 (1916): 14.
4. E. W. Gifford, "Clans and Moieties in Southern California," *Univ. Cal. Publs. Amer. Archaeol. and Ethnol.* 14 (1918): 218.
5. E. W. Gifford, "Miwok Lineages and the Political Unit in Aboriginal California," *American Anthropologist,* n.s. 28 (1926): 389–401.
6. W. H. Rivers, *Social Organization* (New York, 1924), p. 16.
7. A. A. Goldenweiser, "The Social Organization of the Indians of North America," *Journal of American Folk-Lore* 27 (1914): 434.
8. Rivers, 1924, p. 32.
9. Gifford, 1926.

10. S. Powers, "Tribes of California," *Contribs. N. Amer. Ethnol.* (Washington, D.C., 1877) 3: 370.

11. A. L. Kroeber, *Handbook of the Indians of California, Bur. Amer. Ethnol. Bulletin* 78 (1925): 496.

12. R. H. Lowie, "Notes on Shoshonean Ethnography," *Anthrop. Paps., Amer. Mus. Nat. Hist.* 20 (1924): 187–314.

13. Kroeber, 1925, p. 496.

14. L. Spier, "Southern Diegueño Customs," *Univ. Cal. Publs. Amer. Archaeol. and Ethnol.* 20 (1923): 298.

15. F. Russell, "The Pima Indians," *26th Ann. Rep. Bur. Amer. Ethnol.,* 1904, p. 195.

16. Ibid., p. 201.

17. Ibid., p. 196.

18. J. G. Bourke, "Notes Upon the Gentile Organization of the Apaches of Arizona," *Journal of American Folk-Lore* 3 (1890): 119. A. M. Stephen, "The Navajo," *American Anthropologist,* o.s. 6 (1893): 349.

19. P. E. Goddard, *Indians of the Southwest,* 2nd ed., Amer. Mus. Nat. Hist., Handbook Series, no. 2 (1921), p. 169.

20. Ibid.

21. The Franciscan Fathers, *An Ethnologic Dictionary of the Navaho Language* (St. Michaels, Ariz., 1910), p. 422.

22. Goddard, 1921, p. 99.

23. C. Wissler, *The American Indian* (New York, 1917), p. 208.

24. Kroeber, 1925, p. 45.

25. E. W. Gifford, "Dichotomous Social Organization in South Central California," *Univ. Cal. Publs. Amer. Archaeol. and Ethnol.* 11 (1916a): 142–46.

26. Kroeber, 1925, pp. 493, 494.

27. E. W. Gifford, "Miwok Moieties," *Univ. Cal. Publs. Amer. Archaeol. and Ethnol.* 11 (1916b): 294.

28. Gifford, 1916a, pp. 293–94.

29. Kroeber, 1925, pp. 550–51.

30. J. Alden Mason, "The Ethnology of the Salinan Indians," *Univ. Cal. Publs. Amer. Archaeol. and Ethnol.* 10 (1912): 189.

31. The coyote or wildcat skin representing Chinigchinich, mentioned by G. Boscana in Alfred Robinson, *Life in California,* 1st ed. (New York, 1846), p. 549, may bear this out.

32. Gifford, 1918, p. 211.

33. C. G. Du Bois, "The Religion of the Luiseño Indians of Southern California," *Univ. of Cal. Publs. Amer. Archaeol. and Ethnol.* 8 (1908): 148. Also Kroeber, 1925, p. 676.

34. The theory may be based on the fact that in Arizona and lower California a red and black phase of *Coluber flagellum piceus* occurs. It is unknown for California north of Mexico. There is no sex distinc-

tion in color. J. Van Denburgh, *Reptiles of Western North America* (San Francisco, 1922), p. 669.

35. Gifford, 1918, pp. 215–16.
36. Lowie, 1924, p. 283.
37. Russell, 1904, p. 197.
38. E. S. Curtis, *The North American Indian* (Cambridge, Mass., 1908), p. 9.
39. Russell, 1904, p. 197.
40. Curtis, 1908, p. 32.
41. See Gifford, 1918, p. 176.
42. C. Lumholtz, *New Trails in Mexico* (New York, 1912), p. 354.
43. Goddard, 1921, p. 132.
44. Russell, 1904, p. 197.
45. Lumholtz, 1912, p. 354.
46. Wissler, 1917, p. 159.
47. Lumholtz, 1912, p. 354.
48. Wissler, 1917, p. 159.
49. Goddard, 1921, p. 166.
50. Bourke, 1890, p. 118.
51. Goddard, 1921, p. 167.
52. Reichard, Letter of Jan. 27, 1926.
53. W. Mathews, "The Gentile System of the Navajo Indians," *Journal of American Folk-Lore* 3 (1890): 104.
54. Stephen, 1893, p. 349.
55. H. R. Voth, "The Oraibi Powamu Ceremony," *Publs. Field Col. Mus., Anthrop. Series* 3 (1901): 152n4.
56. E. C. Parsons, "Tewa Kin, Clan, and Moiety," *American Anthropologist,* n.s. 26 (1924): 336.
57. M. C. Stevenson, "The Zuñi Indians," *23rd Ann. Rep. Bur. Amer. Ethnol.,* 1904, p. 40.
58. F. H. Cushing, "Outlines of Zuñi Myths," *13th Ann. Rep. Bur. Amer. Ethnol,* 1896, p. 384.
59. A. L. Kroeber, "Zuñi Kin and Clan," *Anthrop. Paps., Amer. Mus. Nat. Hist.* 18 (1917): 94.
60. M. C. Stevenson, 1904, p. 172.
61. E. C. Parsons, "Laguna Genealogies," *Anthrop. Paps., Amer. Mus. Nat. Hist.* 19 (1923): 229.
62. See F. W. Hodge, *Handbook of American Indians,* vols. 1 and 2 *Bur. Amer. Ethnol. Bull.* 30 (1910): 652.
63. J. W. Fewkes, "Tusayan Migration Traditions," *19th Ann. Rep. Bur. Amer. Ethnol.,* 1900, p. 582.
64. See R. F. Benedict, "Review of E. S. Curtis: The Hopi," *American Anthropologist,* n.s. 27 (1925): 459.
65. Parsons, 1923, pp. 211, 232.
66. Parsons, 1923, pp. 135–45.

67. Parsons, 1923, p. 229.
68. Ibid., pp. 231–53.
69. Parsons, 1924, pp. 337–38.
70. M. C. Stevenson, "The Sia," *11th Ann. Rep. Bur. Amer. Ethnol.,* 1889, p. 112.
71. F. Starr, "Census of Cochiti," *Proc. Davenport Acad. Sci.* 7 (1899): 33–45.
72. Kroeber, 1917, p. 97.
73. Parsons, 1924, pp. 337–38.
74. Ibid.
75. E. C. Parsons, "Further Notes on Isleta," *American Anthropologist,* n.s. 23 (1921): 156*n*3.
76. Parsons, 1924, p. 336.
77. Ibid., pp. 337–38.
78. Parsons, 1921, p. 156*n*3.
79. Parsons, 1924, p. 336.
80. E. C. Parsons, "Notes on Isleta, Santa Ana and Acoma," *American Anthropologist* n.s. 22 (1920b): 60.
81. J. Mooney, "Calendar History of the Kiowa Indians," *17th Ann. Rep. Bur. Amer. Ethnol.,* 1898, p. 227.
82. J. R. Murie, "Pawnee Indian Societies," *Amer. Mus. Nat. Hist. Anthrop. Paps.* 11 (1914): 642.
83. P. Radin, "The Social Organization of the Winnebago Indians. An Interpretation." *Canada Geol. Sur. Mus. Bull.* no. 10. Anthrop. Series, no. 5 (1915): 1–8.
84. Gifford, 1926.
85. Ibid.
86. Kroeber, 1925, p. 494, translates this as "dog."
87. Gayton, 1926, field notes.
88. Mason, 1912, p. 189.
89. Kroeber, 1925, p. 547.
90. Ibid., pp. 552–56.
91. Boscana, 1846, pp. 264–67.
92. H. Reid, "The Indians of Los Angeles County," Letters to the Los Angeles *Star,* 1852, letters 1 and 3.
93. Gifford, 1916a, p. 208.
94. Ibid., p. 213.
95. Ibid., p. 202.
96. Gifford, 1916a, p. 213.
97. E. W. Gifford, "California Kinship Terminologies," *Univ. Cal. Publs. Amer. Archaeol. and Ethnol.* 18 (1922): 56.
98. Gifford, 1916a, p. 202.
99. Detailed study of the more westerly of these peoples clearly shows the strong centralizing influence of the Mission Fathers and Mexican government who, desiring responsible native officials, exalted and gave

power to certain prominent clan heads at the expense of the others. An almost tribal organization resulted.

100. Lowie, 1924, p. 283. Also applicable to the northern Shoshone. Lowie, "The Northern Shoshone," *Anthrop. Paps. Amer. Mus. Nat. Hist.* 2 (1909): 206.

101. Spier, 1923, p. 299.

102. Gifford, 1926.

103. T. T. Waterman, "The Religious Practices of the Diegueño Indians," *Publs. Amer. Archaeol. and Ethnol.* 8 (1910): 281.

104. Gifford, 1926.

105. Kroeber, 1925, pp. 741–44.

106. Ibid.

107. Ibid.

108. Kroeber, 1925, p. 794.

109. Ibid., p. 795.

110. Spier, 1926 MSS.

111. Neither the chief's house nor the small sweat-lodge among the Havasupai is used for ceremonial purposes.

112. Russell, 1904, p. 197; Curtis, 1908, p. 32.

113. Curtis, 1908, p. 9; Lumholtz, 1912, p. 354.

114. Russell, 1904, p. 197; Curtis, 1908, p. 32.

115. Curtis, 1908, p. 9; Lumholtz, 1912, p. 354.

116. Gifford, 1916a, p. 176.

117. Lumholtz, 1912, pp. 49–52.

118. Goddard, 1921, p. 166.

119. Ibid.

120. Bourke, 1890, p. 111.

121. Ibid.

122. Goddard, 1921, p. 166.

123. Mathews, 1890, p. 104; Stephen, 1893, p. 349.

124. Reichard, Letter of Jan. 27, 1926.

125. Ibid.

126. Mathews, 1890, p. 106; Franciscan Fathers, 1910, p. 424.

127. Reichard, Letter of Jan. 27, 1926.

128. E. C. Parsons, "Notes on Ceremonialism at Laguna," *Amer. Mus. Nat. Hist. Anthrop. Paps.* 19 (1920): 88n1.

129. V. Mindeleff, "A Study of Pueblo Architecture in Tusayan and Cibola," *8th Ann. Rep. Bur. Amer. Ethnol,* 1891; F. W. Hodge, "Pueblo Indian Clans," *American Anthropologist,* o.s. 9 (1896): 345–52; Fewkes, 1900, etc.

130. Kroeber, 1917.

131. E. C. Parsons, "Contributions to Hopi History," *American Anthropologist,* n.s. 24 (1922): 253–98; Lowie, field notes, 1916.

132. C. Mindeleff, "Localization of Tusayan Clans," *19th Ann. Rep. Bur. Amer. Ethnol.,* 1900, pp. 105–8.

133. Kroeber, 1917, p. 103.
134. Fewkes, 1900, pp. 622–31.
135. Kroeber, 1917, p. 152; also Parsons, 1919, p. 329.
136. Lowie, field notes, 1916.
137. Goldenweiser, 1914, p. 434.
138. Gifford, 1926.
139. Lowie, field notes, 1916.
140. Parsons, 1922, p. 284.
141. Ibid.
142. Kroeber, 1917, pp. 135–45.
143. Lowie, field notes, 1916.
144. H. R. Voth, "Hopi Proper Names," *Publs. Field Col. Mus., Anthrop. Series* 6 (1905b): 68–73.
145. See Benedict, 1925, p. 460.
146. Lowie, field notes, 1916.
147. R. H. Lowie, *Primitive Society* (New York, 1920), p. 117.
148. Kroeber, 1917, pp. 91–134.
149. Parsons, 1923, pp. 226–28.
150. F. H. Cushing, "The Zuñi Social, Mythic and Religious Systems," *Popular Science Monthly* 21 (1882): 187.
151. Parsons, 1923, p. 225.
152. Kroeber, 1917, p. 166.
153. Voth, 1901, p. 82.
154. E. C. Parsons, "Notes on Zuñi," *Mems. Amer. Anthrop. Assoc.* 4 (1917): 259.
155. Parsons, 1923, p. 213.
156. Kroeber, 1917, p. 48.
157. Ibid., p. 48 [?].
158. F. H. Cushing, "Zuñi Fetishes," *2nd Ann. Rep. Bur. Amer. Ethnol.,* 1880, pp. 19, 31.
159. Parsons, 1920b, p. 58 n. 2.
160. Ibid., pp. 67–68.
161. Parsons, 1923, pp. 175–76.
162. Ibid., p. 207.
163. Ibid., pp. 212–14.
164. Ibid., 219.
165. Ibid., p. 180.
166. Parsons, 1918, p. 175.
167. Parsons, 1923, p. 142.
168. This paper.
169. M. C. Stevenson, 1889, p. 19.
170. Parsons, "Notes on Isleta," 1920, p. 64.
171. Parsons, 1923, p. 81.
172. N. Dumarest, "Notes on Cochiti, New Mexico," *Mems. Amer. Anthrop. Assoc.* 6 (1919): 148.

173. Parsons, 1924, p. 334.
174. J. P. Harrington, "Tewa Relationship Terms," *American Anthropologist,* n.s. 14 (1912): 475.
175. B. Friere-Marreco, "Tewa Kinship Terms from the Pueblo of Hano, Arizona," *American Anthropologist,* n.s. 16 (1914): 270.
176. Ibid.
177. Parsons, 1924, p. 334.
178. Ibid., pp. 337–38.
179. Parsons, "Notes on Isleta," 1920, pp. 56–57.
180. Ibid., pp. 60–61.
181. Parsons, 1923, p. 334.
182. See Hodge, 1896, pp. 350–52.
183. Parsons, 1923, p. 228.
184. Kroeber, 1925, pp. 556–57.
185. Boscana, pp. 235–36.
186. Ibid., pp. 246–55.
187. Ibid., pp. 259–61.
188. Ibid.
189. Ibid., pp. 263, 264.
190. Ibid., p. 267.
191. Ibid., pp. 248, 271.
192. Reid, 1852.
193. This paper.
194. *Ma'swut* or *mĩsvut,* was first mentioned in a creation story of the Desert Cahuilla, obtained by L. Hooper, "The Cahuilla Indians," *Univ. Cal. Publs. Amer. Archaeol. and Ethnol.* 16 (1920): 326. Cactus fiber mats in which the Serrano keep their sacred feathers are mentioned by R. F. Benedict, "A Brief Sketch of Serrano Culture," *American Anthropologist,* n.s. 26 (1924): 389. The Serrano call this mat and the sacred feathers *mu'urtch;* the Luiseño, Cupeño, and Cahuilla all use local variants of the term *ma'swut.*
195. Benedict, 1924, p. 389.
196. Kroeber, 1925, p. 794.
197. The upriver Havasupai have no traces of this complex, having no priest, fetish, or dance house.
198. Goddard, 1921, pp. 171–72.
199. Franciscan Fathers, 1910, pp. 329–33; Stephen, 1893, p. 351.
200. Goddard, 1921, p. 167; Cushing, 1880, p. 44.
201. W. Mathews, "The Mountain Chant," *Fifth Ann. Rep. Bur. Amer. Ethnol.,* 1887, p. 438.
202. Ibid., p. 234.
203. Franciscan Fathers, 1910, pp. 496–97.
204. Reichard, Letter of Jan. 27, 1926.
205. J. Stevenson, "Mythical Sand Paintings of the Navajo Indians," *8th Ann. Rep. Bur. Amer. Ethnol.,* 1886, p. 23.

206. Franciscan Fathers, 1910, pp. 496–97.
207. Lumholtz, 1912. J. A. Mason, "The Papago Harvest Festival," *American Anthropologist,* n.s. 22 (1920): 13–25, gives a similar description.
208. Lumholtz, 1912, p. 49.
209. Ibid., p. 49.
210. Ibid., p. 173.
211. Ibid., 53–55.
212. Ibid., p. 173.
213. Ibid., p. 51.
214. Ibid., pp. 102–6.
215. Ibid., p. 52.
216. Gifford, 1916a, p. 176.
217. Russell, 1904, p. 153.
218. Ibid., p. 252.
219. Ibid., p. 106.
220. Goddard, 1921, p. 135.
221. Cushing, 1896, p. 366.
222. Ibid., p. 351; Mindeleff, 1891, p. 111.
223. A. V. Kidder, *An Introduction to the Study of Southwestern Archaeology* (New Haven, Conn., 1924), pp. 123–27.
224. Voth, 1901, p. 86.
225. H. R. Voth, "The Oraibi Oa'qöl Ceremony," *Publs. Field Col. Mus., Anthrop. Series* 6 (1903): 6.
226. Voth, 1905b, p. 73.
227. Parsons, 1922, p. 296.
228. H. R. Voth, "Oraibi Natal Customs and Ceremonies," *Publs. Field Col. Mus., Anthrop. Series* 6 (1905a): 49.
229. Parsons, 1923, p. 177n4.
230. Lowie, field notes, 1916.
231. G. A. Dorsey and H. R. Voth, "The Oraibi Soyal Ceremony," *Publs. Field Col. Mus., Anthrop. Series* 3 (1901): 44–45.
232. Parsons, 1923, p. 177n4.
233. Voth, "Oraibi Oa'qöl," 1903, p. 44.
234. Parsons, 1922, p. 289.
235. Lowie, field notes, 1916.
236. Goddard, 1921, p. 113; also Dorsey and Voth, 1901, p. 22.
237. Voth, 1901, p. 87; Voth, "Oraibi Oa'qöl," p. 15.
238. Voth, "Oraibi Oa'qöl," 1903, p. 11.
239. Lowie, field notes, 1916.
240. Voth, 1901, pp. 78, 88.
241. Voth, "Oraibi Oa'qöl," 1903, p. 12.
242. See Parsons, 1923, p. 216n2.
243. Ibid.
244. Cushing, 1880, pp. 12–32.

245. M. C. Stevenson, 1904, p. 26.
246. Ibid., p. 164.
247. Ibid., p. 125.
248. Ibid., p. 21.
249. Kroeber, 1917, p. 174.
250. M. C. Stevenson, 1904, p. 179.
251. Parsons, 1917, p. 252.
252. M. C. Stevenson, 1904, p. 166.
253. Kroeber, 1917, pp. 167–68.
254. Parsons, 1923, pp. 95, 118.
255. Ibid., pp. 125, 126.
256. Parsons, 1923, pp. 221–22.
257. Ibid., p. 214.
258. Dumarest, 1919, pp. 197–99.
259. M. C. Stevenson, 1889, p. 16.
260. Ibid., p. 67.
261. Ibid., pp. 72–85.
262. Parsons, 1920b, pp. 60–61.
263. Murie, 1914, pp. 641–42.
264. Lowie, 1920, pp. 118–19.
265. F. Boas, "Evolution or Diffusion," *American Anthropologist,* n.s. 26 (1924): 342.
266. Kroeber, 1925, p. 454.
267. The Diegueño attach a color symbolism to the wildcat. Gifford, 1918, p. 169. Among the Mountain Cahuilla of Los Coyotes Canyon a somewhat similar symbolism is attached to the coyote.
268. Boscana, p. 254.
269. Gifford, 1918, p. 216.
270. Kroeber, 1925, p. 578.
271. Murie, 1914, pp. 549–643. It is well to note that the Pawnee moiety is matrilineal.
272. Radin, 1915, pp. 1–8; Wissler, 1917, p. 158.
273. Gifford, 1926.
274. Parsons, 1922, p. 284; Lowie, field notes, 1916.
275. Parsons, 1924, p. 338.
276. Parsons, 1922, p. 289.
277. L. Spier, "A Suggested Origin for Gentile Organization," *American Anthropologist,* n.s. 24 (1922): 487–89.
278. Boscana, pp. 293–95.
279. A. L. Kroeber, "A Mission Record of the California Indians," *Univ. Cal. Publs. Amer. Archaeol. and Ethnol.* 8 (1908): 16.
280. Boscana, pp. 293–95.
281. Kroeber, 1925, p. 574.
282. The Plateau Shoshoneans show more relationship to northern than to southern California; see R. H. Lowie, "The Cultural Connections

of Californian and Plateau Shoshonean Tribes," *Univ. Cal. Publs. Amer. Archaeol. and Ethnol.* 20 (1923): 147.

283. Kidder, 1924, pp. 43, 126.
284. Ibid., p. 124.
285. Kidder, 1924, pp. 126, 127.
286. Ibid., p. 37, fig. 8.
287. Ibid., p. 124.
288. P. E. Goddard, "The Cultural and Somatic Correlations of Uto Aztecan," *American Anthropologist,* n.s. 26 (1920): 247.
289. C. Lumholtz, *Unknown Mexico* (New York, 1902), pp. 171, 173, 311, 353, 365.
290. Ibid., pp. 519–20.
291. Ibid., pp. 461–64.
292. Kidder, 1924, pp. 107, 48, figs. *b, c.*

BIBLIOGRAPHY

Bandelier, Adolph F.
1892 An outline of the documentary history of the Zuñi tribe. *Journal of American Ethnology and Archaeology* 3, no. 4.

Burrus, Ernest J., S. J., ed. and trans.
1969 *A history of the Southwest. A study of the civilization and conversion of the Indians in southwestern United States and northwestern Mexico from the earliest to 1700* by Adolph F. Bandelier; vol. 1, *A catalogue of the Bandelier collection in the Vatican Library.* Rome, Italy: Jesuit Historical Institute; St. Louis, Missouri: St. Louis University.

Cabeza de Vaca, Alvar Nuñez
1944 *Naufragios.* México: Editorial Layac.

Chávez, Father Angélico, O. F. M.
1968 *Coronado's friars.* Washington, D.C.: Academy of American Franciscan History.

DiPeso, Charles C.
1966 *Archaeology and ethnohistory of the northern Sierra.* Albuquerque, New Mexico: Dr. S. H. Dike, 1611 Bayita Lane, NW.

Dutton, Bertha P.
1963 *Sun father's way: The kiva murals of kuaua.* Albuquerque: University of New Mexico Press.

Ekholm, Gordon
1939 Recent archaeological work in Sonora and northern Sinaloa. *Proceedings of the 27th International Congress of Americanists* 2: 69–73.
1942 Excavations at Guasave, Sinaloa, Mexico. *Anthropological Papers of the American Museum of Natural History* 38: 23–139.

Hallenbeck, Cleve
1939 *Alvar Nuñez Cabeza de Vaca: The journey and route of the first European to cross the continent of North America 1534–1536.* Glendale, California.

179

Hedrick, Basil C., J. Charles Kelley, and Carroll L. Riley
1971   *North Mexican frontier: Readings in archaeology, ethnohistory, and ethnography.* Carbondale, Illinois: Southern Illinois University Press.

Hobgood, John
1964   Chalma, a study in directed culture change. Unpublished M.A. thesis, Southern Illinois University, Carbondale, Illinois.

Kelley, J. Charles
1950   The La Junta archives. *New Mexico Historical Review* 25: 162–63.
1952a Factors involved in the abandonment of certain peripheral southwestern settlements. *American Anthropologist* 54: 356–87.
1952b The historic Indian pueblos of La Junta de los Rios. *New Mexico Historical Review* 27: 257–95.
1953   The historic Indian pueblos of La Junta de los Rios (continued). *New Mexico Historical Review* 28: 21–51.
1966   Mesoamerica and the southwestern United States. In *Handbook of middle American Indians,* Robert Wauchope, gen. ed., vol. 4, ed. Gordon F. Ekholm and Gordon R. Wiley. Austin: University of Texas Press.
1972   Archaeology of the Northern frontier: Zacatecas and Durango. In *Handbook of middle American Indians,* Robert Wauchope, gen. ed., Vol. 11, ed. Gordon F. Ekholm and Gordon R. Willey. Austin: University of Texas Press.

Kelley, J. Charles, and Ellen Abbott Kelley
1969   Introduction to the ceramics of the chalchihuites culture of Zacatecas and Durango, Mexico. Part I, The decorated wares. *Research Records of the University Museum, Mesoamerican Studies* no. 5, Southern Illinois University, Carbondale, Illinois.

Kelly, Isabel
1938   Excavations at Chametla, Sinaloa. *Ibero-Americana* no. 14, Berkeley, California.

Kidder, A. V.
1924   An introduction to the study of southwestern archaeology. *Papers, Southwestern Expeditions,* Phillips Academy, New Haven, Connecticut.

Lange, Charles H., and Carroll L. Riley, eds.
1966   *The southwestern journal of Adolph F. Bandelier, 1880–1882.* Albuquerque: University of New Mexico Press.
1970   *The southwestern journal of Adolph F. Bandelier, 1883–1884.* Albuquerque: University of New Mexico Press.

Riley, Carroll L.
1971   Early Spanish-Indian communication in the greater Southwest. *New Mexico Historical Review* 46, no. 4, pp. 285–314.

Riley, Carroll L., J. Charles Kelley, Campbell W. Pennington, and Robert L. Rands, eds.

1971   *Man across the sea: Problems of pre-Columbian contacts.* Austin:
        University of Texas Press.
Sauer, Carl R.
1932   Road to Cibola. *Ibero-Americana,* no. 3, Berkeley, California.
Weigand, Phil C.
1968   The mines and mining techniques of the chalchihuites culture. *Ameri-
        can Antiquity* 33: 45–61.
White, Leslie A., and Ignacio Bernal
1960   *Correspondencia de Adolfo F. Bandelier.* Instituto Nacional de An-
        tropología e Historia, Seria Historia, 6, México.

INDEX

Acoma: Pueblo of, 54, 129, 130
Acuco: Pueblo of, 54
Agriculture. *See* Farming
Alcaraz, Captain Diego, 47
Alvarado, Hernando de, 54, 162
Anasazi, 18, 20, 98, 102, 155
Antevs, Ernst, 12
Apache Indians: reservation of, 70; Jicarilla, 114, 118; Western, 118, 126, 146; White Mountain, 126; Plains, 162; mentioned, 54, 56, 114, 118, 126, 135, 140, 143, 144, 147
Arapaho Indians, 114
Arbolillo: site of, 18
Archaeology: in America, 10; in Central America, 12; history of, 14; modern period in, 15
Archaic: Period, 12, 20; hypothesis of, 15; remains of, 18; in Valley of Mexico, 19; pre-Archaic, 21
Athapascan Indians, 114, 126, 143, 145, 147, 150, 151
Aztec Period: deities of, 27; turquoise in, 87, 88; Priesthood in, 151; feather symbolism in, 165; mentioned, 15
Aztec Ruin, New Mexico, 98, 166

Bamoa: settlement at, 159
Bandelier, Adolph F., xi, xii, 3, 42, 51, 64, 110, 131
Bartsch, Dr. Paul, 168

Basketmaker: chronological position of, 1, 102; costume of, 7; discovery of, 7; burial description of, 7, 8; technology of, 7, 8; naming of, 8; cultural level of, 8, 9; stone tools of, 8, 9; pottery, 8, 17; competition with Cliff Dwellers, 9; graves of, 10, 15; dating of, 12, 13, 98, 103, 105, 106, 107; geographic extent of, 104; Developmental, 155; mentioned, 16, 17, 18, 102, 103, 109, 156
Basketmaker-Pueblo: development of, 1, 17, 102, 155; geographic area of, 98
Baskets: in burial, 7; with clay linings, 8; as ceremonial container, 130, 135, 136, 138, 139; mentioned, 103, 104, 105, 106, 133
Beads: disc, 97; of olivella, 139; mentioned, 7
Benedict, Ruth, 110
Bennett, Wendell R., 15
Berry, Dr. Stillman S., 168
Betatakin: ruin of, 169
Bison. *See* Buffalo
Blake, William P., xii, 86
Boas, Franz, 15
Boatright, Mody C., xi, 22, 24
Boscana, G., 121, 122, 132, 142
Brand, Donald D., xi, 92
Bristol, Miss Viola, 168

183